The Cieszanow Memorial Book
(Cieszanów, Poland)

Translation of
Sefer zikaron le-kehila kedosha Cieszanow

Original Book Edited by: Dr. David Ravid (Shmukler)

Originally published in Tel Aviv 1970

JewishGen
מרכז שולמי לגנאלוגיה יהודית
The Global Home for Jewish Genealogy

A Publication of JewishGen, INC
Edmond J. Safra Plaza, 36 Battery Place, New York, NY 10280
646.494.2972 | info@JewishGen.org | www.jewishgen.org

**MUSEUM OF JEWISH HERITAGE
A LIVING MEMORIAL
TO THE HOLOCAUST**

The Cieszanow Memorial Book (Cieszanów, Poland)

Translation of *Sefer zikaron le-kehila kedosha Cieszanow*

Copyright © 2024 by JewishGen, INC All rights reserved.
First Printing: January 2024, Shevat 5784
Editor of Original Yizkor Book: Dr. David Ravid (Shmukler)
Translated by: Jacob Solomon Berger
Cover Design: Irv Osterer
Layout: Jonathan Wind
Name Indexing: Stefanie Holzman
Photo Extraction: Sondra Ettlinger

Library of Congress Control Number (LCCN): 2023945853

ISBN: 978-1-954176-82-9 (hard cover: 280 pages, alk. paper)

About JewishGen.org

JewishGen, an affiliate of the Museum of Jewish Heritage - A Living Memorial to the Holocaust, serves as the global home for Jewish genealogy.

Featuring unparalleled access to 30+ million records, it offers unique search tools, along with opportunities for researchers to connect with others who share similar interests. Award winning resources such as the Family Finder, Discussion Groups, and ViewMate, are relied upon by thousands each day.

In addition, JewishGen's extensive informational, educational and historical offerings, such as the Jewish Communities Database, Yizkor Book translations, InfoFiles, Family Tree of the Jewish People, and KehilaLinks, provide critical insights, first-hand accounts, and context about Jewish communal and familial life throughout the world.

Offered as a free resource, JewishGen.org has facilitated thousands of family connections and success stories, and is currently engaged in an intensive expansion effort that will bring many more records, tools, and resources to its collections.

Please visit https://www.jewishgen.org/ to learn more.

Executive Director: Avraham Groll

About the JewishGen Yizkor Book Project

Yizkor Books (Memorial Books) were traditionally written to memorialize the names of departed family and martyrs during holiday services in the synagogue (a practice that still exists in many synagogues today).

Over the centuries, as a result of countless persecutions and horrific atrocities committed against the Jews, Yizkor Books (Sefer Zikaron in Hebrew) were expanded to include more historical information, such as biographical sketches of famous personalities and descriptions of daily town life.

Following the Holocaust, the idea of remembrance and learning took on an urgent and crucial importance. Survivors of the Holocaust sought out other surviving residents of their former towns to memorialize and document the names and way of life of those who were ruthlessly murdered by the Nazis. These remembrances were documented in Yizkor Books, hundreds of which were published in the first decades after the Holocaust.

Most of these books were published privately, or through Landsmanshaftn (social organizations comprised of members originating from the same European town or region) that still existed, and were often distributed free of charge. Sadly, the languages used to document these crucial histories and links to our past, Yiddish and Hebrew, are no longer commonly understood by a significant percentage of Jews today. As a result, JewishGen has undertaken the sacred responsibility of translating these books into English so that the culture and way of life of these communities will be preserved and transmitted to future generations.

In 1986, a group of farsighted JewishGenners started a project to pool their efforts together in groups based upon their ancestors from each town and donate money to get the Yizkor books of their ancestral towns translated into English. As the translated material became available, it was made accessible for free at www.JewishGen.org/Yizkor. Hardcover copies can be purchased by visiting https://www.jewishgen.org/Yizkor/ybip.html (see below).

It is our hope that the translation of these books into English (and other languages) will assist the countless Jewish family researchers who are so desperately seeking to forge a connection with their heritage.

Director of JewishGen Yizkor Book Project: Lance Ackerfeld

About JewishGen Press

JewishGen Press (formerly the Yizkor Books-in-Print Project) is the publishing division of JewishGen.org, and provides a venue for the publication of non-fiction books pertaining to Jewish genealogy, history, culture, and heritage.

In addition to the Yizkor Book category, publications in the Other Non-Fiction category include Shoah memoirs and research, genealogical research, collections of genealogical and historical materials, biographies, diaries and letters, studies of Jewish experience and cultural life in the past, academic theses, and other books of interest to the Jewish community.

Please visit https://www.jewishgen.org/Yizkor/ybip.html to learn more.

Director of JewishGen Press: Joel Alpert
Managing Editor - Jessica Feinstein
Publications Manager - Susan Rosin

Notes to the Reader

The images in the original book were reproduced from photographs from the time of the first edition. These reproductions were already of poor quality, being pre-war. As a result, the images in the book are the best achievable.

A reader can view the original scans of the book on the websites listed below.

The original book can be seen online at the Yiddish Book Center website:

https://www.yiddishbookcenter.org/collections/yizkor-books/yzk-nybc313730/ravid-david-sefer-zikaron-di-kehilah-kedoshah-tsyeshinov

OR

at the New York Public Library Digital Collections website:

https://digitalcollections.nypl.org/items/aa9e98b0-66c1-0133-964b-00505686d14e

To obtain a list of Shoah victims from **Cieszanow (Cieszanów, Poland),** the reader should access the Yad Vashem web site listed below; one can also search for specific family names using family name option. These lists are continually updated by Yad Vashem, so it is worthwhile to periodically search these lists.

There is more valuable information (including the Pages of Testimony, etc.) available on this website: https://yvng.yadvashem.org/

A list of all books available from JewishGen Press along with prices is available at: https://www.jewishgen.org/Yizkor/ybip.html

Photo Credits

Front Cover:

R' Aryeh Rubin z"l , the Chief Rabbi of Cieszanow, the son-in-law of the righteous Rabbi and Admor of Cieszanow, R' Simcha Issachar Halberstam.

Back Cover:

Top Left:
The Great Synagogue. On the left side is the bathhouse and mikva in Cieszanow. Standing on the right is the youngest son of R' Leib Sternlicht, Yaakov.

Top Right:
Memorial monument in the Shoah Cellar on Har Zion in Jerusalem to commemorate Cieszanow's victims. Donated by Aryeh Koenig z"l of Antwerp.

Middle Right
Reizl Schmid z"l

Cover Design: Irv Osterer

Geopolitical Information

Cieszanów, Poland is located at 50°14' N 23°08' E 167 miles SE of Warszawa

	Town	District	Province	Country
Before WWI (c. 1900):	Cieszanów	Cieszanów	Galicia	Austrian Empire
Between the wars (c. 1930):	Cieszanów	Lubaczów	Lwów	Poland
After WWII (c. 1950):	Cieszanów			Poland
Today (c. 2000):	Cieszanów			Poland

Alternate Names for the Town:

Cieszanów [Pol], Tzieshinov [Yid], Cheshanov, Tsyeshinov, Tseshanov, Tsheshanov

Nearby Jewish Communities:

Lubaczów 5 miles S
Ułazów 6 miles WNW
Oleszyce 6 miles SW
Dzików Stary 9 miles W
Horyniec 11 miles ESE
Narol 11 miles NE
Cewków 12 miles W
Lipsko 12 miles NE
Łukowa 12 miles NW
Wielkie Oczy 15 miles S
Nemyriv, Ukraine 16 miles ESE
Nahachiv, Ukraine 17 miles SSE
Józefów 17 miles NNW
Bełżec 17 miles NE
Krakovets, Ukraine 18 miles S
Lubycza Królewska 19 miles ENE
Potelych, Ukraine 19 miles E
Tarnogród 19 miles WNW
Mosty Małe 19 miles ENE

Tomaszów Lubelski 19 miles NE
Rava-Ruska, Ukraine 21 miles E
Krasnobród 22 miles N
Cieplice 22 miles W
Sieniawa 23 miles WSW
Yavoriv, Ukraine 24 miles SSE
Radymno 24 miles SW
Jarczów 24 miles ENE
Jarosław 25 miles SW
Skołoszów 25 miles SW
Zwierzyniec 26 miles NNW
Maheriv, Ukraine 27 miles ESE
Uhniv, Ukraine 29 miles ENE
Biłgoraj 29 miles NW
Kuryłówka 30 miles W
Grodzisko Dolne 30 miles W
Mostyska, Ukraine 30 miles S
Komarów 30 miles NNE
Przeworsk 30 miles WSW
Tvirzha, Ukraine 30 miles S

Jewish Population: 2,777 (in 1900), 939 (in 1921)

Map of Poland showing the location of **Cieszanow**

Table of Contents

The Cieszanow Memorial Book
(Cieszanów, Poland)

50°14' / 23°08'

Translation of *Sefer zikaron le-kehila kedosha Cieszanow*

Editor: Dr. David Ravid (Shmukler)

Published in Tel Aviv 1970

English Translation Prepared and Published

Jacob Solomon Berger

Mahwah, New Jersey, USA 2006

Acknowledgments:

**Our sincere appreciation to Jacob Solomon Berger who has kindly donated
his original book to JewishGen for online presentation**

**Our thanks to Sondra Ettlinger for extracting the pictures from the original book,
enabling their addition to the project.**

This is a translation of: *Sefer zikaron le-kehila kedosha Cieszanow* (The Cieszanow Memorial Book),
Editor: Dr. David Ravid (Shmukler), Former residents of Cieszanow in Israel, Published: Tel Aviv 1970
(H, Y 331 pages)

Notes:

o   The complete translation of this book is also available here: The Cieszanow Memorial Book
o   The original book can be seen online at the NY Public Library site: Cieszanow

The Cieszanow Memorial Book

ספר זכרון דקהילה קדושה

ציעשינאוו

Dr. David Ravid (Shmukler), Editor

The Editorial Committee
Zvi Elimelekh Glanzer, Shmuel Zeinvil Tepper, Shmuel Lieberman,
David Langenthal, Ben-Zion Friedman, Sender Schmid

✡

Published by
The Organization of Émigrés from Cieszanow in Israel
Tel-Aviv, 5730 - 1970

English Translation Prepared and Published By
Jacob Solomon Berger
Mahwah, New Jersey, USA
2006

Dedication

Morris Kleinberg, MD
(1910 - 2006)

My late father-in-law, Dr. Morris Kleinberg, was a distinguished exemplar of "The Greatest Generation," whose life was a testament to the struggle of all men for decency, and a right to find their own place in the sun.

He was a firstborn son, on March 20, 1910, to Jakob and Anna Säckler Kleinberg in Berlin Germany, after his parents had moved there from the *shtetl* of Narol in Eastern Galicia, not far from Cieszanow, which is today in southeastern Poland, but at that time was part of the Austro-Hungarian Empire. His parents had moved to Berlin at the encouragement of Jakob's older brother Leon, who helped set up the newly wed Jakob in a butter and egg business. Less than two years later, my father-in-law's younger brother Max was born, though curiously, we find that his mother returned to Narol to give birth to her second son, in 1911. Within two years, Jakob emigrated to the United States to seek his fortune, and sent for his wife and sons the following year. The family settled in Brooklyn, New York, where a year later, the youngest child, Mollie Kleinberg Mandel, was born.

Gifted with intelligence, the young Morris was able to apprehend that education would be the key to making something of himself in this open society. Despite the lack of encouragement to do so, he exercised the initiative to go to college, attending the University of Louisville in Kentucky, from which he graduated in 1933.

The young man, by that time, had set his sights on becoming a physician. However, this was not a good time for a young Jewish boy to aspire to an education in medicine. The infamous anti-Semitic *numerus clausus* was in force, by which the university establishment severely restricted the number of Jewish students that would even be permitted to have access to medical school education. Undaunted, he set his sights on attending medical school overseas. Perhaps because of his German birth, he applied and was accepted to study medicine at Albertus University in Königsburg, then in the East Prussian province of Germany. However, this was 1933, and Adolf Hitler and the Nazis had already come to power in Germany.

It was under these heart-stopping circumstances that he pursued his medical education – a Jew in Nazi Germany, shielded by the thin pages of his American passport. The swastikas in his passport, and on his diploma, granted on September 18, 1938, are a stark and lurid testament to the knife-edge that he walked on, in order to achieve his ambition.

Upon his return to the United States, he began to pursue a career in medicine by joining the staff of the Knickerbocker Hospital in New York City. It was there, in 1939, that he met his future wife, Frances Edith Krantz, of Hartford, Connecticut, who had come to work as a nurse after her own graduation from nursing school in 1937. They married on October 6, 1941, but their budding plans were interrupted by the outbreak of The Second World War.

Dr. Morris Kleinberg saw his duty clearly, and enlisted in the U. S. Army, where he was commissioned as a Lieutenant. Stateside induction and rotational training brought him and his pregnant wife to Shelbyville Indiana, where my wife, Carol Lynn Kleinberg was born on May 26, 1944. By now a Captain, Dr. Morris Kleinberg was sent to the Philippines, where he served as a battalion surgeon through the end of the war, and was honorably discharged on May 16, 1946 and promoted to Major.

Return to civilian life first brought the Kleinbergs to the well-known temporary veterans housing in the Canarsie section of Brooklyn. On October 20, 1947, a second daughter, Susan Janet Kleinberg, today Dr. S. Jay Kleinberg-Flemming was born. The family soon relocated to the newly-built Glen Oaks development in Queens, where my father-in-law would practice medicine for over a quarter century. The family itself, eventually moved into a permanent residence in Great Neck, where the two Kleinberg daughters grew up. Despite an early interest in obstetrics, my father-in-law gravitated to general practice as a matter of economic necessity. However, he would derive considerable satisfaction from seeing his oldest grandson, Dr. Daniel A. Berger, become an Obstetrician-Gynecologist.

My father-in-law was a physician of notable quality. His patients adored him, not only for the obviously good care that he gave them, but also for his genial and compassionate manner, that set them at ease, and gave them a sense of security that they were in the best of hands. And indeed, they were. His quick mind, and mirth-provoking wit, was so effective in being able to dispel anxiety, and communicated a sense of confidence that engendered the feeling that no matter what the problem, he would be the one to set it right.

If medicine was his profession, then golf became his leisure time passion. With time, he became highly skilled at this hobby, and became a fixture at the Lake Success Country Club, along with my mother-in-law. He is the owner of a remarkable accomplishment there: three holes-in-one, two of which were shot on the same weekend. It was noted, in a news article on this accomplishment, that many of the world's leading golf champions have never shot even a single ace. He was an avid bridge player, and up to the last week of his life, would always be trying his hand at the crossword puzzle in the newspaper.

In the fullness of his ninety-six years, my father-in-law saw a great deal, accomplished a great deal, and was privileged to watch his family come to maturity, and see his progeny prosper and multiply. While we take a considerable amount of comfort in his longevity, there is a profound ache in our hearts at his passing, and knowing that this kind, dear, and gentle man is not with us any longer, and must live, from now on, in our hearts and in our memory. We are comforted in the sure knowledge that he will always be a bright and shining star in the firmament of our family ancestry.

Supporters Honor Roll

The following members of our extended family of *landsleit*, friends and well-wishers, provided financial contributions to help make the publication of this book possible. Their generosity assures the preservation of this heritage for future generations, by which they have earned a large measure of our collective gratitude.

Dr. Daniel Berger & Monique Monokoff
David Berger & Dana Spanger
Rachel & Robert Berger
Herbert & Rita Beyenbach
Bruce, Judy & Daniel Brickman
Frank & Uta Catterson
Martin & Ellen Diesenhof
Lee Feldscher & Lisa Mintz
Drs. Nicholas Flemming & S. Jay Kleinberg
Kirsten Flemming
Peter Flemming
William & Roseline Glazer
Richard, Nancy & Eric Goodman
Harry-Paul & Judyth Greenbaum
Dr. Sandy & Abetta Helman
Robert & Dana Isbitts
Allen & Jayne Jacobson
Dennis & Sharon Ann Javer
Herbert & Judith Javer
Jewish Genealogical Society of Great Britain
Frances E. Kleinberg
Melvin & Martha Kosminoff
Bruce Leeb & Rona Eagle
Seelig & Edna Lewitz
Charlie & Peggy Long
Arthur Gary Melnick
Beatrice Melnick
Melvyn & Hadassa Morris
Robert & Stella Plevan
Susan F. Pollack
Jaithirth & Neelambari Rao
Seymour & Leslie Ratner
Ron Rosensweig & Linda Dombrowsky
Larry & Sharyn Rubin
John C. Ryan
Sandra & Larry Small
Sisterhood, Temple Beth Rishon
Lillian Silver
Stephen & Susan Sorkenn
Leonard & Ruth Stern
Stephen & Margaret Taylor
Robert & Susan Walters
Alan & Sue Weber
Gary & Marierose Zwerling

Translator's Foreword

Like the prior books translated as part of this endeavor, *Sefer Zikaron D'Kehillah Kedoshah Cieszanow* is no exception in providing its own unique and special insights, and a variegated set of perspectives, that refresh the history, and add that much more to the record, of what transpired in the Jewish communities of Eastern Europe during the course of their existence.

This sixth translation in a series, provides a memorial to the *shtetl* that is proximate to the ancestral home of my wife's paternal family in Narol – a *shtetl* in the Eastern Galician Province of what is today Poland. At the time I undertook the effort, I did not anticipate that I would come to dedicate this volume to the memory of my father-in-law, Dr. Morris Kleinberg, ה"ע, both of whose parents were natives of Narol. Sadly, there is no *Yizkor Book* for Narol. In fact, only 1,273 volumes of this kind were written after the Second Word War, despite the fact that 6,500 Jewish communities were obliterated. It is fitting that this book carry a synopsis of his life in its dedication pages, because the fulness and the drama of his 96 years is a testament, to the endurance and survivability that has become the hallmark of all Jewry throughout the ages.

This compendium about the *shtetl* of Cieszanow offers us a counterpoint to some of the books we have seen to date. By the admission of the compilers, it is a place that was not unusually distinguished, even though it boasted its own share of outstanding Jewish sages, scholars, and men revered for their holiness and piety. Its special value lies in the portrait that the writers give us of the outlook and feelings of a very typical Eastern European Jewish community, in which the spirit and doctrine of the *Hasidic* movement were dominant.

Yet, despite this, we are also told that, even in this seeming backwater, the winds of modernity could not be kept out. We see an almost anomalous ferocity, on the part of younger, and more enlightened age cohorts, as they give battle to their more recalcitrant elders, unwilling to let go of traditions, forged over centuries of placid and relatively static agrarian life, inexorably being swept away by the forces of industrialization and political upheaval. This is a very valuable record, because the tensions, in *shtetl* life that they describe, are often overlooked, or not documented at all, in conventional histories. Accordingly, an unrealistically idealized view of the *shtetl* often emerges, that does not reflect the rough and tumble contest of ideas that was taking place in Eastern Europe in the century prior to, and leading up to, the Holocaust.

While, again, it is true that the tragic outcome of the telling is known in advance, the record is enriched by the endeavor of these writers, to tell this tale from their own unique perspective.

I am indebted to Tomasz Panczyk and Leon Szyfer for their assistance in assuring that my rendition of Polish names and places, transliterated from Yiddish into English, were done correctly. I am also grateful to my friend and colleague Dr. Thomas Zoltan Fahidy for his help with getting the Russian idioms correctly conveyed in this text. Finally, my thanks also go to Yeshaya Metal, the reference desk librarian at YIVO in New York City, who, as usual, was ever ready with a suitable insight regarding the occasional esoteric word that would surface from time to time.

Jacob Solomon Berger
Spring 2006

Organization Section

"To Enter into the Inner Sanctum"

Dr. David Ravid

Justifiably, this is what the progenitors called it, because, it was not without an aura of the sacred, that we approached this *mitzvah*. And the heavy burden of producing this book was placed on my shoulders, and I carry it with love, and pull on the yoke with commitment, out of recognition for the sacred responsibility that I have taken on.

Apart from this difficult burden, I was laden with the spirituality and the complexity of explanation and organization, such that no item in the organization and explanation did not pass through my hands and be subject to my values in evaluation.

I tried with all my might, and even beyond my might, to do justice to the many, turning nights into days, in order to facilitate and erect this spiritual monument in an esthetic form, that it be worthy to serve as an eternal memorial to our martyrs in the community of Cieszanow who gave their lives in the Sanctification of The Name, the Nation and The Country.

I labored a great deal, I worked at the work of ants, and I did not stint in effort, or expenditure of energy, to uncover information and events in connection with the rich past of the Jews of our *shtetl*.

I wrote down every detail, I conserved and gathered every tale. Despite exhausting myself in this, I discovered very little, but important material from reliable sources, despite the fact that it is evident to me that the additional material is not sufficiently adequate to limn a complete picture that encompasses the history of our community.

Despite this, I have a spiritual satisfaction and an inner relief, that I have accomplished something that transcends my own spirit and capabilities – to discharge my obligation as regards the members of my community, and from all appearances – I think I have laid a foundation to memorialize the glorious past that the people of Cieszanow have left with us forever.

The community of Cieszanow was one of the links in the golden chain of the period of Jewish life in Galicia, that was;, as it known – the flour and oil of European Jewry, that stood as a model and wonder to all the members of the Diaspora during the hundreds of years up to the accursed years of 5639-5705 [1939-1945].

The community of Cieszanow was, however, not one of the famous communities, not a 'Mother City' among Jewry, [and] *Gaonim*, philanthropists, and famous people did not emanate from her. Her history was not recorded and retold from one generation to the next, but nevertheless, she made her own modest contribution to the affairs of the life of Jewry in the first eras, and her place was not submerged in the storms of life that inundated the Jews of Galicia, and she made her contribution to the community movements that enveloped the communities of Israel.

Cieszanow was a typical Jewish community, a *shtetl* of *Hasidim*, Torah scholars and community spiritual leaders, that guarded and observed its *Hasidic*-religious complexion, until the waves of internationalism reached even here.

After the First World War, the leaders of the community could no longer prevent that development, and to overpower the influence of the new era.

[Page 2]

An acknowledged contribution to the change in the complexion of the *shtetl*, in the direction of an international posture, was specifically made by the sons and daughters from *Hasidic* families, and the families of Torah scholars.

One of our important missions, was to awaken among the youth, the feeling of the course of Jewish history, and the obligation to work for the Jewish people, and along with this, to nurse along the feeling of being connected to all of humanity, and to engage in the struggle for the international Zionist and religious ideals.

The international movement introduced a spiritual revolution into the center of the ranks of the young people; instead of spending their time exclusively withing the four walls of the *Bet HaMedrash*, and to withdraw themselves from the realities of life and activities, we committed ourselves – after the international influence was infused into us, to education, to nurturing the Zionist awareness, along with a religious cognizance. Our motto was – the same as the proverb says: "It there is no Torah, there is no flour," also says, "If there is no flour, then there is no Torah." That is to say, flour {i.e. sustenance] and Torah are essential to us simultaneously.

After I had been asked to involve myself in the construction of this spiritual monument, to memorialize our Brethren and Sisters whose souls are in the Garden of Eden, who fell dead in the period of the *Shoah*, the first thing I saw fit to do, was to divide the spiritual material into three parts: Organizational, Historical, and General.

It was my view – that this organization was logical, and despite this, there is no doubt in my heart that part of the community will rebel against me for this, or that, but despite this, I assume the responsibilities of editing and the trials of criticism with affection, and I will not get upset:

> If I heard with my ears,
> And I will certainly know,
> That a certain individual
> Was burdened by my shortcomings,
> Rebelled against my words –
> I say, I forgive –
> Because I was created for you.

When Nahum Sokolov,ז"ל, with his profound skills, fluent and at ease with all of the wisdom of the Hebrew language, and other languages, a scholar in Jewish literature and the literature of other nations, a genius of a writer, whose level is approached by only the very few, sent a piece to the editor of "*HaTzefira*," he garnered the response of the editor in the columns of the paper, to the effect that, "I did not find anything to print."

The reason I included this story at the beginning of those entries that will be printed below, is that one cannot know, that it is possible that future generations, and possibly even our generation, will look upon us with admiring eyes, and will convey gratitude to us for this literary memorial that we are here erecting in memory of our heroes who fell mostly in Sanctification of The Name, at the hands of the German murderers and their Ukrainian and Polish accomplices, ימ"ש.

Lord in Heaven, remember favorably those pure souls, along with the remainder of the righteous of the world, and take vengeance, avenge the spilled blood of Your People.

[Page 3]

A Foreword to the Publication of the Memorial Book

Dr. David Ravid

A feeling of the stirring of the soul, a feeling of sanctity, enveloped us at the time we approached the publication of this *Yizkor Book* [dedicated] to the eternal memorialization of the Jews of Cieszanow who were cruelly exterminated by unclean Nazi hands with help from their bestial accomplices, in the years 5639-5705 [1939-1945].

Years have passed since that time, but the voice of that spilled blood called out, and calls still, from the mass graves, and demands of us to erect a monument in memory of the precious and sacred lives that they gave up.

We struggled with a variety of difficulties because Cieszanow, as a new town, was not blessed with historical monographic documents, and the little that did exist was lost.

We made every effort to gather the material that did remain, and also, we made the effort to stimulate people, who in the past were active in Jewish community life in our *shtetl*, to relate their memories, and in this manner, this book was created.

The soul of the commonplace, rooted, and unique Jewish populace is woven into its chapters, describing its committed, dedicated, readiness and fairness, its joys and sorrows, and its misfortune and annihilation.

For commercial, financial and also technical reasons, we were unable to meet all of the demands of our respected community.

We appear to have two lists:

1.   A list of everyone in Cieszanow according to the recollection of native families.
2.   A list of individual people, whose names were sent to us by relatives; and the names that do not appear in the book, are the responsibility of those people who did not convey the names of their relatives, either through oversight, or not taking this endeavor seriously.

Many pictures were, in the first instance not printable, and many [others] were marred by the printing machine, and we were compelled to removed them from the book, and we were also pressured by the large costs that we absolutely could not cover.

From the many pictures that did come out well, the bright faces of fathers, mothers and children look down upon us , who up to their extermination carried in their hearts – each in their own way – the dream of their personal liberation, and also – the two-thousand year-old dream of the Return to Zion.

We wish to express our recognition to the *landsleit* of out *shtetl* in Israel and in the Diaspora, especially thanking Dr. Beryl Koenig of Antwerp, who, together with his sister-in-law Leah, helped to get this book published with their substantial contribution.

[Page 4]

And This Is How It Began…

Dr. David Ravid

The Members of the Committee

R'David Langenthal   *Dr. David Ravid*   *R'Shmuel Z. Tepper*

R'Zvi Elimelekh Glanzer   *R' Shmuel Liberman*

Ben-Zion Friedman   *R'Sender Schmid*

**Past Members of the Committee –
The Organization of the Émigrés of Cieszanow in Israel**

From Right to Left: R' David Langenthal, ג״י, R' Shmuel Tepper, ג״י, Dr. David Ravid, ג״י, The Chairman, speaking, R' Leib Geller, ע״ה, R' Shmuel Lieberman, ג״י.

R' Dov Koenig

R' Dov Koenig of Antwerp, a scion of Cieszanow, son of R' Moshe, ז"ל, allocated a substantial donation from his personal assets, and because of this, it made it possible for us to publish this book.

May He, who dwells on high, give him his just reward in this world and the next.

The Organization of the Émigrés of Cieszanow in Israel

R' Zvi Elimelekh Glanzer שליט"א, during his speech on Yom HaShoah in the year 5726 [1966] in Tel-Aviv.

Approximately 6-8 years ago, during a memorial service for our martyrs, we surfaced an idea, that we, the survivors of out *shtetl*, **Cieszanow**, who find themselves in the Land of Israel, need to make the effort to publish a '*Yizkor Book,*' dedicated to the eternal memory of our people of Cieszanow, who were brought down by the wicked Europeans.

I, and all the other members of the one-time committee, appealed to our gathering:

    1.   That pictures should be sent to us immediately from every location, that have any relevance to the town.

    2.   To write – biographies, incidents, suffering and joyous stories from the time that our now destroyed town still existed.

    3.   Financial contributions to cover the costs of printing the 'book.'

We waited for long years, and not a single person responded to our call.

However, as has been said – this concept gnawed away at me in my mind, and gave me no surcease.

For this entire time, I felt an emotional pressure, as though this was a sort of sacred obligation, so it seemed to me, that some Divine Oversight had put down the mitzvah of erecting this spiritual monument for the fallen among our near and dear ones.

Initially, I struggled only with myself, and asked only of myself – why specifically you? Why are you responsible for the future generations – more than someone else?

[Page 5]

Everything is already decided, and everything is divinely ordained.

On a certain Saturday, after midday, I am studying '*Pirkei Avot*,' and among other decent and wise thoughts from Hillel 'the Elder,' I study also the familiar maxim, 'In a place where there are no men, strive to be a man' (*Avot, B.*). In simple language, what this means is:

'In that place where there are no men, **you** must strive to be **the man**'

And it was in this fashion that the concept of a '*Yizkor Book*' became crystallized in my mind.

The writer of these lines, upon whom our community, headed by our committee, laid the burden with responsibility for both action and development, became the central force in the creation of the book.

It is natural that in such a gigantic effort, mistakes are also made, and it is also known that the man has not yet been born who does not make any mistakes.

However, my comfort is – as one says in Yiddish:

'When one makes a mistake, it is a sign that one has done some work.'

I immediately invited those members who had signed the announcements to our *landsleit*, and not thinking a great deal, on that very night, we decided to step up to the task, and it must be said to everyone's credit, that we were immediately successful in our difficult but sacred mission.

Indeed, we alone – the members of the committee immediately took on the responsibility, and on the spot, immediately paid in 100 pounds, so that on the spot, the foundation was laid for the large expenditures that the 'Book' would, in time, absorb.

Each member of the committee received his assigned work, we immediately approached our *landsleit* in Israel, and also in the Diaspora.

Here are the three appeals to our community, all were printed in both languages, Hebrew – Yiddish.

[Page 6]

The Organization of the Émigrés of Cieszanow & Vicinity

With the Help, Tel-Aviv, Nisan 5729
April 1969

Dear Friends!

We are honored to inform you, that the committee of our *Landsmanschaft* in Israel,
has decided to publish a '*Yizkor Book*' to preserve
the memory of the martyrs from our town and its vicinity.

We need your help

1. Send us a variety of pictures, of the deceased and also of those who are still
alive, may they live to one hundred and twenty years.
2. Letters, stories, incidents from before the War.
3. The 'Book' will be printed in both Hebrew and Yiddish, and
will be professionally bound, in which everyone will be able to memorialize
his own name, the name of his family, friends and acquaintances.
4. You may send your material in Yiddish as well.

We are appealing to you – to help us in our sacred undertaking, with material
and a substantive financial contribution. We note that the outlays have been
estimated at approximately 10 thousand pounds.

After the 'Book' has been printed, everyone will receive their
original pictures back, and also a book.

The material and financial contributions can be sent to one of the members who has
signed below, who belong to the committee.

With warm regards

The Committee

1. Hirsch Melekh Glanzer, Ramat-Gan HaTikvah 1
2. Shmuel Zeinvil Tepper, Tel-Aviv Rehov Hovevei Zion 31
3. Shmuel Lieberman, B'nai Brak Rehov Levi Yitzhak 7
4. David Langenthal, B'nai Brak Rehov BESH"T 30
5. Ben-Zion Friedman, B'nai Brak, Rehov Yehoshua 14
6. Dr. David Ravid (Shmukler) Derekh HaShalom 95 (Association Headquarters)
7. Sender Schmid, Bat-Yam Rehov Perlstein 31

Donate for the Book !

[Page 7]

Notice Number 2
The Organization of the Émigrés of Cieszanow

With the Help of the Almighty, Tel-Aviv, Sivan 5729
May 1969 (*typo shows 1966*)

Effusive greetings to our friend!

For an additional time, we permit ourselves to turn to you respectfully as follows: the Committee has decided, that in another month, it will turn over the book material to the printer, along with the pictures that it has in hand.

In accordance with our expectations, we anticipate that the book will appear within three weeks; If by July 15 of this year we will not receive a positive response from you, that is to say, a **picture of relatives and a donation**, we will take that as a sign of refusal to participate in this mitzvah.

In this instance, we absolve ourselves of any responsibility, and caution against any complaints after the fact, or that someone should raise their voice that we did not provide a warning to this effect.

Those members of our town that will not participate in this endeavor, will no doubt feel sorry that their families will not appear in this 'Memorial' Book, no picture of their dear ones, and no telling of their good deeds, and most importantly – **that they should not be envious** of those, whose pictures and words of eulogy about their families will be made known in this Memorial Book for all time.

It is worth noting that the book will be decorated artistically, with bold lettering in Hebrew and Yiddish, in a beautiful binding.

(Partly reproduced in Yiddish)
With great respect

In the Name of the Committee

Dr. David Ravid, Chairman   Shmuel Z. Tepper, Secretary

Members of the Committee

Zvi Elimelekh Glanzer Ben Zion Friedman Shmuel Zeinvil Tepper
Dr. David Ravid
David Langenthal   Sender Schmid
Shmuel Lieberman

[Page 8]

With the Help of the Almighty, Tel-Aviv, Sivan 5729

To our friend!

We ask that you please **immediately** convey the names of those who died during the period of the Shoah, that you wish to have included in the Memorial Book.

The Committee

In response to these three notices, 2-3 *landsleit* responded initially, and immediately responses began to appear from individuals, almost all of the Cieszanow residents in Israel and also from the Diaspora, with effusive acknowledgment and blessings for each individual separately, and for the members of the Committee in particular, and with heart and gratitude sent along their donations, many also wrote essays, which were published in the book.

A heartfelt 'thank you' to the members of the committee:

R' Zvi Elimelekh Glanzer
R' Shmuel Zeinvil Tepper
R' Shmuel Lieberman
R' David Langenthal
R' Ben Zion Friedman R' Sender Schmid

For their heartfelt dedication and for their assistance to erect this spiritual monument.

In my own name, and in the name of the Committee, we also thank you, our dear *landsleit*, for your trust in us, and we wish you and your families a long life, nachas from your children, peace upon you and on our dear Land of Israel.

[Page 9]

To the Editor of the Cieszanow 'Memorial Book!'

Dr. David Ravid

With respect, to my comrade and friend, the Chairman and Editor of the 'Memorial Book' of Cieszanow, Dr. David Ravid (Shmukler), our friend, scion of our town, may he live to a good, ripe old age.

The mission of organizing the Book was placed in your trustworthy hands, and it was of you that the line says, 'for all the days when I grew up among sages, and I was covered in the dust of their feet,' in that you demonstrated your power as someone skilled in the Hebrew style, as well as in the creation of the source material and organization of 'The Cieszanow File.'

My dear friend Dr. David Ravid, may your candle burn brightly.

You are a scion of the distinguished Shmukler family, and outstanding scholar, you received your Torah and traditional education, and studied Torah in your youth with ardor, and your name went out to glory and praise. You absorbed Torah and the fear of God from the Rabbi and Leader, Rabbi Simcha Issachar Halberstam of Cieszanow, may the memory of this righteous man be a blessing, and in a like manner, you imbibed your knowledge from the well known teacher R' Zalman Lehrer, Katz, in Cieszanow, and with the outbreak of the First World War, you and your entire family moved to Vienna, and there you continued your secular studies at Gymnasiums and Universities; With your knowledge and wondrous skills, you were privileged to earn a Doctorate in Vienna. After you returned to our town – you continued to be occupied in community matters, and in community and cultural activities, and because of this you extended a helping hand to assure the success of the endeavor to create "The Memorial Book of Cieszanow in Israel."

In my capacity as a member of the Committee, I convey to you the sentiments of gratitude, and to all those who help with their hands, with money, and deed, in order to realize this agenda of memorialization.

Shmuel Sh. Lieberman[1]
Member of the Committee

Translator's footnotes:

1. The JewishGen website, under Lubaczow, makes the following attribution, which is worth noting at this point:

This is a translation of a one-page Yizkor list for Lubaczow. The list, containing close to 860 persons, was finished in 1954, a project of the Israeli Lubaczower *Landsmanschaft* and its chairman, the late Uri Roth. The scribe who wrote the one-page list was the late Samuel S. Lieberman from Tel Aviv, originally from Cieszanow.

History Section

[Page 12] [blank] [Page 13]

The Life of the Jews in Cieszanow
Up to the First World War

Cieszanow, that far-flung corner at the edge of the Russian and Austro-Hungarian border, was sealed off, and closed off within itself.

It did not have a railroad station, and its rigorously pious way of life had not changes since time immemorial, and events that caused upheavals in the larger world did not penetrate into its center, even with so much as a faint repercussion.

The worker, storekeeper, merchant, wagon driver or porter – all arose in the morning to go to the house of prayer or the *Bet HaMedrash*, to slake their spiritual thirst, one with the recitation of the Psalms, another with a page of the *Gemara, Mishnah, Eyn Yaakov*, yet another with perusal of the sacred *Zohar*.

The 'young men' were the enlisted men of the *Bet HaMedrash*, the young married men having their sustenance subsidized by their in-laws, while they engaged in study of the Torah and principles of *Hasidism*.

Hasidism pervaded everything, guided by the hand of the Chief Rabbi, R' Simcha Issachar Halberstam, ז"ל, and by the courtyards of the Rabbinical Leaders from Belz, Czortków, Husyatin, and others. Life revolved about the pivot of faith.

After the outbreak of the First World War in the year 1914, the people of Cieszanow spread out into all ends of the Austro-Hungarian Empire, especially those that reached the capitol city of Vienna, they were imbued with a new spirit that intermingled with the fundamental religious spirit, and young people opened their eyes and, for the first time, saw that a life existed outside of the four walls of the *Bet HaMedrash*.

After the war, along with the rest of the populace, these people returned to their homes, which also included a portion of those who had been influenced by the *Haskala*, and among these, the young generation became especially attached to the new concepts and ideals, and this caused a spiritual revolution in the daily lives of the town. In Cieszanow, from that time forward, they sprouted like mushrooms after a rain, where various political classes were added to the Torah study, and especially the international concept was given foundation, in all its forms: ordinary Zionism, *Mizrahi, Poalei Mizrahi, Agudat Yisrael*, and *Poalei Agudat Yisrael*, etc. etc.

[Page 14]

The Sacred Congregation of Cieszanow

The Editor

The Organization of the Émigrés of Cieszanow in Israel

A Facsimile of the Writing of the Chief Rabbi R' Simcha Issachar Halberstam, ז״ל.

In order to give something of a flavor of the life of the Jews of our town, let us first of all present those institutions and organizations that functioned in the town as indicators.

Apart from the Great Synagogue, there were additionally many other houses of worship, such as: the *kloyz*[1] of Belz, the *kloyz* of Husyatin, the *minyan* of the "Skilled in Hand," the *Bet HaMedrash* of the Mizrahi and the Zionists, whose customs acted as an addition to politics and social services.

In our town, social institutions functioned, each in its own sphere, such as: The *Hevra Gemilut Hasadim*[2], the *Hevra Kadisha*[3], the *Hevra* to provide bread to the poor, etc. From among the political institutions, it is worth remembering the '*Tze'irei Agudat Yisrael*,' the *Bund*, and above all of them, 'Zionist International Histadrut.'

There were also institutions for Torah and education that looked after the study of Torah among the young and the grown up together.

All of this was cut down and destroyed on the accursèd September of the year 1939, when the Nazis, ימ״ש, captured the town, in accordance with the agreement between the two devils, Molotov-Ribbentrop, may the names of the evil rot.

It is worth recollecting the names of a number of people who were scions of our town:

First and foremost, it is my desire to recollect for good, my teacher and Rabbi, the Chief Rabbi of the area, R' Simcha Issachar Halberstam זצ״ל, and his son, the last Rabbi R' Yekhezkiel Schraga, ז״ל, who fell dead after severe and terrible torture in Belzec at the hands of the Nazis, ימ״ש, may his spilled blood be avenged.

As is known, R' Simcha Issachar, of blessed memory, was the *Rebbe* to thousands of *Hasidim* who streamed to him from all corners of the land, to seek shelter in the shadow of his wing, to hear the words of Torah from his mouth, and to obtain his good counsel for their various exigencies of life.

On the Sabbath and Festival Days, we would all gather together with hundreds of *Hasidim* from out of town, to hear his refrains and prayer.

I am not ashamed to confess, that when I go back in spirit and look back at that period, I feel pins and needles

[Page 15]

in my soul; on the one side, I honor and praise the memory of the great Rabbi, ז״ל, and yet, I feel the ache of a pained soul, and ask myself why such a righteous man did not have the privilege of living long enough to personally see, with his own eyes, and to celebrate the great miracle of the establishment of The Nation on the soil of his fathers?

He was a great man in Torah and in good deeds, one of the great men of Jewry in his hour, holy, and pure in body and soul, doing all of his deeds only because of, and for the sake of heaven, and breathed his last on 20 Tevet 5674 [January 14, 1914], at the age of forty-two. May the memory of this righteous man be for a blessing.

His only son, the last Rabbi, R' Yekhezkiel Schraga ז״ל, followed in his footsteps in regards to Torah, piety, and a commitment of his soul against anything and everything that he thought would compromise tradition, and was renown for his good deeds that knew no bounds.

After having recollected these two Rabbis who led the communities, I wish to provide a short overview on the remainder of the Rabbis up to 150 years ago, approximately, who served with sanctity in our town.

I found an old book, whose name is Responsa *"Hessed L'Avraham,"* by the Rabbi *Gaon* of our era, R' Abraham of Zaworow-Buczacz ז״ל[4], First Edition, *Hoshen Mishpat* Sign 45-46, where he writes as follows: To R' Yaakov Teomim, נ״י, Chief Rabbi of Cieszanow.

In regards to the issue of the woman, who prior to her death set up in her will for a certain man to recite 'Kaddish' for the entire year, for a payment of forty silver Rhenish, and after a number of weeks, this man also passed away, and now the heirs of this man are demanding from the heirs of the woman the entire sum that she had provided, the complaint being that since no condition was set up that if he were not to recite *Kaddish* – that the previously mentioned sum would not be conveyed to him, what is the law? The Rabbi of Zaworow rules as follows:

The heirs of the man are to be paid only for those days in which he did recite the *Kaddish*, and one subtracts out the remaining days during which he did not say it.

Zaworow, 29 Nisan 5610 [1850].

The second response that I found is that of the Rabbi of distinguished acuity, Our Teacher, Rabbi Abraham Abba Isserles נ״י, Chief Rabbi of Cieszanow.

In response to the question of the eminent Rabbi in the matter of – a resident of your town who left a will prior to his death, that all of his books are to be given to the *Bet HaMedrash* of the city, and the relatives influenced the bedridden sick man to retract this will and to will the books to his relatives.

The question is – is it permissible to retract the original bequest? The previously mentioned Rabbi *Gaon*

[Page 16]

ends and rules as follows: there is nothing substantial here to be taken as a retraction, and his first bequest still stands, and the books therefore belong to the *Bet HaMedrash* of the Sacred Congregation of Cieszanow.

Signed by Abraham, Chief Rabbi of Zaworow, Menachem Av 5612.

3. Rabbi Dov Berish Meisels, Witness, the Year 5615
4. Rabbi Yitzhak Hurbein, author of '*Be'er Yitzhak*' former Chief Rabbi of Jaroslaw, Witness, the Year 5621
5. Rabbi Pinchas Teomim, Witness, the Year 5639
6. Rabbi Yaakov Frankel, Witness, the Year 5652
7. Rabbi Simcha Issachar scion of Halberstam from 5653-5674.
8. Rabbi Aryeh Leib Rubin from 5677-5685.
9. Rabbi Yekhezkiel Schraga Halberstam, may his blood be avenged, from 5686-the year of the Shoah, 5699.[5]

Among those, that it is also good to recollect, are my teacher and Rebbe, R' Zalman Lehrer, R' Yitzhak Glanzer, R' Aharon Katzbach, R' Yaakov Friedman, R' Herschel'eh Dayan, righteous men that were the pride and glory of our sacred congregation.

The wealthy people of the community were: R' Hanoch Zilbieger, R' Shlomo Shmukler, R' Moshe Koenigsberg, R' Moshe Koenig, R' Mordechai Glanzer, R' Yehoshua Ziegler, R' Nahum Furman, R' Michal Shargil, ז"ע, who knew how to utilize their money in their good deeds, for the benefit of the poor of the town, and for the benefit of its institutions.

The young married men were: R' Leizl[6] Margaliot, R' Yehoshua Shmukler, R' Zusha Twersky, R' Zusha Brenner, R' Asher Dieler, R' Chaim Edelman, R' Michal Halberstam, R' David Dieler, R' Eizik Lempel, and others, all of them suffused and replete with Torah, *Haskala* and good deeds.

It is suitable to recall here, the members of the '*Bund*,' Abraham Futsher, Hirsch Shmukler, the Goldberg brothers, and others.

Here, I will recall an incident that occurred a few days after the German soldiers entered out town, that reveals the character and the tastes of these people.

If I am not mistaken, the matter occurred on the day of, or a couple of days prior to the Rosh Hashanah of 5639 [1939].

I was then a member of the town council, and on the basis of that, the people of the town burdened me with the task of going to the officer in charge of the town, and to obtain permission to pray in the house of prayer of the town. It is permitted to say, that my thoughts were not comfortable with this agenda, and nor was my line of reasoning. I explained that in accordance with our law, it was forbidden to enter a place that was dangerous, and especially – I thought in my heart, that He who dwells on high, would certainly receive our

[Page 17]

plea and prayers during days of peril even from simple places of dwelling, and not necessarily from houses of prayer, which from the days of their creation, were used by us to pour our discourse before Him.

These people of integrity got stubborn with me, and influenced me, despite my opposition, to fulfill their wish, and without an alternative – I went to the officer full of fear and with a broken heart. However, I set a condition that no matter what would happen – to scrupulously follow the decision of the officer in this matter.

To my great fortune, the officer emerged from his room at this moment, and saved me from the German soldier-dogs, and asked me in what matter could he assist me.

At this moment, I did not know his meaning, And I was almost certain that he was concealing some kind of trap with his genteel behavior. I thought I had come to my end.

I had no illusions, nor did I suspect that he had any attitude toward me that was human, and I did not believe that one righteous man could possible still exist in Sodom. After he heard my strange request, he replied:

I do not want you to think that I am a hater of Jews, and therefore – I do not object to you engaging in communal praying on your holiday as a matter of principle, however, my advice is – and this is for your welfare, is not to provide a possible source of incitement to the soldiers; do not go to the houses of worship, lest trouble befall you.

I thought to myself, here are cunning words from the mouth of the *Tzaddik* of Sodom. He shakes my hand, and sends me home.

In my room, people who were of our group awaited me, and when they heard the answer, all responded, "Let us do, Let us Harken."

I was convinced that I succeeded in my mission, and I gave thanks to the Master of the Universe that it was my privilege to guard the lives of these decent people. However, this did not create a [true] respite from the [inevitable] end.

Before dawn, on the first day of the New Month, when I peered through the window that was locked up and shuttered out of great fear – I was able to see how the Jews were going to the houses of prayer – garbed in *shtrymels*, satin *kapotes*, wrapped in their prayer shawls, as if nothing had happened, and without taking into account the bitter circumstances that had befallen us, with the capture of the town by the accursèd Nazis.

In the depth of my heart, I prayed to He who dwells on high, that he guard these of our decent brethren, but – it was all in vain. When it became known to the Germans, that the Jews had gathered in the houses of prayer, they fell upon them with an awful barbarity; they beat these unfortunates from the left and the right, and destroyed everything that fell into their unclean hands.

The decent and pure people who went, never to return, and who, in their death, gave us freedom, and even though they ended their days in smoke – in our eyes, 'They were impervious to the fire of the wicked,' and their memory will flower as an imperative of life forever and ever.

In the end, I beg forgiveness for all that I have forgotten, or about whom I knew nothing at all, and of those

[Page 18]

that I did remember, perhaps I have not made a proper assessment, and perhaps did not do justice to their spiritual position, and the value of their good deeds. You are the forgiveness.

I wish to offer a recognition of thanks and blessing that is due especially to the members of the committee, my friends:

Zvi Elimelekh Glanzer
Shmuel Zeinvil Tepper
David Langenthal
Shmuel Lieberman
Ben Zion Friedman
Sender Schmid

May they all live to see long and good days – who participated in the work, and helped me in my work, to publish this book.

May the purity of the martyrs who are recalled in this book protect me, and them, that we will be satisfied in all our desires for good and blessing.

Translator's footnotes:

    1.   The Yiddish words *kloyz* and *shtibl* are often used interchangeably for a small, clubby house of worship, established by people of a common persuasion and/or custom.

    2.   The traditional charitable institution of a *shtetl*, which not only distributed charity, but also made interest free loans, etc.

    3.   The traditional Burial Society, which was a hallmark of every established Jewish community.

    4.   "…Thereafter the *Hasidic* Court in Buczacz was headed until 1853 by R. Zadoik Rainek, followed by R' Avraham ben Zvi Teomim, author of *Hessed l'Avraham* (d. 1863)…" This reference suggests that the writer may have been a relative of the recipient.

    5.   It would appear that this ruling was endorsed formally by all of the sitting Chief Rabbis of the town. It is not clear why this was necessary.

    6.   A diminutive for Lejzor, or Eliezer.

[Page 19]

The Community of Cieszanow

by Dr. David Ravid

Our town of Cieszanow has been recognized for its Rabbis, Chief Rabbis and Sages for generations.

Our Rabbi, Rabbi Simcha Issachar Halberstam ל"ז, and later his son, R' Yekhezkiel ל"ז, with their *Hasidic* followers, who brought a rich and substantive *Hasidic* way of life to our town, were well known in the *Hasidic* world.

The mutual tolerance, of the various factions of the Jewish populace, was a model for all of the surrounding small towns.

Hasidic balebatim, manual laborers, and merchants, all intermixed under one roof of nationalistic striving, always understood that, in a time of danger, it was necessary to confront an external enemy with united strength.

As is known, our *shtetl* did not lack for anti-Semites, for when our Lisovskis and Szyewskis attempted to act up, they received a suitable reaction from our young people, without regard for their party affiliation. When it became necessary to defend Jewish honor, or Jewish assets, a unity reigned in our *shtetl*, would that such unity existed today among Jewish circles.

Our *shtetl* counted about 500-600 Jewish families, who earned their bread with scrupulous honesty in trade, labor, and in the independent professions. In our community, there were Jewish councilmen. There was a time when a conflict arose between the Polish and Jewish councilmen. The writer of these lines, himself one of the former Jewish councilmen, could write a book about his struggle with the anti-Semitic burgomaster, who only thought about how to compromise the interests of the Jewish citizens of our town.

This is the way we lived both in joy and in distress, until the accursed year of 1939 arrived, and the bands of Germans put an end to our community.

We, those few remaining Jews, who are found in Israel, come together every year, in order to remember this, that which we once possessed.

And we had a great deal. The Jews of our *shtetl*, especially our youth, was an unusual host of intelligent, intellectual and nationalistically aware people in which every cultural people could take pride.

And all this, together with the houses of study, libraries, and other cultural institutions, was exterminated and destroyed by the German murder-nation with their Polish and Ukrainian partners.

[Page 20]

The Cieszanow of Three Centuries

As previously said, I had the honor, or dishonor, for a short time, to be the representative of the Jewish populace of our area, or what was once called a '*Dozor*.[1]'

In this capacity, I had access to community affairs. Among a variety of old, interesting documents, I saw a document that was written in the Old Polish language, the document was dated from the year 1650, meaning, over three hundred years ago.

The following story is told in this document.

In the year 1648, or as I had calculated, to be the well-known sorrowful year of *Ta"kh*, almost all the Enemies of Jesus' to be found on Polish soil, were either driven out or killed.

Two years later, that is, in 1650, three Jews took up residence in our town of Cieszanow, who were saved from the hands of the Defenders of Jesus, these being Hirsch Shabbos, Mordechai Shia, and Abraham Shmukler, the first tilled the soil, the second sold alcoholic beverages, and Abraham Shmukler was a goldsmith, and seeing as there was a law of the land that forbade the Enemies of Jesus to live in the village, they were driven out at the end of 2 years of residence.

The first two Jews, Shabbos and Shia converted to Christianity, and because of this, they continued to remain in residence in our village.

My personal opinion – all of the Shabosowskis and Shiakowskis are descendants of the two [apostate] outcasts Hirsch Shabbos and Mordechai Shia.

I personally had the good fortune, that my great-grandfather of 300 years ago held onto his Jewish faith, and did not convert, but simply left the town which at that time consisted of only a handful of ramshackle houses, and the *Zhukov Gasse*, and he took up residence on the free field approximately 3-4 hundred meters away from the town. Later on, that is, as we read from this document – that after R' Abraham Shmukler built his compound, the spot that we knew as the *Ringplatz* in out town,, and in time, several other Jews took up residence, and it was in this manner that in the fullness of time, with the passage of centuries, that the Jewish settlement in our town developed.

From Cieszanow in Modern Times

I wish to recall, and awaken in the hearts of our *landsleit*, a feeling of both joy and sorrow.

Our town was known as an exception among all the surrounding towns through the worth of its Rabbinical Seat, and its *Hasidic* courtyard, which is reckoned to begin in the year 5653 [1893], that is from the well-know Sabbath of the portion of *VaYekhi*, when the elder Rabbi of Cieszanow, Rabbi Simcha Issachar Halberstam, may he rest in peace, was taken on as the spiritual leader of the community in our town.

[Page 21]

Up to the accursèd month of September 1939, approximately 500-600 Jewish families lived in the *shtetl*. As was the case in all small towns, the Jews derived their sustenance from trade and labor.

The uniquely Jewish trades, the shoemakers, tailors and bakers, would work for their own private gain, and for the market day which was held every Tuesday. Peasants from the surrounding villages filled up the large *Ringplatz*, Jewish merchants buying peasant produce, and the peasants from their side, transacted with the Jews – for clothing, leather, and necessary tools for the fields and wagons. I recollect this today, with mixed emotions, the sound of the iron axes, the ringing of scythes, and of the beer and whiskey glasses broken by the drunken gentiles.

Cieszanow had its Jewish way of life, spiritually rich, and its community social and cultural life was multi-variegated. There were parties from all persuasions, but the Zionist parties had the greatest influence in almost all walks of the community.

The *Bund* had influence over the Jewish workers, and craftsmen. Merchants had their own special class interests, but when it came to the general welfare of everyone, that means, when the community needed to defend itself against the anti-Semitic citizenry, we Zionists, members of *Mizrahi*, and other nationalist elements, would confer among ourselves, including our brethren from the *Bund*, build an iron unity, which the grandchildren of Hirsch Shabbos and Mordechai Shia, all the Shabosowskis and Shiakowskis could not break through with any degree of ease. Who among us does not remember the year of 1924?

It was the time of the resistance, when the *shkotzim*[2] of the surrounding villages gathered in the town, and had a mind to live it up a little at the expense of the Jews.

It began with an iron pot that a *pogromshchik* threw, and indeed, broke the pot on the head of R' Chaim Israel Schreiber, ז״ל.

As if by a secret signal, the entire mass of Jewish young people arose to defend Jewish honor.

If I am not mistaken, I think we laid out 2 *pogromshchiks*, paying no mind to the weak cries of the young priest ימ״ש, who cried out: '*Boze-chrzescijanski polska krew sie leje w polskim Cieszanowie.*[3]'

We just kept on dishing it out – because in a time of trouble, we were all like a bar of steel, forgetting all of our political antagonisms in the critical moment [of danger].

We, the nationalist youth, had our own location with a sanctuary for prayer, the *Bund* [had] a Peretz Library, the *Hasidic* Jew led his own way of life.

The Rabbi's side street, with the Rabbi's yard, the *Belzer Hasidim*, *Husyatiner Hasidim*, the Great *Bet HaMedrash*, was the place where the observant *Hasidic* way of life was concentrated. The Rabbi, R' Simcha Issachar Ber, ז״ל, and later, his unfortunate [sic: martyred] son, R' Yekhezkiel ז״ל, [each] had their adherents. They would come to spend their Sabbaths and Festival days at the Rabbi's table, from various cities in

[Page 22]

Poland, Galicia, and even from faraway Hungary, simultaneously bringing with them a freshening spirit of life into the *shtetl*.

I remind myself, that as a young *Hasidic* boy, of the spiritual and physical joy I felt during the Festivals and Sabbaths that I spent at the [home of] the Old Rabbi, ז״ל.

In his large house, at the time of the Third Meal, it is dark, there is a holy spiritual arousal – literally palpable to the touch, that poured out of the soul like some mighty fountain.

The Purim holidays, the *Simchat Torah* holidays, the joy and the sense of sanctity, can only be understood by someone who had personally lived a life of this kind.

By the final years before the Second World War, Sabbaths were already filled with culture and with Torah.

The bond with worldly Yiddish culture, and the Jew with Torah and Rabbinical tales, and also sneaking in a dance, forgetting that the morrow brings with it new concerns.

We who were on a nationalist platform, with the study of Hebrew, also did not forget to sneak in a lesson in the *Gemara* with *Tosafot*, and a chapter of the *Tanakh*.

And it was this pure and holy life that was annihilated by the German Satan.

Remember, O LORD, what is come upon us: consider, and behold our reproach.
(Lamentations, 5:1)

The Trial of the Scourge Eichmann in Jerusalem

The Organization of the Émigrés of Cieszanow in Israel

The Refined Technology of the German Nation…

"Mine eyes do fill with
tears, my bowels are
troubled, my liver is
poured upon the earth, for
the destruction of the
daughter of my people;"

(Lamentations 2:11)

During the entire time of the trial, I remained silent and held myself back from taking part in the discussion of the bestial inborn characteristics of this loathsome creature with a human visage, called Eichmann. I thought to myself –

so long as this loathsome creature stands before the bar of justice, and the sentence has not yet been pronounced, it is 'sub-judicia,' that is to say, to have uttered an opinion and in this manner is to have mixed into the juridical process affecting the sentence, which is forbidden by all legal codes.

However, after the sentence of the court in Jerusalem, when the dog was sentenced to die, and afterwards, when a variety of so-called 'noble spirits' with feminine soft-heartedness criticized the severe sentence, I was seized by a shudder in my extremities, in reaction to the Galantzes and Bubers, and their ilk.

And so, I permit myself to take a part in the discussion regarding whether the verdict has a just and moral foundation, despite the critique from individual Jews, and despite the elegant, so-called demonstration from the weak-hearted, who put forth their view against the verdict from Jerusalem, trying to enhance their credibility with the analytic reasoning of a Jesuit, saying that when a *Sanhedrin* handed down a death sentence once in 70 years, it was called a 'killer court.' (*Makot*, 7).

[Page 23]

Well – the Galantzes and company, I understand very well, they have their own method of reckoning. Were the loathsome creature to remain alive, he would most certainly write his memoirs, and as business people, they would buy his writings, and millions would fall into their pockets, paying no mind to the fact that through this loathsome creature, it is spilled Jewish blood that is making them rich, because business comes before everything else, but when I read the critical concerns from those who hold themselves out as the righteous people of our generation, and reside in the Diaspora, I permit myself to ask of them, as our teachers, to instruct us: a) Why was Our Teacher, Moses, permitted to carry out the judgement against the Scourge of the Jews called 'Amalek:' '*You shall erase the memory of Amalek from under the heavens.*' And there was no professor or Rabbi to be found that would protest against the just verdict of Our Teacher Moses, even Korah – Moses' greatest protagonist, remained silent. He took a full mouth of water, and quietly consented to the fact that Moses was right. And further – Why was it permissible for the shepherd David to sever the head of that enemy of Israel, Goliath? And at that time, not a single Jew could be found to protest against the judgement that David carried out, and also executed against the Eichmann of that time, on the contrary – the nation was grateful to David, and rewarded him by elevating him to be a king in Israel.

Why was it permissible for the woman, Yael, to deceive the Jew-hater Sisera, and split his skull and through this heroic deed this very woman entered the Jewish folklore history, for all time, even more – she is the recipient of great praise, such as in the *Tanakh*, as it says (Judges 5:24-26): '*Blessed above women shall Yael be, ... she smote Sisera, she smote through his head, yea, she pierced and struck through his temples.*'

Why was Mordechai the Righteous permitted to slaughter tens of thousands of enemies and we celebrate to this day, those miracles that enabled us to take revenge on our enemies, answer me, why, in your eyes, is the greatest enemy of the people of Israel in our long history any better than Amalek, Goliath, Sisera or Haman? These, the enumerated enemies wanted to, but did not live to bring us down, so they were beheaded, this evil man, Eichmann, regrettably exterminated a third of our people by the use if a variety of refined methods of execution, why then, do you take pity on him, on this outcast? And if I am not mistaken, there was not a great deal missing before your heads would have fallen at the feet of this Scourge Eichmann, ימ״ש.

We await your reply………

[Page 24]

The Miracle on the Collective Farm

Fear of Eichmann the Scourge, drove me together with my family into Stalin's regime – where I was one among tens of thousands of Polish Jews, who found themselves at hard labor in various of the Russian steppes.

After something less than a half year, of being incarcerated in a camp deep in the jungle[4] forests beyond the Volga, we were released and each individual fled in whatever direction one's eyes led them. May family and I were flung to a collective farm in Kirghizstan (today: Kyrgyzstan) not far from the three-point border between China, India and Russia.

Living conditions were such, that the best possible outcome was that one could hope to die of hunger. All my efforts to get out of this Hell, met with a categorical refusal both from the N. K. V. D. as well as the Kirghiz director of the collective farm.

For the entire time, they kept an eye on me, as if I were some unusual bargain, so that, God forbid, I should not somehow be uprooted from there. Having no choice, we worked in the Kirghiz rice fields from sunup to evening – for 600 grams of flour.

The 600 grams would have been able to sustain life, but the trouble was, that they were not distributed…day in and day out, we were compelled to work harder and more bitterly, we ate next to nothing, and drank our sweat.

After 6 months of living on the collective farm, my family and I were three-quarters on the way to the next world, but it was then that the great miracle occurred.

After my daily work, every day, I had an added responsibility – to find the Farm Director, and demand the bit of flour that we had earned by our hard labor. However, so that you should not take this incorrectly to mean, or fall into a mistaken belief, I must say to you, that most of the time, I was left demanding from him, and he – was not forthcoming…

And it was in this manner that weeks and months went by. On a certain day, being at the office of the Farm Director in the usual manner, to beg for a bit of flour for my labor, suddenly, a man and a woman appeared in the office with an 'official order' from the People's Commissariat in Tashkent, that in the course of 4 weeks time, our collective fam must construct a bathhouse – 'banya' in the local language.

Upon hearing this order, the Kirghiz (Farm Director) started to run hot and cold. Out of great fear, he turned to me with the following question: Tovarishch David Isiashevich, do you know if among your Polish people, there is a

[Page 25]

construction engineer who could undertake to build this bathhouse?

There is a saying in the world, that need can turn a dumb person into a cantor, and a cantor can become a construction engineer…that very thing transpired with me in that moment. Not thinking a great deal, I answered the Director that I do know a person among our people, who is a construction engineer, an expert, who had constructed the largest houses and factories in Poland, and that person is to be found among us on the collective farm. Hearing such good news, he regained his normal color, and he became lighter in heart.

All I ask is whether they have brought some sort of a plan with them. At my behest, I receive the required plan, and after a few minutes, I say the following to them: Tovarishchi! I, myself, am that great engineer, to which Poland is indebted for its cities and factories. I am the that very expert among experts, and I take on the burden of constructing the bathhouse in the course of 4 weeks, but only under the condition that those 4 weeks shall only commence after the Director will have provided me with all of the building material.

Hearing words like this, the Director, out of great inspiration and affection, gave me such a pat on the back, that I can feel it to this day…he cemented this with a rich Russian 'blessing' and immediately consented to turn over the work to me.

The salary for the work was set at 70 kg of wheat. So it was said, and so it was done.

I took a number of Jewish assistants to me, in order to take possession of 3 portions of wheat, and also arranged for my wife and 6 year-old son to be among them.

We made our own bricks out of clay, drying it under the sun, the roof was covered with 5 mm boards, but there was only one shortfall, according to my calculations the roof required 23 pieces of such board, in which each piece was a square, but I was only given 20 such pieces.

The other three [pieces] were stolen…the Director assured me that in time, I would receive the missing three boards.

The building was completed on schedule, and only a hole remained in the ceiling, the size of three boards…

According to the plan, the bath was built deep into the ground, with the roof aligned over the flat earth… I only want to add that the local climate was very agreeable to the native Israeli. That means, that three quarters of the year there was no rain. Well! The building was completed, as previously mentioned, on schedule. Out of great satisfaction, the Director, this time, kept his word, and turned over the previously mentioned 70 kg of wheat.

Now, good gentlemen, imagine our joy: every day, my wife, she should be well and healthy, cooked 'zacherkehs' – (kasha) and baked 'lepyushkas,' – (pletzl).

It was *Simchat Torah* in our house all week long, until…a misfortune occurred. In the middle of the night, an intense rain fell. Despite the fact that such a rain, in general, was a totally rare event, and especially at that season, when no rain at all falls. Well, imagine my troubles, when in the morning, I see that nothing more remained of my bathhouse than a pile of clay… in order to catch the fish in the net, I, naturally, immediately ran to the Director and appraised him of this great misfortune, arguing that the bathhouse had 'disintegrated' because the three pieces of board were missing in the ceiling, and the water had penetrated within.

Frightened by my words, the Director approaches me with the words: *Tovarishch*, I am making you cognizant

[Page 26]

of the fact that both of us are in danger of being sent off to the White Bears[5], for at least 10 years. There is one course of action by which both of us can be rescued from the consequences of this misfortune.

You must flee this place by this evening!

Afterwards, I will lay the entire blame on you, and I will be vindicated in one blow, and you will be designated as a real crackerjack…

The plan immediately appealed to me, and I consented to it on the condition that he, that means the Director himself, with his full authority, will provide me with a horse and wagon, and provisions for the journey…and this, my dear *landsleit*, is exactly what happened.

At 2:00 AM I packed up my bit of wretched possessions and fled to where the Black Pepper grows[6], together with my family.

The Director remained at the side of his fallen and soaked bathhouse, and I, along with my family, got out of that collective farm 'Garden of Eden' where a certain death by starvation surely awaited us.

A hole in the roof of a bathhouse saved an entire Jewish family from going under.

Translator's footnotes:

1.   *Dozor Bozniczy* is Polish, for Communal Leadership, or a *Va'ad Bet HaKnesset*. It consisted of three people, who, jointly with Rabbi, must work out a budget that meets the needs of community.
2.   The derogatory way of referring to a gentile as an abomination, usually for the manifestation of hostile behavior towards Jews, but not exclusively so. From the Hebrew, *sheketz*, meaning 'abomination'.
3.   Oh, Christian God, Polish blood is being shed in Polish Cieszanow.
4.   The writers, who describe their experiences in Siberia, frequently use the noun 'jungle' to describe their forest surroundings. In the West, this word normally applies to hot and humid regions, however, in this case, it is used to describe wild, densely overgrown forest areas, regardless of climate.
5.   This is one of those marvelously sarcastic Yiddish metaphors for the undesirable places of the world, which in this case is an allusion to the most desolate reaches of Siberia, where only the White (i.e. Polar) Bears are known to inhabit.
6.   The implication is that the family got to India or to an area sufficiently close to India, so that the climate enables spices to be cultivated. It may be Uzbekistan, but in any event, the meaning is clear: they fled to a place well beyond the reach of the communist police.

[Page 27]

Personalities & Pictures

Rabbi Yekhezkiel Schraga Halberstam ז"ל

Stalwarts of the High Heavens, and the Entire Heavenly Host say "Holy."

The martyr, Rabbi Yekhezkiel Schraga Halberstam, ז"ל, the last Rabbi in our town before the onset of the Holocaust, was a well-known righteous man, assuming the place of his father, of blessed memory, in the Rabbinical Chair.

In order to bolster my claim – I will introduce the tale from the Gemara regarding the decree against the Ten Martyrs of the Kingdom.[1]

When the evil decree was promulgated against the Ten Sages of Israel to be put to death, they designated Rabbi Ishmael the High Priest to ascend to the heavens, and to discover whether the decree indeed emanates directly from the Holy One, Blessed be He.

It is written that R' Ishmael purified himself, wrapped in his prayer shawl and phylacteries, and he pronounced the Ineffable Name out loud. The wind immediately transported him to the heavens, where he encountered the Archangel Gabriel, of whom he asked whether the decree was sealed, and coming from the Holy One, Blessed be He. Gabriel said to him, by your life – this is exactly what I heard from the other side of the curtain. And so he [R' Ishmael] said, and for what reason is this? And he replied, the Spirit of the Law stands accusing before the Seat of Honor, and daily says:

Have you not written anything in the Torah, that contains one letter that is invalid?

For is it not written in your Torah: He would steals a human being and sells him shall die, and have not the ten tribes sold Joseph, and you have not taken an accounting from them, and it is because of this – the decree was promulgated.

R' Ishmael said to him, to this time, the Holy One, Blessed be He, has not demanded an accounting for the selling of Joseph, and only sees fit to exact this from us? And he said, from the day that Joseph was sold, The Holy One, Blessed be He, has not found such righteous men in one generation as yourselves, and therefore, he is taking an accounting from you.

R' Ishmael immediately descended to earth, and informed his comrades that the decree had been promulgated and sealed. It is written: And while on one side, they bemoaned the fact that the decree was promulgated against them, they also were happy that The Holy One, Blessed Be He, had selected them specifically, to compensate for the sin of selling Joseph.

[Page 28]

And the two fates are equivalent, as was the case then, [so it was] at the time of the Holocaust, it was a decree of The Holy One, Blessed Be He, that our sainted Rabbi should be killed and was designated to be a martyr, and in his death, there would be an expiation of the 'sin' of the generation that had pursued a corrupting ethos, abandoning the Torah of Our Fathers, instead adhering to the lore of the 'Edomites,' that resulted in the ascendance of underlings to the position of sovereignty, and because of whose satanic sovereignty, tens of millions of men, women and children were exterminated in general, and six million of our brothers and sisters in particular.

Our Rabbi was the son of the Sainted Rabbi and Community Spiritual Leader R' Simcha Issachar, ז"ל; despite the fact that he died while still a young man, he was called 'The Old Rabbi' – the grandson and great-grandson of the Rabbinical Leaders of Zanz, Belz, the *Gaon* of Leipnik[2], going back to King David, ע"ה.

Rabbi R' Yekhezkiel Schraga ז"ל was endowed with many talents, a Sage, a man of substance, an exponent of law, who engaged in charitable activities, and dedicated his life to goodness, and did not stint so much as an iota on the ideas and views that he had, all of which were focused on strengthening traditional Judaism.

May his benefit, and the benefit of his sainted forbears guard over us and all Israel.

May His Soul Be Bound Up In The Bond Of Life

Rabbi R' Aryeh Rubin ז"ל

Rabbi R' Aryeh Rubin ז"ל, the Chief Rabbi of Cieszanow, the son-in-law of the righteous Rabbi and Head of Cieszanow, R' Simcha Issachar of the Halberstam family, זצ"ל

A personality full of grace, a phenomenal Torah scholar, alert, and whoever came in contact with him became bound up with him with all the elements of his soul. This righteous man, the son of a righteous man, was one of the greats, with a big soul, a treasure trove of goodness, and full of sensible and direct sayings, which lit things up like the rays of the sun. He was the master of rich spiritual vigor, full of joy and gladdening of the soul.

May His Soul Be Bound Up In The Bond Of Life Under The Wing Of The Holy Spirit

Rabbi Sholom Yekhezkiel Schraga

The youngest son of R' Leib Sternlicht ז"ל, Yaakov, נ"י who is in Israel

The Great Synagogue, on the left side is the bath and mikva in Cieszanow

[Page 29]

Seven of the good men of the town of Cieszanow, after the First World War. engaged in the repair of the wall around the cemetery
From Right to Left: R' Moshe Glanzer, ג"י; R' David Goetz, ג"י; R' Berish Schuster, ע"ה; R' Shi'keh Starkman ע"ה; R' Joseph Tanenbaum ע"ה; R' Koppel Goldberg, ע"ה; R' Shmuel Tepper ג"י

At the Time of the Repair of the Cieszanow Cemetery

Standing from Right to Left: R' Moshe Glanzer, ג״י; R' David Goetz, ג״י, r' Abraham Langenthal, ג״י, R' Yehoshua Starkman, ע״ה; and R' Joseph Tanenbaum ע״ה

Rabbi R' Yekhezkiel Schraga, may he live a long, good life, is a Rabbi in Brooklyn.

He is the son of Rabbi R' Aryeh Rubin ז״ל. It appears that the apple does not fall far from the tree.

The son, Rabbi Sholom Yekhezkiel Schraga, שליט״אalso provides the services of clergy in the Diaspora. He is a sharp Torah scholar, and a righteous man, in the tradition of his father, of blessed memory, as well as a talented individual, including the talent of an accomplished Scribe.

The compiler of this *Yizkor Book* had the honor of visiting this Rabbi, שליט״אat his home in Brooklyn, and I am not ashamed to say that during my visit, I felt a celestial joy in my soul, that in the moment, returned my soul to the days of my youth in Cieszanow, when I still adhered to the Old Rabbi and Leader ז״ל with all my soul, in order to study Torah and *Hasidism*.

May we be worthy of earning a true peace, peace on all of the people of Israel, and on the State of Israel.

Rivka Shmukler, Her Son Shimon, & Daughter Chana, ע"ה

This righteous woman met her end in the jungle forests of Russia. From the mouths of people who spoke with her in the camp, I became aware that she died from hunger, and from diseases that seized upon her in the freezing cold of the place to which she was exiled by the Stalinist armed forces. She was engaged in charity and good deeds for her entire life. There was not a family in the town, that was in need of support, that did not receive a package from her every Friday, for the requirements of the Sabbath and Festivals. With this, never did she reveal the name of the needy withing our earshot, the ears of the children. Charity, she would say, needs to be given with the greatest discretion.

The life story of the deceased is a long list of good deeds and a variety of experiences. The task of documenting this, and eulogizing her, is especially difficult for me, because, after all, she was my mother, and I – apart from the fact that I respected her boundlessly, I also lauded her as a wise woman, enlightened, of good heart, and full of lofty, spiritual and soulful sentiments. She was the daughter of the Rabbi R' Yerakhmiel Hertzberg ז"ל, of Lubaczow. Of which the Rabbi of Belz ז"ל said in his time: there are yet missing nine other Torah Sages to be added to this R' Yerakhmiel, in order that the enabling act be decreed... the coming of The Messiah. This woman who was exterminated in the Holocaust, was a woman of understanding and sympathy, possessed of a clear and strong conviction, a daughter of *Hasidism*, modest, and held in esteem by all.

[Page 30]

Her son, Shimon, and daughter Chana, were both killed in the city of Volodymyr-Volyns'kyj, being buried alive together with hundreds of their Jewish townsfolk.

May God avenge their blood, and may their pure souls be bound up in the eternal bond of life.

Reizl Koenigsberg, Two Daughters, & Brother Mordechai

Together with the sisters, Rachel Shapiro, Gitt'l Dornberg, Tzivia Bessekhs, Hinde Atlas, Chaya Weinberg, and their mother Ethel Koenigsberg, all were killed in the year 1942 in the Janowka-Lwow camp.

The elder lady, Ethel, was an intelligent woman, sensible, and good-hearted, a scion of the well-known Rapaport *Kohanim.*

Her youngest son, Pinchas Aryeh, was killed in battle, with the Germans, on the shores of the Volga River.

May Their Memory Be For A Blessing

May God Avenge Their Spilled Blood

R' Baruch Bessekhs & His Wife Tzivia Koenigsberg
A Scion of Cieszanow, Daughter of R' Moshe & Ethel, May They Rest in Peace

R' Baruch was a Torah Scholar, God-fearing, and an ardent devotee of the Old Chief Rabbi, ז"ל, and was someone who could lead prayers with consummate ability. His home was open to anyone who had a need. He, and his entire family were killed in the year 5704 [1944] by the Nazis in the 'Janowka' Camp in Lwow.

May God avenge their blood.

R' Mordechai Glanzer, ע"ה & the Members of His Family
Reizl Koenigsberg, Two Daughters, & Brother Mordechai

R' Mordechai Glanzer, ע"ה was known as a donor and giver of charity, with his heart open to assist the community. A God-fearing man, and an enlightened man, the son of R' Yitzhak Glazer ע"ה was a formidable Torah Scholar and a *Hasid.*

With roots deep among the leading families, he was considered to be very important among the people of our town, and he was considered to be among the more gifted minds in the town.

Sitting, from the right: His son, R' Elimelekh and his wife, R' Mordechai and his wife, their daughter Tamara and sister-in-law Faiga.

Standing from the right: The daughter of R' Leibl'eh Zandbank of Lewkow, his son, Moshe, Daughter Brachia, and the daughter of his brother-in-law R' David ז"ל.

Translator's footnotes:

1. Memorialized in the Yom Kippur prayer "Eyleh Ezkerah," recited during the repetition of the Musaf service on that day.
2. Today Lipnik in Moravia.

[Page 32]

R' Asher Dieler ז"ל, his wife Dwora and their son

Our outstanding friend, R' Asher Dieler, ז"ל, his wife Dwora and their son, all of whom were exterminated – after forced labor and severe illnesses – in the forests of Russia.

R' Asher was a scholar, a *Maggid-Shiur* of the *Gemara* in the *Bet HaMedrash* of the Zionists, which he did without pay, an ardent Zionist, observing the mitzvot both difficult and easy, in harmony with all about him, respected and held in esteem in all parts of the city.

May the Lord Avenge Their Blood.

R' Abraham Shmukler and his family

Sitting, from right to left: His wife, Charna, their grandson, and R' Abraham, ע"ה
Standing from right to left: Their daughter Zelda, their son Joseph with his wife, Reizl, ע"ה , and their youngest daughter, Sarah

Reizl Schmid ע"ה

Reizl Schmid, ע"ה. This righteous woman was a beacon among the women of the town, being involved in charity work, and guarded to ember of tradition in her own home, raising a family, along with her husband, R' Yehoshua, that was the pride of the city.

R' Abraham Goetz, ע"ה

R' Abraham Goetz, ע"ה was a Torah and Mezuzah Scribe, and ardent *Hasid*, God-fearing and an honest and straight man, always conducting himself with integrity and working honestly, one of the most important of the *balebatim* of our town.

[Page 33]

The lady, Rachel Lieberman from Lubliniec near Cieszanow

This righteous woman was incinerated as a martyr in Belzec, may God avenge her blood.

May her soul be bound up in the bond of life under the wings of the Holy Spirit.

A Handiwork of Shmelka Lieberman, Tishri 5730, B'nai Brak, Israel

This is a memorial scroll, configured as a triptych, and is translated as follows:

Yom HaShoah

10 Tevet 5703 has been set aside for the generations, as that bitter day, when we unite ourselves with the souls of our beloved martyrs, in order that future generations that come after us shall know to seek vengeance on their behalf for all time

Within the Star of David

Write down the memory
In the Book
And Put It in the Ears of your Sons
As a Memorial to the Martyrs of Lubliniec

Remember what Amalek did to you, and erase their name.

Text

In memory of the Paluh family from Lubliniec, ל"ז, R' Leibusz David Koren and his wife Shprinza, ל"ז, their son, Moshe and his family, ל"ז. Their daughter Reizl, and her husband Zelig, and their son, the young man Moshe, allegedly having died in Russia, ל"ז, may God avenge his blood, R' Dov Tepper and his wife Frieda and their children Mekhl and Chaya, ל"ז, The Graff family, ל"ז, The Kleinfeld Family, ל"ז, The Rosenblit Family, ל"ז, The Weltzer Family ל"ז, The Wertzel Family ל"ז, The Rubin Family ל"ז, The Schenk Family ל"ז, The Shtrigler Family ל"ז, R' Itcheh Meir Liebeh's and his family, ל"ז, The Lehrer Family, ל"ז, R' Yerakhmiel Bumal ל"ז, Leibusz David (Zilber) Koren, and his wife, who were killed in an accident on the road in Paris, and brought to burial in Jerusalem, the Holy City. May the light of the firmament always be the portion of the martyrs, and the spilled

[This panel is a variation of the *El Moleh Rakhamim* Prayer, usually recited at funerals, or annual visits to the grave sites of relatives, and is used in commemoration services for victims of the Holocaust]

The blood of your brethren cries out to me from the earth.

Text

In memory of my father, and teacher, R' Baruch ל"ז, and my mother and teacher, Rachel, ל"ז, my brother R' Chaim Eliezer and his wife Chaya, and their grandchildren, ל"ז, my brother R' Yaakov and his wife, Mindl, and their children, ל"ז, my sister Faiga, and her husband Moshe Lempel, and their children, ל"ז, my brother R' Elimelekh and his wife, Frimet and their children, ל"ז, and my daughter the young girl Chaya Sarah, who died on 19 Marheshvan in the year 5703 in Russia. My uncle, R' David Yaroslavitz and his wife Faiga, ל"ז, their son, R' Menachem Mendl, ל"ז, their daughter Reizl Shmukler, their grandson, R' Elimelekh ל"ז. My uncle's son, R' Chaim Sholom Yaroslavitz, ל"ז of Lubliniec. My uncle's son, R' Aryeh Leib and his wife Rachel and daughter Tzila, ל"ז. My uncle's daughter Shayndl Ratseh, and her husband Yaakov and their children, ל"ז. R' David Lempel and his two daughters, Chaya and Rivka, their husbands and children, ל"ז. Miriam Lempel of the Zaltsberg family, Dwora Lempel of the Bratt family and her son, the young man, Benjamin (Bennie), who fell in the discharge of his duty in the Sinai campaign. To the memory of all the residents of the community of Cieszanow, may their memory be for a blessing, those who were exterminated in the diaspora. May God avenge their blood. – May their souls be bound up in the bond of life.

[Page 34]

In the Takhkemoni School

The young people of the Takhkemoni School, in the middle – the Teacher, Mr. Fallig, currently a scribe and involved in community affairs in Argentina.

'HaTzofim' in Cieszanow

From the left, standing: H. Bluestein, R. Gershtenfeld, Kh. Schmid, M. Greenberg
Sitting: Sh. Brenner, Y. Goetz, Sh. Ziegel, B. Schlaf, may God Avenge their Blood

[Page 35]

R' Eliezer Taubenblatt and his wife

Aristocratic people from among the respected members of the town, may their memory be for a blessing.

The Tzigler Family

In the first row, from right to left: The son of R' Yaakov, R' Yaakov, R' Shlomo, R' Yehoshua, their brother-in-law, Mr. Weinberg, the second son of R' Yaakov.

The wife of R' Yehoshua – Miriam Yehudis ע"ה

R' Shlomo, R' Yehoshua, and R' Yaakov Tzigler were known as scholars and God-fearing men, ardent *Hasidim*, and lovers of good ways and charity.

R' Yehoshua ז״ל was especially exceptional in this regard when it came to the celebration of the Purim festival, and was a wonder that served as a model to the entire area.

Poor people streamed into the town from the entire area to take part in the Purim feasts of R' Yehoshua Tzigler, and after they had eaten and drunk to the point of insensibility, every one of them received a generous gift of charity as well.

The Tzigler family was one of the most respected families in our area.

May Their Souls Be Bound Up in the Bond of Life

R' Yitzhak Kaufman, שליט״א

A Seminal Thinker, A Visionary and Highly Gifted Torah Reader

[Page 36]

R' Leibli Sternlicht, ז"ל

"A Man's Wisdom Illuminates His Face," the prophet says. The wisdom of life poured forth from the countenance of R' Leibli Sternlicht, ז"ל. A Jew who was a scholar, a God-fearing man, he was one of the members of the *aliyah* drawn from the important populace of Cieszanow.

He was privileged to establish himself in the *Holy Land*, with almost his entire family, and derived ample nachas from his talented children.

He passed away in Tel-Aviv after a serious illness. May his soul be bound up in the bond of life.

The Kaufman Family

One of the Aristocratic Families of the City

On the right – the wife of R' Yitzhak, נ"י – Dina, ע"ה, a descendant of a rabbinical family, a perspicacious and good-hearted woman, died in Tel-Aviv approximately 18 Av 5723
On the left – Her daughter Faiga with her husband, Mr. Weissberg, who were exterminated at Belzec, may God avenge their blood

ת.נ.צ.ב.ה

R' Nahum Furman, ע"ה

R' Nahum Furman, ע"ה. among the most important of the *balebatim* of the city, a good man, loved by all. All matters that were difficult and complicated were brought before him, and with his acuity, he conveyed his point of view to the satisfaction of the sides involved. His home was open to all who were in need.

May God Avenge his Blood.

Rachil Neshi Furman, ע"ה

Mrs. Rachil Neshi Furman, the wife of R' Nahum, ז"ל.
One of the aristocratic women in the city, a righteous woman, and known for her
good deeds.

ת.נ.צ.ב.ה.

[Page 37]

An Israeli Hero – I

Yitzhak Isaac Stremer, the grandson of Yitzhak Isaac Stremer from Cieszanow – Zokov.
Fell on the altar of the State of Israel on 18 Tishri 5727, in the destruction of the "Eilat.[III]" May God avenge his
blood.
ת.נ.צ.ב.ה.

An Israeli Hero – II

Binyomin Lempel, ז"ל, the son of Mordechai and Dwora from Lazow beside Cieszanow, who fell in the Sinai
Campaign on the 26 day of Adar II 5717 (1957). His final resting place is in Kiryat Shaul.
ת.נ.צ.ב.ה.

The Rapaport Family – The Kohanim

From right to left: R' Joseph Rapaport, ז"ל, a scion of Cieszanow – during the war years he was in a labor camp in Siberia, working at forced labor, became run down, and fell sick from many physical and emotional agonies, and after a short while – after he returned from the Red Hell, he passed away in Paris.

His wife, sits opposite him, a righteous aristocratic woman, and at her side – their son. Both were killed at Auschwitz.

Beside R' Joseph, ז"ל, is seated their only daughter Shoshana-Rosa, may she have a long life, who lives in Paris and is known for her good deeds.

R' Joseph's permanent residence was in the city of Krakow, a city that in the past was a 'Mother of Israel,' and he was among the most important citizens there.

ת.נ.צ.ב.ה.

[Page 38]

R' Baruch Aryeh Kalechman ז"ל

An ardent Hasid, a scholar, a scion of an aristocratic family, esteemed by one and all.

The Goetz Sisters

Faiga and Rachel Goetz, the wife of Yaakov Goetz, were exterminated in Antwerp during the years of the Shoah. Faiga was the daughter, and Rachel the bride of R' Abraham Goetz ז"ל, a Torah Scribe from Cieszanow.
ת.נ.צ.ב.ה.

R' Joseph Tanenbaum ז"ל

In the perspective of years gone by, things appear to us in memory that are different perhaps from how they actually happened. Despite this, I wish to present several lines appropriate to the picture of R' Joseph.

The man was dedicated to his town with his heart and soul, and community matters kept him occupied day and night, and the issues of Cieszanow were at the forefront of his concerns. He served as the head of the community in the years before the Second World War, up to its outbreak.

At his death in 1942, he was only 53 years old. Several months before he died, his wife Dwora died, as well as his oldest daughter Adela, and her only son, David.

תנצב"ה

Two Righteous Women

Who saves even one single soul, it is as if he saved an entire world (Sanhedrin 37)

Reizl Shmukler, ע"ה (right) Chaya Weber ע"ה (left)

Reizl Shmukler, ע"ה distributed her money to charity and for good deeds. In the labor camps in Russia, during the war years, she helped the weak and sick with all she had, and thanks to her help with money and food, many survived.

Mrs. Weber was the daughter of R' Pinchas Mendl Tanenbaum ע"ה, and died on 25 Shevat 5722.

ת.נ.צ.ב.ה

[Page 39]

R' Abraham Ber Starkman, his wife and grandchildren ה"ע

[Shown are] R' Abraham Ber Starkman with his wife and their two grandchildren, Sabina and Shlomo, the children of their son, R' Chaim Starkman, נ"י.

This family was one of the most important and visible – because of their good deeds – in our town.

Grandfather and grandmother, and both grandchildren were killed by the German murderers. God – take revenge for their innocent blood that was spilled.

May their souls be bound up in the bond of life under the wings of [God's] holy spirit.

The Najman Family

The Najman Family was known for its nobility and the breadth of its heart. They were traditionalist, who observed the lesser mitzvot as well as the more important ones, ardent *Hasidim*, and followers of the Chief Rabbi R' Yekhezkiel Schraga, ז״ל, the last Rabbi before the Holocaust. May God avenge their blood.

May their souls be bound up in the bond of life, so they can stand to be judged at the End of Days.

The gravestone of a woman who was born in Cieszanow, who passed away in the Holy Land: Frieda daughter of Yehuda Buchholz, peace be upon her.

R' Moshe Lempel and Family

R' Moshe Lempel ז״ל, his wife and their children – All exterminated in Belzec – May God avenge their blood.

R' Yerucham Fishl Zeuerman

R' Yerucham Fishl Zeuerman ז"ל, killed by the Germans, may God avenge his blood.

[Page 40]

R' Simcha Schweber ז"ל

This perspicacious and understanding Jew earned his place with his entertainment during festivals in the house of the Old Chief Rabbi ז"ל of Cieszanow, of whom the deceased was an ardent follower. Murdered by the Nazis, ש"ימ.

His son Eliezer, ע"ה fell in battle against the German Satan in the year 1942.

God will avenge their blood, and may their memory be for a blessing

R' Mordechai Schrieber & his wife, ז"ל

R' Mordechai Schrieber ע"ה died in the *Holy Land* in 5726, and his wife Faiga died in 5722. Very dear and quiet people, they went in the way of the Torah and tradition.

The late Faiga was recognized as a person of exceptional spiritual qualities. On every Friday, or on the eve of a Festival, she would gather foodstuffs and distribute it to the needy of the city.

May Their Memory Be for a Blessing.

[Page 41]

The Schneider Family

From right to left: Reizl Schneider, her son, Mordechai, R' Yukel Schneider, ז"ל
Standing: R' Joseph Schneider נ"י, and the youngest in the family, Zvi

A Repentant

M. Joseph Schneider, the son of R' Yukel Schneider ז"ל, writes to me from Brazil, and beseeches me to reveal his 'transgression' in the *Yizkor Book*, and his error in believing the false Red world leaders, in whom he – and his comrades believed the way a pious Jew believes in the Messiah, without them, meaning only the Reds will bring salvation to all of humanity and among them the hapless Jewish people.

His emotional articulation, filled with heartache, cry out from his soul and from every written line, from every word, and from every letter.

His disappointment is so enormous, and his heart is so embittered against the Communist leaders of the world – to the point of bursting. and foremost, his bitter cry is directed against the Polish bandits whom he recollects even to this day, their irrational, murderous assault against the defenseless youth in Cieszanow, to whom the letter writer belonged, and who – as he writes, felt – in school, in the street, on the job, and at every turn, their feral incitement and their cry of '*Zydy do Palestina*' '*Parszywy Zyd*' etc.[2]

After decades of being in the so-called free land of Brazil, and after so many years of believing in the Red doctrine of that bandit and murderer Stalin, ימ"ש, he concluded that there was not any great difference when it came to Jews – between Hitler's brown [shirt] murderers and Stalin's Red anti-Semites, both ideologies are built on Jew-hatred, evil, abandonment and neglect of personal freedom, and careerism at the expense of all humanity.

Our friend, Joseph Schneider portrays his younger years in Cieszanow and comes to the conclusion that the children of the *balebatim* were correct, who recognized that Poland , Germany, Russia, was not the place for the hapless Jewish people, and even not Brazil, where the writer lives now, allegedly – in peace, but only in the Land of Israel – only in the State of Israel, can a Jew live out his life proudly, as a Jew and a human being, not to be insulted by anyone – as a Jew, and not to have to put up with all manner of abuse from such primitive and murderous bandits such as the German Nazis, Polish pigs, or Ukrainian beasts.

Translator's footnotes:

1.   In October 1967, the Israeli destroyer and flagship *Elat* was sunk by a missile fired from an Egyptian ship docked in Port Said; Israel retaliated with the destruction of Egyptian oil refineries at Suez.
2.   These were epithets, commonly hurled by anti-Semitic Poles at Jews. These two translate as 'Jews to Palestine,' and 'Mangy Jews.'

[Page 42]

From the People of Our City

A group of people, almost all of whom, excepting the first one standing in the first row, Mr. Joseph Shmukler, and the first reclining on the right, Mr. Chaim Starkman, may they both be granted good lives, are no longer alive. Most of them were killed in the Holocaust era.

ת.נ.צ.ב.ה.

From right to left (Standing): Joseph Shmukler, His wife, Reizl, Moshe Shmukler, the daughter of Wolf Schmid, Sarah Shmukler-Hordhowski, Melekh Nadel
The second row: Chaim Starkman, currently in Argentina, Mikhl Shmukler, and the son of Hirsch Drayman

Cieszanow Children

A group of Cieszanow children – girls at a Purim Ball in the year 1937

In the Hebrew School

The boy and girl pupils of the Hebrew School in Cieszanow under the direction of Mordechai Kaufman – now in Argentina

From the Intellectual Youth of Cieszanow

From right to left: Schreiber, Kaufman, Spiergel, Eichbaum, and Tanenbaum
Sitting: Sali Tepper, Shoshana Ravid – an actress in 'HaBima'

R' Mordechai Schreiber,יח', and his wife, Eidel ז"ל

R' Mordechai ben Chaim Israel Schreiber, long life to him, and his wife Eidel, who passed away on 11 Adar 5720 in Tel-Aviv. May Her Soul be Bound Up in the Bond of Life Under the Wings of the Holy Spirit.

[Page 43]

The Rabfogel Family

family of Shlomo and Rivka Rabfogel and their son, who were privileged, after physical and emotional tribulations and suffering, to settle in the Holy Land.
May the Good Lord look over them, and may they be privileged to enjoy plenty, nachas from their children, together with all of the residents of The Land, in peace and tranquility.

R' Joseph Eichler, Chana Eichler

R' Joseph Eichler and his wife, Chana, may they rest in peace,
were killed by the Nazis in the year 5703, may God avenge their blood.

R' Joseph ז"ל was a man of pleasant demeanor, God-fearing, a gifted leader of prayer, who educated his children in Torah and the [Jewish] tradition.

ת.נ.צ.ב.ה

The Rabfogel Daughters

From right to left: Chaya, Leah-Blume, and Ethel, May God Avenge Their Blood

R' Zvi Rabfogel and his wife Tova, may they rest in peace, were killed in the Holocaust in the city of Cracow, together with their daughters, Chana-Riva, and those who appear in these pictures.

This aristocratic family was one of the most respected families in the city, known for its good deeds, in the giving of charity and good works.

May Their Souls be Bound Up in the Bond of Life Under the Wings of the Holy Spirit.

David Ravid and his wife

The Editor, Dr. David Ravid and his wife Sarah,
née Koenigsberg, after their marriage

[Page 44]

A Memorial Candle for Our Mothers

One of the most sensitive responsibilities assumed by the 'Organization of the Emigrants of Cieszanow in Israel,' is to eternalize the memory of their sacred community that gave its life in the Sanctification of the Name.

In the ranks of this sacred duty, we have provided a series of articles which record and provide a permanent memory of a number of the prominent people 'personalities,' Rabbis, scholars, community activists, and the like, but the dearest of all the dear are our 'mothers,' whom we have forgotten, but the feeling of honor and respect makes it incumbent upon us to recall our 'grandmothers' who earned a good name for themselves through their warm hearts, with their tireless activity on behalf of the common good, for the benefit of the large number of the poor, and sick, who could be found in our town.

Among the countless groups that dispensed charity, which had an impact in Cieszanow, it was the women who occupied the important positions with their activity. Their home was always open to the needy, and their objective especially was to give 'charity in anonymity.'

May my few lines [here] serve as a memorial candle for their holy souls. Their names will remain in the history of our town of Cieszanow as a symbol of charity, justice and gentleness, compassion and a good heart.

[Page 45]

My Little Town, Cieszanow

by Dr. David Ravid

Fragments and Memories from the Life of Cieszanow Families

The Evil Spirit, '*HiSta-Khrumika*' Dominates the World

It is the year 1912, two years before the outbreak of the First World War, and I find myself, on a ordinary hot summer Sabbath, after noon, at the table of my sanctified *Rebbe* – humming along the sorrowful melody of 'Rafschein-Sanzer' the liturgical tune of the '*Eitkanu-Seudasa*' for the *Shaleshudes* [The Third Meal].

The heat was terrifying in the large house where the *Rebbe* presided over his *Tisch*[1], and the dense air was literally palpable to the fingers, mixed with the odor of sweat, onions and herring, which intoxicated the senses. Meanwhile, the familiar *Shaleshudes* darkness oppresses the soul.

The *Rebbe* Speaks the Law

A fiery flame circles above the heads of the *Hasidim*, and they think – that maybe they are really seeing angel fluttering and hovering over them, with their pure white wings, over and about the Rebbe's face, pale and white as chalk lime.

Suddenly, the Rebbe throws back his great round and noble head, as handsome as a round egg, dreams off – and it becomes as still as a grave in the house.

All that is heard is the buzzing of a fly which dances about on the window pane, which is located not far from the Rebbe's seat.

In the meantime, seconds and minutes go by, and the gathering of *Hasidim* is anxious to the point of bursting. Just as a clap of thunder comes unexpectedly, so did a wild cry come from the Rebbe's mouth, 'Jews, Repent!' – Jews, you sons of compassion, if you were to know what a sorrowful time is drawing near, especially for the Jewish people, you would bury your heads in the earth, in order not to see and to feel the coming reign in the world of the Evil Spirit, '*HiSta-Khrumika*.'

For nearly a half century, his *Hasidim* broke their picks trying to understand these esoteric words of prophecy from their Rebbe.

These plain words from their Holy Rebbe began to reveal themselves immediately with the onset of the First World War in their bare full effect, with the pogroms of Petlura, and other enemies of the Jews of Russia, Ukraine, Poland and other lands.

Only after such beings as: Hitler, Stalin, Khrushchev, Mao Tse-Tung and Castro dominated nearly the entire world, and after these previously mentioned beasts killed off tens of millions of innocent people, among them

[Page 46]

six million Jews, did the *Hasidim* understand the key to the prophecy of their Rebbe: "The time of the Devil's '*HiSta-Khrumika*,' draws nigh."

The esoteric expression of their *Rebbe, HiSta-Khrumika*,' was an acronym for the five world leaders who, with their nations bear the responsibility for the majority of the millions of men women and children who were murdered, and among these guilty, through the greatest recognized enemy and murderer of the Jewish people in our long history, Hitler ימ״ש.

The writer of these lines will attempt to portray images from his young years, when he was rooted in the Galicia of [The Emperor] Franz Joseph.

These will be portraits of Jewish generations in Galicia "who are now cut down at the hand of the so-called 'Nation of Culture,' in front of the eyes of other 'Nations of Culture,' who are partners in this crime."

I also wish to attempt to preserve these personalities and all their experiences, in their struggle for existence, in their way of life, in their good deeds of scholarship, loyalty, and their constant yearning for a good life, and a striving for a higher spiritual level.

In my telling of this tale, the life of a young man from a family of *balebatim* will play itself out, from the time of the First World War (1914-1918), the Second World War (1939-1945) and to the last, an active participation in the Arab-Israeli War (1948-1949) in the Land of Israel.

I will also communicate something of the intellectual and emotional atmosphere of this past era, especially that of the former Austrian Galicia.

I want to make the effort, on behalf of my readers, to portray for them, and display to them, a rich gallery of personalities, of the communal. psychological and emotional forces that altered the face of the world, and thereby positioned it for the extermination of a large part of humanity.

Every type of personality presents a different aspect of the mosaic of the altered society to me.

* * *

An uproar , a groan, a sigh rises from the town of Cieszanow, on the border between Czarist Russia and Austrian Galicia, where Jewish men and women cannot find a place for themselves.

Ye Gods! What does one do? To where can one flee?

Precisely at Passover, the Magistrate of the town ordered the Rabbi along with the head of the community, R' Pinchas Rosenblatt summoned to him, and advised them that on the following day, that is to say, precisely on the first day of *Hol HaMoed*, they have to provide ten young Jewish men for the draft, which is to take place in the town.

In accordance with the size of the Jewish population in the town, year in and year out, the requirement was, that ten Jewish soldiers were to be provided to the Czarist army.

No amount of weeping and pleading is of any help, ten Jewish boys have to be provided by the community.

[Page 47]

Jews have a folk-saying: "With each misfortune, comes a bit of good luck."

The community had the right to send anyone that it wanted to as a soldier, because the Czarist authority only demanded a contingent from the locale, and the contingent for the town of Tomaszow was ten Jewish soldiers, and if they were weak or sick, this was no liability to 'Ivan,[2]' the foremost thing being that it was required to present ten 'Yevreis' on the spot.

The community *khappers*[3] knew exactly from which house to grab a candidate, once given the nod from the head of the community.

The decree had no impact on the sons of the 'beautiful Jews,' they sleep in their beds at night, they study Torah in the during the day, without fear, as if the bitter decree does not refer to them, and that the specific line written does not apply to them.

This decree of the regime applies only to those Jews of Tomaszow that live in the crooked alleys behind the bathhouse.

By happenstance, the sons of Abraham Wassertreger (The Water Carrier), Beryl Schneider (The Tailor) and Mekhl David Schuster (The Shoemaker) found out in a timely fashion that the community *khappers* were going to make a run through their streets, to tear those sons from their mothers' arms that had been designated as the sacrifice for all those 'beautiful' little boys to go serve the Czar as soldiers.

The town of Tomaszow lies in a valley, and just as God had sent a tribulation to the Jews, and it becomes necessary to flee from that tribulation, God also provides a cover, a teeming rain mixed with thunder and lightning, precisely in the middle of the night, when frightened young boys are fleeing the town.

An antediluvian flood rain storms over the town.

The streets of the place are flooded with water and mud, it is cold and wet, and ever body member trembles from the cold.

Eyes become blinded by the naked bolts of lightning, and after each such lightning bolt, eyes become doubly darkened.

What is the Jewish expression: "At a time of trouble, when one seemingly has no options, the fool becomes a wise man, and the weak becomes strong."

Ignoring the rain and the storm, they ran as if from a fire.

[Page 48]

A fourth boy was swept up with the three youngsters, also he Shlomo, from a poor home in Tomaszow, found out about the great secret, that there will be seizing of boys after the first days of Passover.

Shlomo, a healthy young lad, a marketplace merchant, dealt in flax, swine hair, chickens, geese and grain, but few blessings remained for him from all of these endeavors.

The poverty in Shlomo's home was so great, that he was compelled to become a merchant when he was ten years old, in order to help his mother to make a living, his father having died when Shlomo was a year old. At the age of ten, Shlomo was compelled to leave the *Heder*.

Shlomo never went to synagogue, first – as previously mentioned, he needed to assume the burdens of making a living while still young, but more to the point, was fear of the hooligan gentiles.

Shlomo was a decent, law abiding and quiet person.

Just as he was physically strong, massive and primitive, his soul, by contrast, was pure, gentle and good.

Shlomo demonstrated his complete gentle beauty immediately at the time of fleeing from the town, in the rain, mud and cold.

It happened, as often does happen in such a tragic moment, that one of those who fled, became sick from great exertion and exposure to the cold and wetness, and contracted a severe fever, and could not move from his place.

The Polish road that stretched from Tomaszow to the Austro-Galician town of Belzec was surrounded by thick forests of pine trees.

Many sawmills, called '*tartaki*,' were to be found in these forests, which on the Polish-Russian side belonged to the Graf Czartoryski, and the Austro-Galician Baron Watmann on the Austrian side of the border.

These sawmills were largely in Jewish hands.

The *balebatim*, employees, and overseers of the lumber industry in this locale, were all our brethren, Jews, in contrast to the forest watchmen, hewers of wood, wagoners and cutters, who were poor peasants from the area, since the sons and daughters of the village families were distanced from their poor father's heritage by their older brothers.

And these self-same sawmills are worked intensively, the chute in the sawmill does not rest either by day or night.

In a pile of cut timber, almost up to half a body length, stands the worker, Kaczynski, who with his strong hands keeps on pushing the six-meter blocks of wood into the chute, and on the second side, in the same position, stands the worker Pietruczka, pulling the cut boards out with his strong hands from the chute.

The owner of this sawmill, R' Gedalia Schreiber, a Jew with a bit of a belly, wanting to make an impression on his appointees and workers, wraps his corpulent body in a heavy sheepskin, despite the fact, that come Passover, the frosts are already in the past.

[Page 49]

He appears in front of his forest workers in this sort of a pose, and with a good word, a sharp bit of wit in Polish, or a wink in his eye to a young female worker, he endears himself to this gentile coterie.

In the 'night shift' of the first days of Passover, R' Gedalia was forcibly called to the sawmill, since a well-known lumber merchant had arrived from Byten, who wants to close his big transactions exclusively with the owner of the mill, and not his director, R' Moshe Honigsberg who had that authority in the name of R' Gedalia, to conclude all possible business.

Out of respect for this important guest from Byten, Herr Neumann, R' Gedalia made the effort, ignoring the fact that a frightful weather reigned in the streets, a rain mixed with snow – a sign that in Heaven, it had not yet been decided whether this night would belong to the winter just passed, or to the coming summer.

In the middle of this, R' Gedalia ordered his wagon driver, Fishl, to get the wagon ready, and be prepared to be on the way in a half an hour.

The road, which had been paved by Austro-Galician peasants, meanders for twenty kilometers from R' Gedalia's town of Cieszanow to the forest.

The conveyance on which R' Gedalia rides, driven by his wagon driver, Fishl, glided along this stone-paved road.

Riding along the way, an intensive discussion developed between R' Gedalia and Fishl the wagon driver, regarding a variety of social questions.

Time passed, the clock showed eleven o'clock – it is already twelve, and they ride, and ride, absorbed in their conversation, they failed to notice that the horses had strayed off the road, and they found themselves in the middle of the forest.

Suddenly – they hear a man calling from the thick forest – '*Stehen-bleiben*!'

They were frightened to the depth of their souls, not knowing who was calling to them, and what is wanted of them.

They thought, at midnight in the forest, this can be no other , and they were immediately certain, that this was not just anybody, but rather the 'Wayfarer' and well-known robber, Mayevsky, who was known by all, and a terror to all the residents of the area.

As usual, when Jews find themselves in danger, they take a long time to get down from their wagon, first – one looks for one's *tzitzit*, to assure that –God forbid – a thread is not missing – '*Shema Yisrael*' is recited seven times, then one spits, and says: 'It hasn't occurred, hasn't happened – The Angel Who Redeems Me from All Evil[4].'

A person, stepping quickly, draws near from the distance, and from the silhouette of the person they noted that it was a man, tall, broad, strong, with firm feet and hands.

[Page 50]

There remained no doubt with them that this was none other than the robber Mayevsky.

In this critical and dangerous moment, R' Gedalia went through an accounting of all his deeds to the present, coming to the conclusion that since the end has arrived, a Jew must naturally repent for all the transgressions he had committed during his life, and as it seems, R' Gedalia had a heavy load of past sins on him, because according to his vigorous striking of the heart while saying '*Al Khet*,' during the recitation of the confession, and thereby also pouring out a river of tears, it would appear – that this burden was very significant.

When two Jews find themselves in danger, assaulted by a murderer, a dog, or a gentile hooligan, the more refined Jew hides himself behind the coarser Jew, such that the coarser Jew stands exposed first with his face towards the oncoming danger.

Saying '*Al Khet*,' R' Gedalia slowly pushed himself behind the back of his wagon driver Fishl, waiting for the murderer Mayevsky.

Fishl had driven R' Gedalia in his wagon for his entire life, and therefore had great respect for him.

Fishl also was seized with a fright. But, alas, he had no one behind whom he could shove himself, their ears could hear the beating of their hearts.

In that moment – they hear a call from the man, who in the meantime was now standing by their coach – '*Jews!*'

R' Gedalia and his wagon driver, opening their eyes, which they had shut tightly, in order that they not see – how the murderer Mayevsky was going to stab them in the heart with his long knife, in the first instant did not know what was going on.

They were almost certain that it was all over for them… that they were in the World to Come, as a sign – an angel was asking them, in Yiddish no less, '*Are you Jewish*?'

R' Gedalia immediately touched himself on the forehead and noted that a cold sweat was pouring down his brow, and it is as if he had just emerged from the *mikva*.

Not being entirely certain, and despite this, he stretches out his right hand and says '*Sholom Aleichem a Yid.*' Shaking, and with teeth chattering out of great fear.

He receives a warm reply: '*Aleichem Sholom.*'

Shlomo wants to say something, but R' Gedalia, immediately assuming his arrogant pose, knowing almost with certainty that this is not the robber Mayevsky, he asks a question directed at no one in particular, well my dear sir – tell me something huh? Are you not one of the no-goods? Well, yes? You should know that in my *tzitzit*, not one thread is missing, and each and every erev Shabbat, my *mezuzot* are inspected by R' Aharon the Scribe, and, if all of these virtues are for you, 'Devil' insufficient, I will shout out in my loudest voice, '*Shema Yisrael*,' and you will be transformed instantly into ash and dust.

Shlomo immediately grasped the correct condition of the emotional wreckage of the two frightened Jews.

[Page 51]

Shlomo attempted to calm them down, and himself began to recite the *Shema*, and in this manner, reading through the entire portion, he drew closer to them, and in this manner, asking R' Gedalia with a warm and friendly voice – well, my fellow Jew, are you calmed down yet?

What I mean, says Shlomo, is that you no longer need to have misgivings about my 'humanity' because a 'Devil' doesn't read the *Shema*.

Did you understand?

Their normal physical and emotional state righted itself immediately after Shlomo explained himself. R' Gedalia re-boarded the wagon, straightened out his feet, again assumed his hauteur, and with arrogance, asked of Shlomo – Nu? What does a Jew require?

I must tell you, my dear Jews, Shlomo responds – that God does not sleep, he sent you at the correct moment, like an angel to help us.

I find myself here in the forest, with a friend of mine, who became ill along the way, fleeing from the *khappers* in our town.

Shlomo relates further, two of our comrades have abandoned us at the minute that the sick one could not continue moving by himself, and I carried the sick one on my back until I crossed the border.

Coming to the forest in the middle of the night, not knowing where we were, exhausted, hungry and frozen, I laid my sick comrade down under a tree.

Now, I have come to you to ask for help, you must ride over with the wagon about two kilometers from here, and take us to a place where your people live.

Asking no one, Shlomo jumped into the carriage, he tugged on the reins, shouted *"Via!"* in the direction where his friend Abram lay.

True – R' Gedalia did not oppose this, in his heart he took pleasure in the fact that God had specifically sent him to perform this great and valuable *mitzvah*, to rescue a sick Jew from two evils with one blow, from illness, and from the hands of gentiles.

However, really deep in his heart he was not completely convinced that Shlomo was really human, and Jewish to boot, who knows, he thought to himself, what sort of joke the 'No-Goods' and the 'Devils' are capable of perpetrating?

Realistically, it is the middle of the night.

Apart from this, he thought, and this irreligious thought also occurred to him, that the 'No-Goods' in these times are of a sort, that they do not fear *tzitzit* that are ritually correct, *mezuzot* that are kosher, and not even the *Shema*.

In the meantime, Shlomo asked no questions, and only drove the horses, the horses running over the paths, along the ways and around the bends, in order that he arrive more swiftly to rescue his friend, he needed to

[Page 52]

act in this daring manner, even though it was against his normal behavior, and contrary to his effacing character.

Arriving at the tree, Shlomo ran to Abram with quick strides, and lifted the ill man in his strong hands, and like a heap of straw, he tossed him into the wagon.

R' Gedalia took off his heavy sheepskin coat, covered the sick man, and before they even moved off from the spot, R' Gedalia took out a bottle of Slivovitz from his purse, and poured a bit of these bitter drops into Abram's throat, ordering his wagon driver Fishl to find the fastest way possible out of the forest, in order to be able to meet with Herr Neuman at the earliest possible time, who expected to catch the Lemberg-Vienna-Berlin express train at seven o'clock in the morning after leaving the sawmill.

He clock showed half after two past midnight.

When Fishl gave the horses a whip in their rear legs, the wheels of the wagon started forward with a splash of mud and water, with three at half right, and with a violent pull, exited from the forest, drawing close to the road that would lead to the sawmill in Belzec.

In the meantime, the ill Abram warmed himself up considerably, lying covered up with the heavy sheepskin, but it appears that what really warmed him up was the Slivovitz that R' Gedalia Schreiber poured into him at the time that Shlomo laid him in the wagon.

Gradually, Abram came to, and until R' Gedalia and his wagon driver got themselves oriented out of the confusion of the events, the wagon, and its entire complement arrived at the village.

At the gate of the sawmill, which was illuminated by a weak electric light, which was powered by a small generator owned by the sawmill itself, stood a watchman wrapped in a heavy overcoat.

As soon as he took note of his Jewish boss, he opened the gate with an expansive, '*Dzien Dobry Panu*!' And they vanished into the courtyard of the sawmill which was full of mounds of split blocks and boards.

* * *

Abram lay in R' Gedalia's sawmill for a week's time, his comrade Shlomo attended him, and cured him, the village *feldscher* ordered that Abram be treated by cutting a blood vessel behind the ear, and putting eyelets, cups[5] in mustard [plaster] and other such remedies.

Shlomo carried out everything in accordance with the *feldscher's* orders, and after eight days, Abram improved to the point that they decided to leave the sawmill, and to travel further in the Austro-Galician province, until such time that God will provide them with some means of earning a living, or an appropriate

[Page 53]

wedding match.

Here, on Galician soil, they a little more free, that means that they were protected and secure from the Czar's forces, and they had no great fear of the Austrian gendarmerie with their green feathered tall hats, because firstly – because they learned from the Galician Jews, that the gendarmes had an explicit order from the Kaiser, Franz Joseph, may his glory be elevated, to 'look through their fingers' at Russian Jews who flee across the border from Russia to Austria.

But what satisfied them the most, and calmed them, was the fact that Franz Joseph's gendarmes spoke almost a Yiddish-like language, so because of this, they thought that in the worst case, that even if a gendarme tried to take them up, they will be able to reason with him, using familiar phrases. How does a person not take pity on a Jewish refugee, even if he is a gendarme?

Simultaneously, he would ask the gendarme, what is it to you if we choose to live in *Froyim-Yossel's*[6] country?

These thoughts strengthened the will behind their mission, and with confident steps, they traveled deeper into the new land.

Dragging themselves over villages and towns, they – meaning the two friends, Shlomo and Abram, arrived Wednesday morning in the first Austrian town with the musical name of Cieszanow.

The Austrian owner of the entire area resided in this town, the so-called '*Bezirkhauptman*.'

This Master, appointed to his post, was something of a minor king.

To be able to see the *Bezirkhauptman* personally, with one's own eyes, was tantamount to a holiday for the lower classes, a privilege.

However, this privilege was extended to them only twice in the year, on the eighteenth of August, which was the birthday of the Kaiser Franz Joseph, on which day, all of the residents of the town gathered together in the marketplace, and there, several days before, the children of the town would gather old things, douse it in kerosene, and on the night of the Emperor's 'Name Day' light a great fire.

When the '*Bezirkhauptman*' approached the bonfire, everyone took off their hats, and with great earnestness, as was the case in the synagogue during prayer, sang the Austrian [national] anthem, '*Gott Behalt, Gott Beschutze Unser Kaiser, Unser Land.*'

When the assembly finished singing, the '*Bezirkhauptman*' bowed his head with great dignity, and left the location.

The second time this nobleman appeared before his citizens on the anniversary of the date when the Empress

[Page 54]

Elisabeth was assassinated.[7]

On that day, the Jews would assemble in their houses of worship, recite Psalms for the soul of the Empress, and the Rabbi and the Head of the Community would hold forth with speeches, the finale of those annual patriotic speeches was every year nearly always the same.

The result of this was a song of praise for all the three 'K's' The Kaiser should live, the *Kommandant* should live, and also the '*Koymenkerrer*' [the Chimney Sweep] should live. Bravo…bravo… everyone shouted, and clapped their hands out of great joy.

It was on one such holiday that the two former Russian Jewish boys arrived in the town.

The boys opened their dreamy eyes, like eight-day old children suckling at their mother's breast being awakened to the tumult of reality.

They began to think in a practical manner, and Abram being a watchmaker by trade, didn't need to think very long, went off to the big city, and it appears he succeeded there.

By contrast, Shlomo was a merchant, meaning that he had never acquired a trade in hand, and because of this, he, in the end, was forced to remain behind in the town of Cieszanow.

The first days in the town were a denouement for Shlomo, without relatives, without acquaintances.

People, by Shlomo's thinking lived in an entirely alien 'milieu' relative to what he was familiar with, and were a great novelty to him, as if they were people from a different planet.

The songs of praise, and good words being offered for their Emperor, and just the officials, was a novelty to him, and deep in his soul, he mocked what he considered to be the naive Galician Jews, and thought to himself – it is not for nothing that in Russia we refer to them as '*Kira Mak,*[8]' and he simply could not comprehend how a Jew could suddenly love his king.

Only a Jew who was a fool could do this, he thought, or a person with a screw missing upstairs.

Under no circumstances could Shlomo understand that it is possible for Jews to be great patriots of their land, if the gentile citizenry does not carry out pogroms against them.

But the real difference between the Russian Jews on the other side of the border, and the Galician-Austrian

[Page 55]

Jews on this side of the border is that – with the Russians, a real so-called '*numerus-clausus*□ was in force, as regards Jewish young people, and from time to time, a bit of a pogrom was thrown in as an addition, but there was no lack of ways to make a living, and not only a livelihood – there were even quite wealthy Jews in 'Ivan's' land, as opposed to *Froyim-Yossel's* Jews, were the situation was fundamentally different – education, freedom – as much as you want, but a livelihood – next to nothing.

So many beggars, paupers, unfortunates, and ordinary genteel Jews without so much as a Kreuzer in their pocket, you would not find in the entirety of the Russian Empire. this is what Shlomo concluded after creating an acquaintanceship between himself and the village sage, Mendele Hammer.

What do we have, argued Mendele Hammer further, from our 'doctorates' in tailoring and shoemaking, or from the *shtrymels* worn by our wagon drivers together with their silken *kapotes*, when we are prepared to bite off a finger for a single Austrian Kreuzer.

Despite this, Shlomo acclimated himself to this world that was so alien to him, he rented a room from R' Jekuthiel Einbinder – a Jew with a black long beard, black curly side locks, a *Hasidic* Jew and a great Torah scholar – and immediately began thinking about making a living.

Shlomo was never an idler, and he thought and thought.

Ln the first market day in the town, which for years would take place on Tuesday, Shlomo gave his luck a try.

He went out to carry, bought flax, swine hair, eggs, chicken, and other goods, which he used to trade with in his home town of Tomaszow.

Shlomo spoke a good Polish, not like the native Galician buyers, who spoke with the peasants half in *Deitschmerish*[9] and half in Polish.

The peasants, especially, wanted to deal only with '*Szlomko*', and Shlomo really succeeded.

Immediately, Shlomo set up a store near R' Jekuthiel's little house, where he lived, in which he kept the merchandise that he bought.

The young girls of the town immediately took a shine to him, because in town, it was gossiped that Shlomo had become a wealthy man, but the truth was that Shlomo did not have the time to allocate to the girls of Cieszanow.

His businesses took all of his time, during the day he would travel to the fairs in surrounding towns and villages, and at night he would sort out his merchandise and sell it.

* * *

A sister of R' Jekuthiel Einbinder also lived with him, who was called Mirl, a very chaste young lady, with all the virtues, but she had two minor shortcomings, those being a lack of a bit of money, and a lack of

[Page 56]

feminine charm.

The dwelling of R' Jekuthiel, in which Shlomo lived, consisted of three rooms, which in reality was one single room, divided into a kitchen, a bedroom, and a sitting room.

Mirl sleeps in the kitchen, and R' Jekuthiel in the bedroom, and in the sitting room, R' Jekuthiel binds his books during the day, and at night, it serves a bedroom for Shlomo.[10]

Naturally – when three adult people live in such close quarters, there is no lack of minor conflicts.

Every morning, Sholom had only one thing to do: Get going, there being no difference as to where, primarily – to get out of the room and the quicker the better, in order that Mirl be able to crawl out of her bed, in order to mover about the house earlier, and not to be thwarted by Shlomo.

The principal reason why Mirl always went around looking gloomy was, that there was a young, healthy, fresh man moving around in the other room, a merchant with all the virtues – and because of this, she thinks to herself: Go ask the Rashb"a a question?

Why, dear God, and for how long, must the virgin Mirl drag herself around, and sleep alone in her room?

Shlomo, wanting to exit the room, hears how Mirl suddenly shouts after him: say there, young man – which side of the bed did you get up on today? On the right side, or, perhaps altogether on the left side?

On both sides – Shlomo smiles cynically.

On only one – Mirl notes, on her way over to her brother Jekuthiel – on the side he laid down, her brother rumbled to her under his nose.

Ha, ha, ha. Jekuthiel shoots out a laugh at her.

Tell me, indeed, Shlomo – which side did you get up on today?

Shlomo casts a poisonous look at Mirl.

Do you understand? – he says to Jekuthiel.

This situation becomes increasingly more difficult and more complicated, complications manifest themselves – whether one wants them or not.

Three grown people in one room?

Here I mean – said Jekuthiel, defending Shlomo, and says to Mirl: we are not treating Shlomo correctly.

Shlomo, says Jekuthiel to Mirl, is a very familiar person to us, practically a relative.

Well, that is precisely what I don't want, Mirl answers sharply.

[Page 57]

It is not proper that Shlomo should remain in the family.

That is complete nonsense, Jekuthiel thinks to himself in his heart, I really and truly don't know why the silly goose holds herself so haughtily?

Does a young woman speak like this, who is waiting for a husband? Jekuthiel says this bitterly and quietly, but categorically to his sister.

Mirl becomes sad and serious instantly – and speaks directly to her brother as if he had just awoken from a sleep.

Do you mean, Jekuthiel, that I love Shlomo any less than you do?

Listen to what I will tell you Jekuthiel.

And this time, once and for all – the fact that we have Shlomo at home here is interfering with his private life, and deprives him of his will to become that which he must and has to become, he is becoming more and more of a bachelor, and he is becoming increasingly enamored of his bachelorhood, that is – being *alone*, and living *alone*.

Did you understand that? Mirl asked.

Jekuthiel agreed with Mirl, and he gave a sigh and said: this is possible.

Mirl said with conviction, we need to handle this differently.

We have to say to him frequently – give him his way, let him go where he wants to.

Not waiting for Jekuthiel's answer, Mirl gives a groan like someone who has fallen down from the attic – and maybe, Jekuthiel, perhaps it is more suitable that you find another place to live?

Jekuthiel smiles thereby, but Mirl retorts with a very specific and serious demeanor: Men do not understand women, they are flighty creatures.

Shlomo went off on his various ways, not thinking about Mirl, because – firstly, his days were taken up with traveling to the surrounding villages.

On Monday, to begin with, Shlomo was the first one in the village of Khatilov, Tuesday he spent the entire day conducting business at the market fair in Cieszanow, and every Wednesday, he had things to do with the peasants in the village of Lubliniec, Thursday and Friday in the other villages.

And in this fashion, months and years went by, and with every passing year, Shlomo grew more prosperous, until a certain Sabbath day in the summer, at the time of the afternoon prayers, when Shlomo, along with the ordinary rank and file Jews of the *shtetl*, were returning from the Little Synagogue of the '*Yad-Kharutzim*,' with a full belly of instruction over the Pentateuch and *Rashi* commentary – thinking over, at the time, the incident of 'Zimri ben Salu' and what he did with the young girl 'Kozbi bat Tsur,' the daughter of the

[Page 58]

Midianite chieftain, with whom the young Jewish man sinned[11], and he was suddenly seized with a fright and fear.

It is possible that such an occurrence could take place to him, God forbid, because a man is after all, only made of flesh and blood, he thought.

And what if, God forbid, the Evil Inclination should be stronger than him? What can become of this?

Additionally, he reminded himself, that during the past winter, he heard with his own ears, in that very same little synagogue, and from the very same R' Yossel'eh Melamed, a portion of the Pentateuch, in which God, Blessed be He, commanded the Adam, the first man, and said to him, as follows: 'Therefore shall a man leave his father and his mother, and shall cleave unto his wife: and they shall be one flesh.[12]'

After such thoughts, Shlomo took stock of himself.

Perhaps, he thought, the young women are right? It is necessary to do a little thinking about getting married.

Money, he thought, I have enough of, to rent a place and support a wife with children, is not the most difficult thing to do.

Most oppressively weighing on him were the dark Sabbath later afternoons, before nightfall.

The other nights of the week – even Friday night, kerosene lamps burned in the houses, and it was more or less light enough to see, but it was only on the Sabbath, late in the afternoon, that is, about the time of the Third Feast, a dark fear descended on him, because the entire town was engulfed in the darkness of an Egyptian plague, and on the *Bombesgessel*, as it was called – [the street] on which Shlomo lived, it was doubly dark because of the lack of space, and the poverty, and it was because of this, that Shlomo especially at the time of the Third Feast, was in an unhappy mood.

Arriving at his shared residence, he threw himself on the bed out of great aggravation, closing his eyes in the dark house, and making a merchant's calculation – that perhaps it would be easier if there were two?

It actually might cost a bit more, but what is one to do? Perhaps the Pentateuch text is right?

A man should not, and must not, sit alone, a man must get married?

Laying down, and sunk in his thoughts – he did not notice that someone had quietly stolen into his little room, which was now dark.

Suddenly, he felt that something was tickling him under the nose. Once, then again.

Not opening his eyes, he wipes the underside of his nose with a finger of his right hand.

[Page 59]

Shlomo again contemplates his options: to marry, or not to marry?

Something tickles him again under the nose, and again he wipes it – again he thinks – and again a tickle, and this goes on for quite a few minutes, until finally, Shlomo tries one more time, but this time with his entire hand, to grab the nasty stubborn fly under his nose, and to his astonishment, instead of a fly, he feels a thin hand which he had grabbed in his own.

In the first second, Shlomo was a bit frightened, but he immediately saw that it was Jekuthiel's hand.

He calmed himself, and asked, Jekuthiel? Is it permissible to recite the evening prayer yet, and light a candle? I am literally being asphyxiated by the darkness.

No, Shlomo, Jekuthiel replies – we need to wait another quarter of an hour.

Shlomo, Jekuthiel says further – I want to have a conversation with you about an important matter, and as you know in our Holy Writ it says, that at the time of the Third Feast, it is a time to show compassion, and since we still have a quarter of an hour, it is appropriate to ask you something of this nature....

It was difficult for Jekuthiel to articulate verbally that which he had inside of him.

Instead of speaking plainly, he obfuscated and stammered, and asked an aimlessly directed question: what is your opinion, Shlomo, of the repulsive story of the Jewish young man and that girl Kozbi bat Tsur, the Midianite princess?

As previously mentioned, Shlomo was no fool, and he immediately grasped 'В Чём Дело' as they would say in Shlomo's home,[13] and he immediately understood that Jekuthiel wanted to discuss a serious matter with him. In order to ease Jekuthiel's soul, Shlomo suddenly says – Well, Jekuthiel, will you be satisfied? I agree to take Mirl to wife.

I tell you the truth Jekuthiel, Shlomo says further, hearing the story in the Pentateuch, about all that can befall a man, I was simply overcome with fear.

As a practical matter, I understand that the life of a man can follow two ways – the crooked way, for example, as the way in which the young man went in today's Torah portion, and a more straight way – simply as all good and pious Jewish young men go, one clarifies a wedding match, one gets married after erecting a wedding canopy.

Jekuthiel didn't let Shlomo finish, and he burst out with a sentiment of great joy, and out of the depths of his heart he cried out: Mazel Tov!

Shlomo was not in love with Mirl, but rather, the tale in the Pentateuch made such a strong impression on him, that he immediately decided to get married.

Since Jekuthiel was the first one to broach the marriage proposal, Shlomo didn't think about it for long, and while still under the weighty influence of the story, he immediately decided to become Mirl's bridegroom.

[Page 60]

In the morning, the entire town of Cieszanow reverberated with the news of the betrothal of Mirl and Shlomo.

Shlomo immediately bought a vacant location right on the Ringplatz, and immediately built a stone-walled house.

* * *

In time, Mirl bore Shlomo 5 sons and 2 daughters. and in between, Shlomo grew even more prosperous, and he was made Head of the community in the *shtetl*.

With the exception of Yusha[14], Shlomo's sons all were built like their father, meaning, solid, massive, salt-of-the-earth Jews, good and simple.

By contrast, Yusha was very delicate, sitting and studying Torah day and night, reading *Der Freier Zeit* and the Vienna paper, '*Neue Freie Presse*.' helping his parents in their business affairs which prospered even more.

All of Shlomo's children became the sons-in-law and daughters-in-law to simple, yet prosperous *balebatim*, with Yusha, by contrast, the son-in-law of R' Paltiel Schwartzberg, known in the entire district as a Torah scholar of reputable descent, and a great *Hasid*, but at the same time, someone of more modest means.

R' Yusha's wife, Faiga Ruchama, a renown beauty, genteel in her soul, with good aristocratic manners, and a good character, managed to attract people from all walks of life into R' Shlomo's house through her proud bearing and modest way of life, and it was because of this, and her good fortune that R' Shlomo's businesses prospered even more.

Shlomo immediately bought the 'Profinancia,' meaning the franchise for all manner of alcoholic beverages in the entire district, and in addition to this, he had the warehouse of '*Akotzshimmer*' Beer, renown throughout all of Austria, and as an extra – a saloon with the only modern guest house with walls on which were hung pictures of the royal family of the Viennese courtyard.

R' Shlomo's kept his skilled son Yusha, with his even more talented daughter-in-law, Ruchama in his own home, from whom he derived substantial gratification.

From time to time, Ruchama's father, R' Paltiel the well-regarded *mekhutan* of R' Shlomo, would come to visit his daughter and son-in-law.

Walking with the *mekhutan*, R' Paltiel in the street, Shlomo felt himself to be highly honored, and would at that time introduce his *mekhutan* to anyone he would encounter in the street – this is R' Paltiel Schwartzberg, the great Torah scholar of such prominent descent – my *mekhutan*. At times like this, Shlomo would literally fall into a so-called '*Mania Grandiosa*.'

In the meantime, years went by.

Yusha and his wife Ruchama lived in the corner of the big house on the Ringplatz, which R' Shlomo had

[Page 61]

built.

Their dwelling consisted of a room with heavy massive furniture, a large table, on which stood a heavy oil lamp covered in a large globe, a bureau with sacred texts in it, that Yusha would consult every morning, a large, massive oven, made of white tiles, and on the side, an inside primitive telephone, which connected all of the rooms in R' Shlomo's house.

Near their room, there was a kitchen that served the entire residential premises, and also cooking and baking was done their for guests – merchants, who resided in Shlomo's hotel.

The walls of the kitchen were hung with a variety of brass and copper utensils, which gypsies would sell to Shlomo or exchange for a glass of strong drink.

In the kitchen, there was a dumb waiter which was used to send the cooked delicacies to the guests in the large dining room which was known throughout the area as the 'big house.'

The room also served as a community meeting place, a place for political gatherings, and also in this room, the only place where the Lemberg theater troupe would perform their '*Hinke-Pinke*' or a '*Moyd a Flam*' with which they would grace the town almost every year.

The attendants and waiters, who worked on the first floor, then sent the emptied dishes up the dumb waiter to be cleaned.

Among the many rooms on the floor, there was a small reserved room off at a distance to the side, which was known by the name 'The wedding Room,' with a sexual undertone, or as R' Shlomo's grown up grandchildren used to call it, 'The Intercourse Room.'

This room served R' Shlomo's children and grandchildren as the first night's bedroom after the wedding ceremony, which would take place in the large dining room.

All the rooms of the house were connected by a common plumbing system, the water coming through pipes from a huge storage tank which stood at the highest point of the house, which every morning, was filled by Abraham the Water Carrier, who would carry the water with his pails yoked across his scrawny shoulders, from the large well which was found in the very same Ringplatz of the town.

R' Shlomo very greatly enjoyed traveling to the city of Prague, on his return from the familiar Carlsbad, where, ever year, in the style of a wealthy man – he would travel tov repair, the gas lamps – which lit the hotels there.

Not giving it much thought, he bought luxurious lamps of this kind for his own hotel.

These new lamps indeed did make a strong impression on the town, it being as light in R' Shlomo's house, and the locals would say among themselves that it was as light in his house as if from the sun on a day in Tammuz, and they would come from all over the province to see this great wonder.

R' Shlomo's residential premises, in the meantime, grew in length and breadth, and with each passing year, his family extended itself further, sons, daughter, sons-in-law, daughters-in-law, and tens of grandchildren

[Page 62]

of both sexes, all of whom lived under the patronage of their father-grandfather.

Just as success pursued Shlomo in all his undertakings, he would modestly take pride – that whatever he touched – turns to gold, so – as the devil would have it, the angel of success distanced himself from his sons and sons-in-law.

Almost every year in, and year out, R' Shlomo would have to cover the debts of his sons and sons-in-law.

He had to do this, he once poured his heart out to his old acquaintance and friend, R' Gedalia Schreiber.

First, he argued, it simply doesn't look good for such a grand Jew, who is also wealthy, to be the object of finger pointing about his son, Beryl' eh, or his son-in-law, R' Luzer, who was the son of R' Pinchas, the former head of the community of his former Russian home town, the very same one who ordered the *khappers*, and also put Shlomo onto the list of recruits for 'Ivan's' soldiers – regarding their obligations.

It was an embarrassment for him, that his children were called – bankrupt, or debtor.

He was terrified at the mere thought of it – it is necessary to also understand this.

In 'Kira's-Land' someone who went bankrupt was not one of the better regarded business people, as was the case in 'Ivan's' country, there, in Ivan's territory, Shlomo said, a bankrupt was treated exactly like someone with a toothache, that when one extracts the painful tooth, it eases the soul, and the one who is ill is cured, but in 'Kira's' such a 'Bankrupt' as he was called in the Galitzianer dialect, would be aggravated to death by the children.

At every turn, a group of little folk would yell at the 'Bankrupt,' and they would work over the unfortunate individual so long, until he would uproot himself from the town, and his wife would be left abandoned forever, or they would simply drive him crazy, and he had to be committed to the so called '*Fiaren*' in Lemberg, the well-known Insane Asylum, from which no one any longer emerged alive.

About thirty to forty 'Kaiser Franz-Josephs' and a large number of 'Rothschilds' loitered about in this '*Fiaren.*'

All these sick people where cured in such a way, that they never lived to see the beauty of God's world ever again, apart from which, R' Shlomo said to his friend, simultaneously – their houses, mine, – their good for my money, which they squeeze out of me, whether I want to or not.

If I don't give it to them graciously, I must give it to them grudgingly, they scandalize me, and not only once has my daughter Baylah Rachel knocked out my window panes.

Which ever one of them needs to pay off a note – comes to me – Father, pay.

So it is more appropriate that I pay graciously, without scandal – and discreetly.

And so years passed for R' Shlomo, with joy and grief, but more joy than grief.

Every Monday and Thursday, A bit if a happy occasion – today a Brit for a newborn grandson, tomorrow,

[Page 63]

consummation of a wedding contract, the day after tomorrow, a Bar Mitzvah, and in short order, weddings of his sons and daughters children descended on him, and also the various unmarried young ladies of the family.

R' Shlomo's dining hall was often busy with the happy occasions arranged by his children, naturally – at their father's expense, even his grandchildren knew how to hit up their grandfather for presents.

At the end of each summer, when R' Shlomo returned from Carlsbad, he brought back with him, a large trunk with a variety of presents, for the women, silk for clothing, for the men, silk for caftans, and also high plush fur '*Hilkehs,*' hats; for the grandchildren a wooden stereopticon from Carlsbad with a magnifying glass in the middle, through which one looked with an eye to see pictures of the city of Carlsbad.

He brought separate valuable presents for his beautiful and well-bred daughter-in-law Faiga Ruchama, or as she was called in town, '*Rukhamchi-Shlomo'leh's,*' and for her oldest son, Chaim-chi.

From all of his grandchildren, he derived the greatest nachas from two, [one] from the middle son, of his son-in-law R' Luzer, Chaizikl.

R' Shlomo had an extra sentiment for this little boy, first - because he, Chaizikl, was also the grandson of the former community head and his current *mekhutan*, but the essence of why he derived such nachas from Chaizikl, is because he was the outstanding one nearly from all of the grandchildren.

Chaizikl was a talented student, and a boy of whom it was said 'Torah and commerce together with shined shoes.' a well-known Galitzianer expression for aristocratic, *Hasidic* and studious young boys.

Also, the grandson, Chaim-chi the son of Ruchama, was a scholar, and a modern *Hasidic* boy.

Chaimchi was completely wrought in his mother's image, handsomely developed physically, blond silken hair, with two blue eyes that shined like stars in the sky, a face of white alabaster, around which two short curled side locks bounced about.

From these two grandsons, their grandfather R' Shlomo waxed along all dimensions, deriving pocketfuls of nachas from them.

Between them, these two little boys got along well with each other, but deep in each of their hearts, each wanted to outperform the other.

It was a genuine envy between two scholars.

When Chaizikl completed the study of the *Talmudic* tractate '*Moed Katan*' in a matter of four weeks, Chaimchi applied himself strenuously, and completed his study of the tractate '*Hagiga*' in a matter of only three weeks.

When Chaizikl engaged in a casuistic discourse in front of the young people of the town – scholars, R' Shia'leh Frenkel, R' Mikhl'leh Halberstam, R' David Dieler, and others, and literally integrated 'East' with 'West' Chaimchi was so strongly motivated, that he sat for several Thursday nights, delving deeply

[Page 64]

into a number of Gemara texts, with the commentary of the *Tosafot*, *Maharam*, and *Maharsha*, until he was able to deliver a simple discourse that not only integrated 'East' and 'West' but 'North' and 'South' as well.

When Chaimchi celebrated his Bar Mitzvah, all of the distinguished Jews of the town attended the grand feast for that occasion.

Chaimchi's second grandfather, R' Paltiel Schwartzberg, came to the festive occasion with a whole regiment of relatives, genteel young men with sharp *Hasidic* minds, the older relatives with not insubstantial waistlines, and on their Gaonic heads, fur hats, with yarmulkes protruding.

The Bar Mitzvah boy, adorned for his full length with golden watches, bracelets, and just plain golden jewelry, gave a very analytical discourse, both grandfathers carrying on a sharp discussion between themselves, his father R' Yusha and his mother Ruchama exuded nachas from their talented darling.

The Rabbi of the town, R' Issachar Dov, a great Torah scholar and also a well-known 'Rebbe' to thousands of *Hasidim*, who never would attend the festive occasions of such *balebatim*, made an exception for Chaimchi.

The Rebbe, in all his splendor, accompanied by his *Gabbaim* and *Hasidim* came to the Bar Mitzvah feast of little Chaimchi.

Hearing the analytical discourse from Chaim, the Rebbe, for so was his custom, in order not to permit the Evil Eye to gain control, specifically engaged the young man, and deliberately tried to catch him making a mistake.

Chaimchi, however had a good and genuine *Talmudic* head on his shoulders, and he wriggled like a fish in the water, and extricated himself from the substantial trap into which the great and respected Rabbi had tried to lead him.

And it was in this way, that life went on, and R' Shlomo's premises increased and fructified with nachas and happiness, until God mad a war, and drove his people Israel to all four corners of the world.

* * *

On a beautiful July day in the year 1914, in the city of Sarajevo in Bosnia-Herzegovina, the Austrian Heir Apparent, [Archduke Francis] Ferdinand was shot [and killed] by the Serbian student [Gavrilo] Prinzip.

The shot in Sarajevo destabilized the life of the Jewish populace in the Austro-Hungarian monarchy.

Since the year 1866, the year of the war between Austria-Hungary on one side, and Italy-Germany on the other side, forty eight years of peace had elapsed.

During those years, the Jewish populace in the Austrian country, under the rule of the fanatically clerical, but good Emperor Franz Joseph, lived in great tranquility, and became substantially emancipated.

Up to the tragic shot in Sarajevo, a factual and positive equality reigned for the Jewish populace in this country, and when, on the day of July 28, 1914, the so-called 'Manifest' to my people was published by the Emperor, the Jews of Galicia, upon reading this 'Manifest', shed rivers of tears, not, God forbid, because

[Page 65]

the land was threatened by war, along with its unforeseeable sorrowful consequences, but rather simply – out of pity for their elderly Emperor, Franz-Joseph, who was compelled in his old age, to engage himself in order to lead a war.

The patriotism of the Jews grew stronger daily, young and old ran to the mobilization points, to present themselves for military service.

R' Shlomo, at that time had already passed away, as also had his son, R' Yusha, who was no longer alive, the businesses, however, primarily the saloon and the hotel, were managed by his daughter-in-law Ruchama, with the assistance of her little son Chaimchi, who was already a that time grown to be a fourteen year-old-boy.[15]

Immediately in the first days of the war, all manner of military units began to stream through the town of Cieszanow, from all of the Austrian nations who lived on Austro-Hungarian territory.

The town was found in border territory, and indeed the Austrian-Russian 'front' was not far from the town.

There was an unending march of military units – day and night. Infantry was seen to be immediately on the move, after them – artillery accompanied by the famous Austrian aristocratic cavalry, in which almost all of the officers were princes, dukes, barons, and so forth.

In the third day after the outbreak of the war, on the way to the front, an entire brigade of mounted dragoons arrived in the town, with their golden insignias on their decorated uniforms, and with feathers in their tall hats.

These dragoons disembarked to rest on the large Ringplatz of the town, in contrast with the officers who quartered themselves in the fine Jewish houses.

Two officers quartered themselves in Faiga Ruchama's house, one was the grandson of the Emperor Franz-Joseph, with his high name and title of Oberleuetnant Prinz von Windisch-Graetz, and his companion was a Jew from Vienna with the his own also aristocratic name of Leutenant Baron von Rothschild.

The two young officers were so-called friends, or at least that what it looked like to the observer, but what actually went on in the heart of the Catholic Prince in regard to this seeming friendship with the Jewish Baron, remained his secret, which a few days later, as a result of a Russian bullet that found its mark, he took with him to his grave.

From a conversation overhead by happenstance, in the form of a dialogue between the two officers, which took place in the presence of a Jewish waiter in Ruchama's hotel – who had served the two officers, we can construct a picture and understand how the true collegial friendship between the two aristocrats appeared:

[Page 66]

> The Prince: Today is Sunday, today we go to church, right?
> The Baron: Not I.
> The Prince: Aha – *Jude*.
> The Baron: I am proud to be a Jew.
> The Prince: I would not be so proud to be a Jew.
> The Baron: I am not certain if Jewish blood does not also course in you.
> The Prince: God forbid – I am a pure Aryan.
> The Baron: Almost all Aryan Europeans are descended from Jews.
> The Prince: That is an exaggeration.
> The Baron: Also, your God, in whose name you shame us, comes from Jews.

Suddenly, in the middle of the conversation, Rothschild notes that one of his boots is torn, and he asks of the waiter, to covy the boot immediately to a shoemaker for repair, but he also wishes that the shoemaker should return the repaired boot to him personally, because he wishes to see, he thinks – with his own eyes, what a Jewish shoemaker from a small Galician town looks like.

An hour did not pass, and R' David Schuster[16] brought the repaired boot back.

Rothschild was greatly amazed by the shoemaker, and the truth be known, there really was something to be amazed at.

R' David Schuster was no ordinary little shoemaker, he was 'also a shoemaker,' but more importantly, he was a handsome Jewish man, with a wide beard, and in addition to this he was a *Hasid*, and a bit of a scholar.

Ignoring his trade as a shoemaker, the prominent *balebatim* condescended to him, and did not keep their distance from him as was their habit with other working people in the town, and especially with regard to shoemakers.

Baron Rothschild, holding the boot in one hand, didn't know what to wonder about first, whether the good, clean workmanship, or the one whom he thought to be – a Rabbinical shoemaker.

He has heard, that in ancient times, among the Jews there was such a shoemaker, who was called *R' Yohanan HaSandlar*, and because of this, he was fortunate to have the privilege of seeing a latter-day replica of the ancient shoemaker, R' Yohanan.

Out of great inspiration, Rothschild extracted a fifty crown note from his wallet, and gave it to R' David for his work.

It was the first time in his life that R' David had ever seen a denomination of this size, for which, in those times, one could purchase a small house.

Exiting from Rothschild's room with the bank note n hand, R' David didn't know for what to thank God first, for the privilege of being so close the legendary Rothschild, and in his residence, or for the great fortune, for the fifty crowns which he received from the Baron.

[Page 67]

The entire town rang with this news almost immediately, and a big hullabaloo ensued, from the double news, first that Rothschild is located at the home of Faiga Ruchama, and more to the point, that the rank and file Jews were intensely envious of R' David's good fortune.

As was to evolve later, the 'Fifty Note' was not all that lucky for R' David personally, because first, he suddenly acquired a host of 'friends,' and all, as one, even the *balebatim* who occupy seats at the East Wall of the synagogue, at once became 'good brothers' with R' David.

Every one of them sought to do R' David a favor, and give him good advice on how to spend this huge sum of money.

R' David, a Jewish man who was no fool, thought – Good.

Let them all flatter me as much as they like, but 'money' from me – let's move very slowly with the horsecart.

It took a strenuous amount of energy every day to separate himself from he 'new friends,' and he quietly let it be known that the town banker, R' Shia Kigler, should pay him a call at home one evening.

The note, that is the Fifty [Crowns], he turned over to R' Shia, and for it, he received a pretty red booklet from his bank.

The Fifty Crown note was put to good use by R' Shia, because it didn't take long before 'Ivan' invaded 'Kira's' country, and all the Jews fled to wherever their legs could carry them, one to Prague, a second to Budapest, but in the main, the Galitzianer Jews felt close to Vienna, and indeed, the larger part to off for Vienna.

R' David never saw the money again with his own eyes, and on that occasion, the folk proverb was realized that said: '*Nie byles panem i nie bedziesz panem.*[17]'

Also, Ruchama and her children fled in fear before 'Ivan's' Cossacks.

The echelon that led to the west, deposited a portion of 'refugees' in each Austrian country, in Bemen, Merren, Hungary, but in Lower Austria, Burgenland, overall the communities took in the Jews very favorably.

A large portion, who could show that the had enough capital, were permitted entry to Vienna.

Ruchama, with her children, on arriving in the middle of the night at the '*Nordbanhof*' in Vienna, were not cordially permitted to debark from the train cars by the local police with their shimmering mirror-like helmets on their heads, and the snow-white gloves on their hands.

They, the police, had an order regarding the remainder of the refugees found in the echelon, to be sent on to a city with the comical name, 'Hatzen.'

Suddenly, an outcry and a shout was heard throughout the station: we want to remain in Vienna, only in

[Page 68]

Vienna – only in Vienna.

No – no, you are traveling to Hatzen, only on to Hatzen, the elegant, cordial, but firm Viennese police replied.

In the middle of this, a giant confusion and panic ensued.

The Galitzianer Jewish refugees, from the first moments of the war, looked to the Viennese like a pathetic burned out relation, indeed, a distant relation at that, but still a relation, and it was through this that the President of the Vienna police took pity on those who fled, and issued a new order, that whoever among them can demonstrate a level of capital of at least one thousand crowns, which can even be in the form of a bank book in the above indicated amount, will be admitted to Vienna without impediment.

Ruchama did not lack for money, and she immediately reached into her bosom, and pulled out a packet of Thousand Crown Austrian notes.

Her neighbor R' Moshe Honigsberg was able to do the same, incidently, an enlightened Jewish man, and a Torah scholar of important pedigree, and an even more important extensively branched family.

This R' Moshe, later became the *mekhutan* of Ruchama, and the father-in-law of her little son, Chaimchi.

All the others who did not have such a sum of money to show, needed to drag themselves on further to the place known as 'Hatzen.'

Crying and pleading were to no avail. *'Nach Hatzen – Nach Hatzen'* the police commanded, a whistle from the train, and off we go, to Hatzen.

The meaning of 'Hatzen' remained as a cognitive among the Galitzianer Jews for a 'place of exile' for those who were [forcibly] sent there.

The name and meaning of 'Hatzen' among Galitzianer Jews was no different that the name and meaning of 'Siberia' to Russian Jews.

In the meantime, one made a living, ate *'meissbrot'* and baked *'meisskuchen,'* that is, the Yiddish expressions for bread and rolls made from corn.

As is known, a great famine reigned in Vienna at that time, and no other produce could be obtained, and so one made do only with maize.

During the day, one was occupied with the 'black market' and at night, one gathered for the communal feat on maize.

* * *

The young Galician boys were still free from having to go off to military service, as well as the young girls, and, for the time being, they made use of the time to throw themselves into lower and upper schools, with an enormous thirst for education.

[Page 69]

The studies did not pose any great difficulty to them, and neither was acceptance in the schools.

As mentioned, in the Austrian country, no *numerus-clausus* existed for Jewish citizens, as was the case in 'Ivan's' land, secondly – the German language was not foreign to them, for them it was a second mother tongue.

Almost ever Galitzianer boy or girl, knew half of 'Schiller, Goethe or Heine' by heart, at every opportunity, a Galitzianer girl or boy would quote from *'Die Glocke'* by Schiller, the *'Disput von dem Rebbe und Mensch'* by Heine, and above all, the famous *'[Liebes] Leiden dem Jungen Werthers,'* by Goethe.

It was not only one sentimental girl who shed rivers of tears at the reading of this heartbreaking fantasy.

The intellectual level of a groom, or a bride was judged by who remembers more poetry by heart. from these so-called 'heavyweights' from the above mentioned German poets.

Chaimchi also took stock of himself. and he thought to himself, that a suitable time had come for him to become a doctor, professor, or possible a Professor of Medicine altogether.

The easiest, he thought to himself, would be to study at a Teacher's Seminary, first – this profession was not unfamiliar to him, because while yet in his Galician home, he had learned a great deal from the pedagogical texts, and second, he found himself in a pedagogical milieu in Vienna, who largely drew him into religious study, that is to say, to Holy Writ and less to secular study, such as: medicine, technology, or other secular occupations.

Chaimchi took to his studies with a ferocious intensity and temperament, before dawn, he studies at the large well-known 'Schiffschule' with Rabbi Yeshayeh'leh Furst, the Rabbi of that synagogue, after noon, in the famous Teacher's Seminary of Professor Hayot, the Head Teacher of Vienna.

For almost three and a half years, Chaim'l studied Jewish subject matter, in these two places of study, which were very well known to the larger part of Galician Jewry.

In the meantime the God of War did his thing, and wrought deeds.

Each year, the war consumed millions of innocent people. Fathers, sons, brothers and brothers-in-law, fell like flies on the various fronts.

The war machine behind the front was compelled to continue working ceaselessly. It worked day and night, each month, others were called to military service, so that the new recruits could take the place of those who fell in the ranks.

The turn of Chaim'l also came.

And the day came, on a beautiful Sabbath in the morning, an order was published in the city of Vienna, that all men born in the year have to immediately present themselves to the so-called '*musterung*,' meaning a call-up to the military.

Chaim'l found himself among those, who needed to object to the commission, to drop his studies in the

[Page 70]

middle to which he was so strongly committed.

Paying no mind to the great patriotism that reigned among the Jews towards their Emperor, Chaimchi, despite this, did not have any great desire to lay his young head on the altar of war.

As a result of this decision, Chaim'l took upon himself the enormous responsibility and placed himself in the greatly dangerous position of a 'deserter,' that is to say, someone who avoided military service during wartime, for which there is the threat of either a death penalty or life imprisonment, and despite this great danger, he hid himself for eight months in a place where it was not easy to find him.

Translator's footnotes:

1.   This word for 'table' has something of a ritual connotation when connected with the home of the *Rebbe*, who 'presided over his table' during mealtime, much in the manner of holding court.

2.   It is important to take note that this is a 'translation' of the Yiddish, '*Fonyeh*,' used as an epithet to describe the Czar. In particular, Czar Nicholas I, a notorious anti-Semite, earned the sobriquet of '*Fonyeh Gonif*,' which stuck to all of his successors as well.

3.   The nefarious occupation of *khappers* (Yiddish, for kidnappers), grew out of the ukase of the anti-Semitic Czar, Nicholas I. These were fellow Jews, who typically victimized poorer Jewish families, by grabbing their children, in order to satisfy the military quota set by the Czarist regime.

4.   Taken from Jacob's blessing of Joseph's two sons, in Genesis 48:16

5.   As opposed to *shtelln bonkes*, which involved the placement of cups to draw out 'evil humors' through the skin, this is the somewhat less common, but more severe process of *hakn bonkes*, where an incision is made in the body before the cups are applied, so the blood can be accessed directly. In either case, it is somewhat dubious as to whether salutary results were consistently obtainable.

6.   An endearment, used by the Galician Jews, to alter Kaiser Franz Joseph's name into Yiddish, implying their gratitude for his tolerance towards them.

7.   On September 10, 1898, Austria's Empress Elisabeth died from wounds inflicted during an assassination attempt.

8.   There are two sobriquets here. In Russian, 'mak' is a poppy. This allusion may be to foolishness. 'Kira' comes from the Hebrew acronym for '**K**aysar **Ya****R**im **H**odo,' an honorific applied, in this case, to the Emperor Franz-Joseph, which means, 'The King, may his glory be exalted.' No doubt, this also is a reflection of the affection in which 'Froyim Yossel' was held by his Jewish subjects. Put together, the '*Kira Mak*' become the 'Galician Poppies,' or people with no sense.

9.   An informal patois which consisted of a mix of German and Yiddish.

10.   We see here, that his last name, Einbinder, is related to his trade as a bookbinder.

11.   See Numbers 25

12.   Genesis 2:24

13.   Russian for 'What's really going on.'

14.   Seemingly yet another variant of Yehoshua.

15.   From the previous section, which describes the Bar Mitzvah of the boy Chaimchi, we see that R' Shlomo and his son R' Yusha were very much alive. Yet here, where Chaimchi is reported to be fourteen years of age, we are told that both of men – father and son – have passed away. It is curious that the writer offers no details as to what the circumstances were surrounding their demise.

16.   This is, once again, an instance of a name (perhaps the official last name) that is taken directly from the person's occupation.

17.   You never were a rich man, and you will never be a rich man.

[Page 70]

On This Day, I Recall My Transgressions

Translator's Note: The reason for the placement of this piece is not clear. It appears to be an insertion into the flow of the narrative that has gone on before, and that is subsequently resumed.

In the year 1916, I was a student at the Rabbinical Seminary in Vilna. Despite the various dispensations that were in place to excuse students of theology in the country of Austria, I was compelled, by law, to enlist in the army, although I enlisted a year late.

As was the case with many others, I decided not to get near to the war, in which the sparks of Aryan racism were already evident and that were already shooting about in Germany at the hands of the then Chief of Staff, General Ludendorff, a partner of the Satan, Hitler, ימ״ש.

According to the law of the land, anyone who avoided military service during wartime, was exposed to placing his life at risk in the most severe manner possible, because the law said, in this regard: anyone who deliberately avoids enlistment, or military service during wartime, his sentence will be death or life imprisonment at hard labor.

I did not enlist on time for a number of reasons. A) I wanted to complete my studies. B) Despite the ardent patriotism of the Jews of Galicia, toward Franz Joseph, I didn't find it appropriate to sacrifice myself on the altar of strangers, that is to say, non-Jews. Specifically, I relied on the words of Our Sages, who said: Anything for the benefit of the wicked is bad for the righteous (*Psakhim*, 103). And being that the ally of the good Emperor was an anti-Semite, who hated the Jews, Kaiser Wilhelm [sic: II], I didn't see any value for Jews to help the German nation win the war by putting their lives on the line.

As was usual, those who transgressed in this respect were brought before a field tribunal (*Feldgericht* in local language). The field tribunal for my area was in the city of Sziget.

On one clear day, I was handcuffed, and two armed soldiers transported me to the previously mentioned court.

I waited in the gigantic corridor of the building, until I was called to appear before the judges. In the meantime, hours went by, and the pounding of my heart did not stop for a minute, due to my fear of the sentence.

[Page 71]

I saw, in the courtyard, how they were escorting soldiers who had been sentenced to death, being taken out for execution. I was almost certain that I would be sentenced to this punishment, however, from the minute that I entered the hall of the court house, some sort of premonition seized me, and I felt some sort of lightening of the pressure in my soul, and to this day, I cannot give myself an explanation of this feeling.

Twelve officers sat in judgement with an aged general at their head.

The Chairman asks me: Why have you not enlisted on time? Are you unaware of the severe penalty that the law imposes on deserters?

With tears in my eyes, I replied: 'Excellence! After I read '*Die Liebes Leiden des Jungen Werthers*,' by Goethe, I sank into the world of romance, a world where everything was good, and I completely forgot that there was another world, that is to say, the real world, practical, a world in which people kill each other without knowing for what or why.'

My answer made such an impression on the old general to the point that he began to smile (it appears, that at that moment, he remembered himself as a young man, and what he did), and in the midst of his remarks, was transformed from a prosecutor to a defender, tuning to his colleagues and saying: we see here before us a matter regarding a person who is yet immature. It is my thought, in this regard, to lighten the sentence to the extent that is possible. He ordered me to leave the room, and after a quarter of an hour, they summoned me to hear their sentence.

It is interesting that, the emotion that took hold of me at the moment I entered the corridor of the court building, did not betray me. The court handed down a sentence as follows:

"*Sie werden verurteilt zu zwei Monate Kerker. Jedoch im Falle ein tüchtiges verhaltens vor dem Feinde, wird Ihnen die Strafe teilweis oder gänzlich nachgesehen.*"

"We sentence you to two months of imprisonment, on condition, that in the instance of distinguishing yourself in the face of the enemy, the command is given the discretion to set the sentence aside, either in part, or completely."

As you can understand, I endeavored to be a good soldier, and a model in my appointment. However, this was only in an office setting, and not at the front, and I was lucky in two respects: A) That year, I received an amnesty from the sentence, B) And this is the core, thanks to God, I successfully was able to get out of the hell that was called The First World War, heathy and whole.

* * *

There is an expression in the Province of Galicia, that "Strife is borne to the point until one's ear is torn off."

Chaimchi was hidden for a period of time, until one fine day, he was nabbed, and thrown into jail., and on the morning, was taken that popular place in Vienna which was a center for the production of cannon fodder.

This place was a primary '*Musterungsamt*,' and was located in the third level of the '*Landstrass-Hauptstrasse.*'

[Page 72]

The commission consisted of senior officers headed by a doctor, who in Chaim'l's eyes appeared to be no minor anti-Semite.

The doctor examined Chaimchi, and palpated him with sullen eyes, touching him here, there, and concluded shortly and sharply 'eligible,' meaning that he was fit to become one of *Froyim-Yossel's* soldiers.

Chaim immediately became a soldier in the land of soldiers, with a feather and patriotic medallions in his headgear, singing along such German military songs as 'How beautiful are the girls of 17 and 18 years of age.'

Chaim was trained in the art of killing people for a month, and he was assigned to a company that was scheduled to be sent to the Italian front.

From the first minute on, Chaim'l gained favor in the eyes of his commandant, who was a Jew with the secular name of Dr. Epstein, a Viennese lawyer, and a very refined person.

A day before Chaim'l marched away to the front, he received a six-hour liberty in order to make his farewells with his family and friends.

His mother, Faiga Ruchama, with her younger children, in the meantime had been sent back to their home that had been liberated from the Russians, and in Vienna, there only remained those whose homes were still occupied by the enemy, or had been entirely burned down.

In the middle of the night, the military transport, in which Chaim'l found himself, chugged off to the front in the direction of Italy, to the sounds of a military orchestra, and patriotic exhortations, from Evangelical, Catholic and Jewish clergy, and with cries of 'Hurrah' being shouted.

The railroad track led to the Italian city of Udine, which was occupied by Austrian troops.

From Udine forward, everything had been torn up, burned and laid waste by the operations of the war which were being carried out by hostile armies.

From the city of Udine to the front, was a walk of ten to twelve kilometers, which had to be done on foot, thereby having to withstand great danger.

Rifle and cannon shells whistled over the heads of the marching soldiers, and not only one of the unfortunate was left lying with a head that was split open, and didn't even live long enough to see the real front.

Chaim'l fell sick out of fear from the very first 'report' that he heard, coming from the other side of the front, getting a severe diarrhea, a disease called 'Dysentery,' which was highly contagious, and therefore it was necessary to send him back to the city of Udine, to be treated at the local hospital there.

In the meantime, the military situation on the western front got worse, and gradually, everyone was evacuated to the east.

To Chaim'l's good fortune, after having been in the hospital for less than two weeks, the turn came for his hospital to be evacuated eastward.

[Page 73]

There was a so-called 'epidemic-hospital' in the *shtetl* of Lubaczow, which was merely seven kilometers from Chaim'l's birthplace, where soldiers were treated from all of the fronts who had contracted all variety of contagious diseases, typhus, cholera, dysentery, and others.

Chaim'l, with his good sense, understood that were he fortunate enough to be admitted to this hospital, it may become possible for him to survive the war.

Some special Providence followed Chaim'l when he found himself in need, and almost at the last minute a salvation came to him.

He thought through and reasoned in such a way, that the chief doctor had to send him for further treatment, and specifically to this hospital which was so close to his home.

Chaimchi was not mistaken, there was an order. that all of the soldiers who were in the present hospital and had returned to good health, were forbidden from returning to the front, but they, as 'immunized,' meaning that they who could no longer contract the contagious disease, should be used as nurses or other jobs among those soldiers who were ill from epidemic diseases, who were send to be cured here on a daily basis.

Chaim'l immediately became a fairly important member of the hospital staff.

As an assigned officer in the hospital chancellery, he served his Emperor '*Kira*' until the bitter war ended, and the legendary '*Kira*-Empire' ceased to exist.

* * *

The news of the establishment of the Polish '*Rzeczpospolita*' had the same effect on the spirit of the Galitzianer Jew as a sudden 'eclipse of the sun' on a fine clear summer day.

The mood of the Jews in Galicia was altered immediately, and they began to think of themselves as a sort of lower class relative, which the higher class community had distanced itself and segregated itself, and this new coterie of uncultured sorts were not to their taste, and was beneath their dignity as someone with whom to associate, especially as regards the unfamiliarity and distance between their culture and way of life.

The best definition of the emotional and physical transfer of the Jews of Galicia to their new Polish country was given by R' Shlomo'leh the Dayan's.

Some beautiful exchange we've made, R' Shlomo'leh argued in front of the Master of the Universe in the *Bet HaMedrash*.

Dear Sweet Father, you took away Prague and gave us Krasznik, we lost Budapest and found Frampol, bargained away Vienna with the Emperor, and acquired Chelm with her well known 'sages[1].'

Truthfully, the Galitzianer Jews were, in the initial period, not satisfied with the exchange, and this was for

[Page 74]

many reasons that are superfluous to reiterate.

The foremost reason is, that even before '*Jasza*' felt like the legitimate owner of the Galician Province, he immediately showed what he is capable of, one little pogrom giving way to a second, a Jew suddenly lost his personal name, and for *Jasza*, 'hate' became the collective name for all the Jews.

In the newly established Poland, there was no other name for a Jew other than '*Parszywy Zydze*.' It was then that the Jews understood, what wise men had once said: 'Better to be the tail of a lion, than the head of a fox.'

The loving '*Jaszas*' not only didn't let the Jews be a 'head,' they spared no effort to bar the way to them from even being a tiny tail.

On the day that the Austro-Hungarian Empire disintegrated, our hero Chaimchi found himself at his daily work.

Not grasping what was going on outside the hospital, Chaim'l attempted to exit the through the great gate, as he was used to doing every early morning, to take part in the little *Bet HaMedrash* for soldiers, which was on the second side of the street, as a center for a minyan.

How great was his astonishment, upon seeing a group of young gentile hooligans in civilian clothes, old rifles on their shoulders, with red and white insignias on their helmets, drunk as Lot[2], staggering along with uncertain steps, and drawing closer to him.

Not asking any questions, they tore off the Imperial Insignia from Chaim'l's soldier's hat, and at the same moment, pinned on a white-red ribbon with a metal eagle, which, with his sullen, murderous stare, stabbed Chaim'l through the heart.

Chaim'l's healthy instinct immediately set him on the right course, he immediately oriented himself to the real situation, reacting with a favorable look to this unfriendly act, sticking his hand into the hands of each gentile individually, and with a seemingly satisfied little smile, blurting out a hearty '*Czesc Bracia*[3]' with the addendum of '*Niech zjye Polska*.'

This lucky thought really did save Chaim'l from a variety of troubles, that other Jewish soldiers had to put up with in the first days of transition.

[At this point} Chaim'l no longer sought to go into the little *Bet HaMedrash*, turning himself about to the barracks with their Polish insignias, quickly entering his room, packing up his bit of impoverished belongings, and with quick strides, left the last of the Austrian territory on the way to his birthplace in the *shtetl* of Cieszanow.

Entering the *shtetl* in full uniform, excepting that instead of the old Austrian markings, wearing the Polish white eagle, he was received with great respect by the local residents, they were taking pride in the fact that

[Page 75]

Chaimchi was, so to speak, a good Polish patriot.

He found great favor in their eyes, personally, he seldom felt their brutal animosity as did the other town Jews.

The took great pride in him, and treated him like he was one of their own, saying to him, in very sincere terms, that it was truly a shame that he was a Jew, and simultaneously, using various forms of compliments and flattery, demonstrated to him that they did not detest him.

This was the way Chaim'l managed to stroll through World War I.

* * *

In 1914, Chaim'l left behind a well-to-do home, which was aristocratic, with all good things, but when he returned in 1918 to his home, he didn't find any home, only a wreck, a desolation.

From all of the houses in the *shtetl*, among them Ruchama's houses, almost nothing remained, burned down, wrecked – everything lay in a heap of garbage.

Only with strenuous effort, was Chaim'l able to clean out a room in one of Ruchama's houses, in which she had lived with her children, and also served a s a guest room in the saloon residence house.

Thanks to Chaim'l's good relationship with the new Polish gentry, he was able to obtain a license from the new constabulary for his mother's businesses.

In this little room, they began to live as if from the beginning, in new effects, with new furnishings, with new laws, and with new people, who were spiritually alien to the Jews.

The condition of the Jews became catastrophic, various epidemic diseases ran rampant, and the resistance of the ill to disease grew weaker with every passing day because of the great hunger which reigned in the Jewish homes.

The larger portion lived nearly in the streets, under the open sky, and were it not for the immediate aid by the 'Joint' from America, which became visible in the Galitzianer Jewish homes after the war, the larger part of the Jewish populace would have perished.

Also the relationship between the Galitzianer Jews and their new Polish neighbors were not very normal.

The larger part of the Polish populace, immediately from the first minute of the transfer of power, manifested a bestial and sadistic hatred toward the Jewish part of the citizenry whom they had taken over in their Austrian legacy, and the more the Jew strove to align himself to the new situation, to serve his newly found fatherland, and to be a good and decent son of Poland, the new rulers pushed them away brutally, insulted them, encumbered their economic position, and from time to time, honored them with a bit of a pogrom.

Up to the San River, Galicia did not officially belong to Poland, despite this, when the Polish-Ukrainian War broke out, and the Poles did not in concert mobilize the young Jewish boys, also not from the part of Galicia that belonged to them, the larger part of the young boys did not protest, but like good loyal Polish

[Page 76]

citizens, they took part in liberating all of Galicia up to the Prut River.

Also, Chaim'l did not protest when his local Polish comrades took him out of his house in the middle of the night, and with a group of Jewish youths, transported him over to the self-same barracks in the *shtetl* of Lubaczow, in which Chaim'l had just finished World War I just five weeks before.

To tell the truth, his new-found military colleagues related very well to him.

They permitted him to retain the rank that he had brought with him from the Austrian army, even honoring him by giving him [a promotion to] a higher rank, handling him with great tolerance, almost like one of their own.

The one-time Yeshiva boy immediately extracted himself from his former German cultural circle, in which he was sunken with head and feet as if in the 49 gates of uncleanliness, immediately orienting himself in the new reality, and with his acute temperament took to 'Mickiewicz-Sienkiewicz[4]' and in a short time, he became a 'Pole of the Mosaic faith' with all the i's dotted and t's crossed.

His gentile friends derived great pleasure and satisfaction from him.

At every opportunity, they boasted about '*Nasz Chaimczu*,' and put him forward as a model before the general, who had organized the assault on the Ukrainians, in which Chaim'l's division took part.

On a certain Friday at nighttime, about twelve o'clock, a trumpet alarm [sic: bugle call] sounded through the barracks, mixed in with [the sounds of] rain and storm.

Outside is a darkness like the plague sent at Pharaoh's time, wet, cold and dank. A chill cuts through the bones of everyone standing in rows with all their gear.

The general holds forth with a patriotic speech, the well known song '*Jeszcze Polska*[5]' is sung, and an immediate order [is issued]: 'March.'

The assault against the Haidamak bands, under the leadership of the Bandit [Semyon] Petlura, who brought tragedy, had begun.

The stalwarts of Petlura demonstrated their might, but only against unarmed and innocent Jews, but when these big heroes, and even bigger anti-Semites, heard the first shot from the opposing side, they would scatter like mice, and take out their anger on the innocent Jews.

Chaim'l was so strongly taken up with what his own eyes had seen, and despite the fact that his own Poles were not exactly righteous people, they also beat Jews and cut off Jewish beards, robbed and abused, but it didn't begin to compare to the deeds of the barbaric Ukrainians.

Not that, God forbid, '*Jasza*' loved the Jew any more than '*Nikita*,' but simply for the reason that many Jews

[Page 77]

were serving in the Polish army, and it was not always that '*Jasza*' could do with a Jew what his befouled heart urged him to do, if he was in the presence of a Jewish officer, noncom, or even plain soldier.

In every eastern Galician *shtetl* occupied by the Poles, the first objective was, instead of searching out spies and Ukrainian gangs who fought against them with arms in hand, was to search Jewish homes for so-called illegal merchandise.

During such searches, the 'troublemakers,' מי"ש would confiscate everything that begins with 'A,' 'A silver Sabbath candlestick,' 'A Hanukkah Menorah,' 'A covering,' 'A fur coat,' and similar things.

After such a search in the *shtetl* of Kalisz, Chaim'l's comrades stole everything from the Rosenbaum family that they could lay their hands on.

Blood dripped in Chaim'l's heart, when he was passing by and he had to witness what was being done with his brethren.

Not being able to control himself, out of great frustration, he threw himself at the three gentile hooligan soldiers, and with an authoritative shout drove them out of the Jewish saloon.

A similar incident happened to Chaim'l marching with his division on the road between Stanislaw and Kolomyja.

In a village they were passing by, a Jew was standing and harnessing his horse in the field.

A soldier, who could not tolerate the fact that a Jew could own his own horse, left the marching division, and specifically wanted to forcibly take the horse away from the Jew.

The Polish hooligan, however, encountered a Jew who was obdurate, who resisted vigorously, and in the midst of this, Chaim'l noted what took place, not thinking, he went with a pennant to the 'war hero' and gave him a not insubstantial whack across his filthy mouth, and in this way, he rescued the Jewish horse which was perhaps the last [possession] that the Jew had.

During all this time, Chaim'l had one plea to The Master of the Universe, that he should be able to take vengeance upon Petlura's bands.

The lust for vengeance was not derived from his love of the opposing side, but rather from hatred of Haman.

In that era, the Polish anti-Semites, with the 'Haller' faction and the 'Poznan' factions at their head, appeared almost as *Tzadikkim* in the eyes of the Jews, in comparison to the wild and murderous 'Petlura' bands.

The Jewish-Polish soldiers had an expression that cholera is worse than typhus, and this was truly the right definition and assessment of the situation of trying to refrain from engaging one's self with the two new sets of neighbors in Galicia, in relation to the Jews.

It was in this condition that Chaim'l marched day in and day out, into a village, out of a city, and his heart broke, observing the destruction heaped on the Jews which both parties strove to deepen and enlarge.

[Page 78]

He saw so much evil with his own eyes, hatred, brutality, and barbarity, that this refined and genteel young man was transformed into a beast thirsting for vengeance.

He thought to himself – Oy, Master of the Universe, if such a Petlura beast would fall into my hand, I would take my revenge on him for the innocent Jewish blood that has been spilled.

Chaim'l lucked out in the *shtetl* of Kossow and was able to get his hands on such a Petlura beast.

In his chancellery, which was found in the house of the local family, Kez, a soldier armed with a gun always stood at a post.

As it happened, on the day that the incident took place, a Jewish soldier from Chaim'l's town of birth was on the post.

The soldier, known throughout the entire company by the name 'Elali,' was small and thing, more uniform than flesh, with his hat always down over his eyes, the rifle almost double the length of himself.

On that day, a gentile hooligan, of sizeable stature, fat, broad as Og, the King of Bashan, with a wild, unkempt forelock, attempted to enter Chaim'l's room.

In response to the question posed by 'Elali' at the post, as to what he wanted, he got a punch in the ribs from the gentile hooligan, and without asking, burst into Chaim'l's chancellery.

Entering – he requested from Chaim'l a 'passport' to be able to travel to the fair at Kolomyja, not grasping that before him was also a Jew, thinking that he had before him a pure Pole, relying on Chaim'l's Aryan features.

The Ukrainian follower of Petlura exudes a cynicism in front of Chaim'l, and simultaneously mocks the 'Zyd' that stands at his post, who had wanted to bar his way from entering the chancellery to Chaim'l. and with what strength he assaulted the *Parszywy Zyd*, and gave his a good shot in the ribs.

The gentile hooligan had not yet finished his nervy description, when the soldier 'Elali' entered Chaim'l's room, his face, which was no bigger than a tiny bouquet, white as chalk, the gentile hooligan gestures arrogantly towards him.

'Here is the *Zyd*, and envelopes himself with a pleasant laughter, Ha…Ha…Ha…'

At that moment, 'Elali' wanted to tell the seated Chaim'l about the incident, but it was no longer necessary for him to do so.

Chaim'l immediately oriented himself towards what was taking place here.

Chaim'l's first act was to lock the door, so that the bird does not fly away, ordering 'Elali' to call in two soldiers to assist, and that they should bring along a leather '*nagaika*.[6]'

[Page 79]

The Petlura bandit was bound hand and foot, thrown on the ground, the two Polish soldiers – themselves gentiles, held him firmly by the head and the feet, and Elali received an order from Chaim'l to administer twenty five lashes to the gentile hooligan's bare bottom.

The two Polish goons, not satisfied with Elali's weak blows, requested permission from Chaim'l to deal with this beast.

The Pole, with his entire might, and beastly murderousness, counted out twenty five lashes anew.

The Petlura bandit no longer was able to get out on his own two feet, and the two gentiles carried him out into the street, ordering a peasant who happened to be conveniently standing not far away, with his wagon, to convey the gentile hooligan to the train station, and from there he was transported to the well-known Lemberger '*Brigidas*[7],' from where, it appears, he did not survive to emerge.

* * *

In the meantime, the Poles occupied the entire area, meaning the vicinity of 'Kossow – Kolomyja – Zhabe,' the corner of Eastern Galicia up to the Rumanian border city of 'Wizniec' beside the Czeremosz River.

Chaim'l, with his company, wandered about the high mountains around Kossow and Zhabe.

This area reminded Chaim'l of the legendary persona of the *Baal-Shem-Tov*, who some two hundred years before, had also wandered here like him, eating *polenta* and milk.

The mountains, the forests, the beasts, and separately the people, look, in reality as if they were created for a *Hasidic*-mystical life.

Even the so-called village '*guralehs*,' with their broad round fur-covered hats on their heads, and thick white woolen coats, with small, almost bursting close-fitting pants, which they wear all year round, even during

[Page 80]

the hottest summer months, their '*kibitkas*[8],' and especially their primitiveness, everything taken together – the local Jews in their integrity and modest lives, conjures the natural picture of the times of the *BESH"T*.

The clear sky, the houses are also identical to the ones in the Cabalistic city of Safed, it appears that the sacred teachings of the 'Holy AR"I[9]' who had studied them with the residents of Safed two centuries ago, were later studied by the *BESH"T* with his *Hasidim* in the towns of Kossow-Kuty which lie deeply imbedded in the sacred hills located there.

A Jew who is well-versed in the Kabbalah, can see here, as well as there, with only a good look from his eyes, how angels, the souls of the righteous, and all the other saints, clamber about in those heavens so full of mysticism.

It is not for nothing that the Holy *BESH"T* selected this vicinity for his labor on behalf of The Creator.

The *BESH"T* like atmosphere of the area made a strong impression on Chaim'l, and in the meantime, he forgot that apart from being a *Hasid* influenced by the *BESH"T*, he was also a Polish officer.

Secondly, he was sunken into a trance of higher worlds, Kabbalah, and mystical dreams.

On a nice winter's day, descending from a such a mountain, imbued with the spirit of the *BESH"T*, in a sleigh, the driver, at a curve, made a strong turn to the left side, at the point when the horse was at full gallop, and he couldn't hold them back, and at that same moment, the sleigh capsized, and people, along with the horse, rolled down the side of the hill with an enormous amount of force, not being able to separate themselves, either from the sleigh, or from the horse, which rolled together as a single unit, with the single destination of falling with a violent force for several hundred meters into the deep Czeremosz River.

In this critical moment, when Chaim was threatened with danger to his life, and when it was a t a point, which he thought of at the time, that there was only a little hope that he would remain alive, in his thoughts, he pleaded for himself, that the good will of the *BESH"T* be with him.

And, indeed, the good will of the *Tzaddik* indeed by him.

As if by command, the sleigh slammed into a telegraph pole, which stood in its way.

Chaim, instinctively sensed that it was now or never, and with both hands, grabbed onto the telegraph pole with the last of his strength, and remained hanging in such a position in mid air.

Behind him, in the meantime, the sleigh, with the horse, together with the driver, fell the hundred meters deep, with a violent shudder, into the river that laid in their way.

Nothing further was seen other than several eddies of water that was churned up. and everything together vanished into the cold deep river forever.

[Page 81]

Chaim, the only one to come back alive from this catastrophe, got banged up severely during the time that he wrapped his hands around the telegraph pole, and specifically, he banged up his head, and because of this, he fell into a deep faint, drenched in blood, and he lay in a deep sleep lying on the snow-covered road between heaven and earth.

At this moment, Chaim'l thought that before him stood a very radiant-looking Jew, wearing a white kaftan, with a *gartel* bound around his loins, half shoes with long white socks, with the face of an angel, and he presses on his head with his soft, skillful hands, and murmurs something of a prayer.

Chaim'l hears, as if the Jew is praying with an intonation, and says I, 'Israel ben Hodel' decree that Chaim ben Faiga Ruchama shall remain alive, and that health should be restored to him soon.

And lying so – Chaim'l sees how this holy *Tzaddik* suddenly wipes him across the eyes with his right hand, and Chaim'l sees how he stands besides an enormously large table of ice and snow.

On the table, there stands a fiery set of scales, with two gigantically large deep plates.

On the right plate, in fiery letters, are etched the letters of the word, '*Zchus*' and on the left plate the word '*Khova.*'[10]

Near the scales lies an old and thick volume, ravaged by age, with yellowed pages.

Opposite the scales, the old man sits, still looking very fresh and healthy, with red cheeks, and a long white beard, with two large penetrating black eyes.

From his shoulders, two large white wings emerge.

A small angel shakes out – immediately onto the right scale dish, immediately onto the left scale dish, white, red, fiery small round beads.

The right scale immediately pulls down – so the angel adds from the red beads to the left plate, – and the left plate pulls over because of the weight.

And so the game proceeds back and forth.

First the right side of the scale up, and the left down, then the left up and the right down, and then the reverse.

In the meantime, Chaim'l's head is splitting from the pain, he sees and thinks, but he can't apprehend, and he wants to cry out – but he cannot.

Soon, he perceives that a small white angel has come, riding on a small horse, and approached the scale with a great haste, where the good deeds and transgressions were being weighed out.

The little angel dismounts from the horse like a bolt of lightning, grabbed it, and flung it into the right side

[Page 82]

dish of the fiery scale.

In that blink of an eye, a great rejoicing occurs around the table of ice.

Chaim'l hears, how the old man with the white beard calls out in a loud voice, which rang like the reverberations of an orchestra:

Chaim ben Faiga Ruchama – to Life!

At that minute, Chaim'l opened his eyes, and saw that he found himself clean and fresh in a bed, a doctor and a nurse in white uniforms – with a variety of vials in their hands, gauze, cotton and bandages, – they are winding it around him, and are occupied in binding his wounds.

The doctor asks Chaim how the catastrophe with the sleigh took place.

Instead of answering the doctor's question, Chaim'l asks that the *Baal Shem Tov*, R' Israel ben Hodel be sent in to him.

He must – he says – talk with him.

Chaim'l's body is burning like a furnace, and he says further to the doctor that he wants to ask the *Baal Shem Tov* who was the small angel with the tiny horse, who added for him to the right side of the scale, and because of this, cause the scale to tip in favor of life.

Chaim– lying ill with a forty degree [sic: Celsius] fever, received an injection from the doctor with a narcotic, and the sick Chaim'l immediately fell into a sleep, and once again saw the same *Baal Shem Tov*, R' Israel.

Now, Chaim'l thought, he must reveal the secret which weighed so heavily upon his soul.

Tell me – Holy *BESH"T*....

The *Baal Shem Tov* cuts off the remainder of Chaim'l's remark, and it seems to Chaim'l that the *BESH"T* is cramming an *esrog* into his mouth, and because of this, he cannot get out even a single word.

But the saint does not leave Chaim'l, he tells and reminds him of the day ten months earlier, when he and his company marched past a village between Stanislaw and Kolomyja, and a Polish soldier from his division saw fit to steal a horse from that Jew, who was grazing it in the field.

The *BESH"T* coughs slightly – and you, Chaim'l literally were prepared to give your life away – a solitary Jew among an entire band of Polish anti-Semites, and you put your life on the line, saving the horse, from which the poor village Jew earned a living to feed his wife and six little children.

And, the holy *Baal Shem Tov* said with a sigh, had you, God forbid, not performed this great mitzvah, that Jew, his wife, and their six children would have perished from hunger.

In the sacred book of the kabbalah, the *Zohar*, it is written, the holy *Baal Shem* says further to Chaim, that He who sits on high, punishes and rewards man measure for measure, that means – said the *Baal Shem Tov*,

[Page 83]

adding in his own beloved Ruthenian tongue, '*kakoi rabotu – takoi ploto*,' and you, Chaim'l have to your credit, a good '*rabotu*,' despite the fact that you found yourself in danger, your life, at that time, literally was hanging by a hair.

At the time when they were weighing and measuring your sins and good deeds, in the two dishes of the scales, they swung up and down, down and up, almost equal, and the Heavenly Court Above could not decide whether guilty or innocent.

Know then, Chaim'l – that in that critical, and for you dangerous moment, that tiny, beautiful angel came flying on your behalf, riding on the little horse, which at that time, you had rescued from the Poles' hands.

This little, good angel, not asking questions of anyone, threw the little horse into the dish marked for 'benefit,' the right side dish, which with difficulty, like an arrow from a bow, buckled and descended downwards.

It is thanks to this 'Little Horse' that it was ruled that you should live.

I assure you Chaim'l, the *Baal Shem Tov*, adds further, that you will soon get well, and you will be released from gentile hands.

At that precise moment, Chaim'l opened his eyes, it was a cold, wintry, dry, sunny day, with a covering of icy frost on the windows.

The fever vanished suddenly, and for the first time since the incident, Chaim'l felt good and fresh.

The nurse immediately came to his side, to his bed, with a small sweet smile on her Polish lips, a glass of warm milk in her hand, and with a pious religious emotion, asked Chaim'l the meaning of the word '*Pshem*?' which you did not let go from your mouth during all the time you had the great fever.

Chaim thought to himself, go explain to a gentile Polish woman a story involving the *BESH"T*.

In order to get her away, he told her that it wasn't '*Pshem*,' but '*Baruch HaShem*,' that he had said, meaning, 'Blessed be the Name of the Lord,' meaning that he had asked of God that he be granted his life.

Upon hearing the name of God, the gentile woman crossed herself three times, and left the room.

* * *

What lay heaviest on Chaim'l's soul were the Fridays before sunset, all of the Jews of Kosow sat at their Sabbath feasts, together with their near ones, and he found himself in a room, with his gentile comrades, in which there was the suffocating odor of non-Jewish kielbasa and the odor of sauerkraut made the air stuffy, and it was possible to almost literally feel the texture of the air.

Chaim'l had requested from his commandant many times, that he be released from duty on Friday, and that he would take the duty of a Christian on Sunday.

The commandant did not want to release him as a matter of principle, and to rub salt in the wound – set him

[Page 84]

to a variety of orders towards Friday evening.

Chaim'l suffered this silently, and ground his teeth, for, after all, did he have another choice?

He suffered this up to the point that God presented him with the incident of the sleigh, and because of this, he was admitted to the hospital for several weeks.

After Chaim'l was discharged from the hospital, the commandant chose to turn a blind eye to the fact that Chaim'l disappeared each Friday towards evening.

Chaim'l made the acquaintance of a Jew, who was a scholar, a so-called man of thought. This man's hat was always on backwards.

When he spoke, he would always point his index finger to his right temple, and lose himself in thought.

With it all, this did not prevent a new child from being born into his family every year.

Despite his eccentric nature, the Jew was a Torah scholar and a *Maskil*.

Chaim'l pleasure was to sit with this Jew, and spend hours with him in discourse about the Torah.

Upon entering into the home of this Jew on a certain Friday evening, he found him in a very upset and distraught state.

What happened? Chaim'l asked the Jew.

My dear Esther'l gave birth to twins today.

Mazel Tov to you, Chaim'l shouted out with glee, and at the same time, out of simple curiosity, asked the distraught happy father, what kind of twins are they?

The distraught Jew replies, I think a boy and a girl, and immediately puts his index finger to his temple and says, excuse me, I am not so sure, but it is possible that it is a girl and a boy.

Chaim immediately understood that this Friday night was lost, he wished him a Good Shabbos, and returned to his soldier comrades, who lay on their general hearth, not their 'berth' deep in sleep, gurgling and snoring, in various hoarse voices, like a symphony of inebriated and incompetent musicians.

It was then that Chaim'l saw the great disaster of the Jewish people.

Petlura, and his bandits, burned, abused, and murdered the Jewish populace in every village and every town where they were only able to set their unclean feet.

It is hard to imagine the fear of the distraught and lifeless eyes in the pale and exhausted Jewish faces, at the time that the Polish soldiers marched into their town.

They had endured enough from the Ukrainians, who were their masters up to this point, and they thought,

[Page 85]

now the same tragic story will be repeated at the hands of another beast.

Immediately at dawn, Chaim took a stroll through the *shtetl*, the windows and doors of the plundered and partly burned Jewish homes were locked up 'with seven locks.'

Neither a Jewish man, nor a Jewish woman trusted to poke their heads out onto the day lit street.

Chaim'l in going from street to street, notices that on a number of locations, dried human blood, here a broken up bed with torn up, dirty and bloodied clothing, bedding and other rags, there an emptied and broken bureau, feathers and bed stuffing was being blown about almost over the entire town.

It was in this a state, that Chaim'l encountered his Jewish brethren on the other side of the border.

Despite this, he was obdurate, and thought, I must present myself and speak with a Jew, in order to strengthen them, and calm them a bit.

Thinking in this way, he espies, with his sharp eye, that from a nearby house, a human finger protrudes a couple of centimeters from a shutter that covers a window.

He stopped by this window, and shouted into the window in Yiddish: 'Dear Jews, no fear, I am also a Jew, I wish to speak with you.'

A deathly silence reigns, there is no voice and no response, silence, nothing moves, and he sees nary a person with his eyes.

Chaim is not discouraged, he knocks, and offers many pleas, that they should open the door – but it is still, and there is no response.

At that very moment, it occurred to him to try the familiar stratagem which united all Jews tribes in all the lands of the world.

He shouts *Shema Yisrael*! into the window, and a miracle occurs, a woman with a bare head, hesitantly showed herself behind the shutter, and asked: Are you really a Jew?

I am a Jew, a good Jew, Chaim'l replied with a sympathetic voice, do not be afraid, my dear lady, let me into your house, I have brought something for you and your family, to give you some sustenance for your hearts, and especially your souls.

Hearing these kind of words, a man with a pointed beard, and gentle Jewish features, immediately opened the door carefully, and with a Russian '*Pozhalusta*' requested that Chaim'l enter his home.

The first thing Chaim asked for was a pair of *Tefillin*.

At the moment, the Jew did not believe his own ears, *Tefillin*? And he thinks to himself, perhaps all this is some sort of a dream?

Chaim'l put on the *Tefillin*, and faced to the east, praying out loud, in order that the frightened people be able

[Page 86]

to hear, and to be certain that he is a Jew and not a Pole.

After prayers, Chaim asked that everyone be seated at the table, he pulled a bottle of 96-year old brandy out of his rucksack and recited a blessing, treated the *balebatim*, and immediately wished that there should be peace on all Israel, and that all enemies of the Jews, on both sides, should soon have a downfall.

Two loaves of bread, and three cans of sardines, which Chaim'l placed on the table, was not adequate for the family, which consisted of three people.

The dear people begged Chaim'l's pardon for the speed with which they ate, they confessed to their guest that this was the fourth day that they were hungering, Chaim'l wished them all good things, and promised them to visit periodically, and at that time, not to forget to bring something with him.

During this time, the Jewish man had a conversation with his guest.

From word to word, Chaim'l became aware of the fact that this Jew was a member of the illustrious Rabbinical *Hasidic* family of 'Twersky,' and is an uncle to R' Zusha Twersky, the son-in-law of Chaim'l's Szczecin Rabbi Rav

Simcha Issachar of the house of Halberstam ל"ז, with whom he studied Torah, before he was transformed first into an Austrian, and then later, a Polish soldier.

This connection, and the recollection of his old good days, so warmed Chaim'l that he emptied his rucksack of everything that he had, and gave it to the people, repeatedly giving them encouragement and comforting them, and after a couple of hot tears, which Chaim'l unwillingly shed, and embarrassed him, took his leave of this Jewish home that had been wrecked by anti-Semites.

After he had seen what the wild Ukrainians, and even the so-called European Poles had done to the Jews, he became disgusted with the entire world, and attempted however more quickly to bring his military service to an end, and be rid of his nearly five years of service to his various 'Fatherlands.'

During all of this time, Chaim'l knew that his being drawn into the Polish army was accomplished by not entirely legal means.

His *shtetl* lies on the east side of the San River, and this part of Galicia was at this time still referred to a 'no-man's land.'

He persistently complained to his colonel, but he was laughed at, until a genius of an idea occurred to him, to make his way to Geneva, to the 'League of Nations' and demand an intervention by the Polish regime to immediately discharge him from the military.

A miracle out of heaven occurred, and a month later, by way of an order from the Warsaw-based Ministry of War, Chaim'l was discharged, his commanding officer sought to detain him at the last minute by making a variety of threats, but it was for nought, and Chaim demanded a discharge.

The dog, left with no alternative, was compelled to let him go.

And it was evening, and then morning, and Chaim'l ended the First World War.

* * *

[Page 87]

Chaim'l returned to his birthplace in Cieszanow two days before Purim, discharged after nearly five years of military service.

The *shtetl* lived on its reputation in the past.

For generations, this very *shtetl* was renown for its Rabbis, rabbinical leaders, Torah scholars and *Maskilim*.

The last Rabbi of the *shtetl*, Rabbi Simcha Issachar of the house of Halberstam, ל"ז, with his full entourage of *Hasidic* adherents infused the *shtetl* with a substantive *Hasidic* way of life.

The mutual tolerance of the various parts of the Jewish populace was a model for all of the other area towns.

Hasidic balebatim, manual laborers, and merchants, all intermixed under one roof of national aspirations, understood that in a time of peril, it was necessary to stand together against an external foe.

When the local anti-Semitic hooligans attempted to perpetrate something in the *shtetl*, they received an appropriate set of desserts from the young people of the *shtetl*, without any difference regarding party or position, when it came to defending Jewish honor or Jewish property, [because] at times like that, a unique unity of purpose reigned among the youth of the *shtetl*.

Several days after Chaim'l returned to his new 'old home,' after all his male and female comrades arranged a picnic celebration in his honor in a nearby woods, on an official day, it happened that a group of the village hooligans forced their way into R' Chaim Yisrael's nearby business location, on the pretense of wanting to buy something, but really to beat the Jew, for no good reason.

As if by a command order, the entire population of menfolk in the *shtetl*, under the order of R' Fishl the wagon driver and Paltiel Sztam, took a stand against the hooligans, and with various implements which came to their hands, stepped out to defend Jewish honor.

R' Fishl the Wagon Driver tore a 'Sign' off of his wagon, and wielded this implement among the hooligans to the extent that he could.

Since that incident, it was truly tranquil in the *shtetl*, these reprehensible troublemakers restraining themselves from carrying on at Jewish expense, which regrettably was not the case in other area towns.

This R' Fishl, *Balegolah*, a Jew possessed of a round, heavy build, with a friendly and perpetually laughing broad face, with strong evidence of the Mongolian race, but with a warm Jewish heart.

R' Fishl himself was a rather simple man, he had never had any schooling, and was compelled to go to work as a young boy, because he came from very poor parents.

When Fishl was discharged from Franz Joseph's military service, where he had served three years with the heavy "Howitzers" as he used to boast, he thought that it was time for him to begin creating a home [and family].

[Page 88]

This did not come easily to Fishl for a variety of reasons.

The daughters of the craftsmen, such as tailors, and others, did not want to have Fishl as a husband. first, being a wagon driver was not something they viewed favorably, they had hoped to get a young man who worked at the same trade as their father, and their argument to Fishl was that a craftsman was a greater blessing.

Fishl thought, let them all go to blazes, and first of all, he built himself a house, bought two horses like lions, and when he cracked his whip, and with his deep booming voice, gave a yell to his two beasts, '*Viyoi*!' the whole street shuddered, and this made Fishl famous among the merchants, nobility, and others, who had recourse to a 'Teamster.'

When all the other wagon drivers had nothing to do, Fishl didn't know what to do with all the people that wanted to ride with him, and specifically only with him.

In the *shtetl*, there lived – can one really say lives?

All anti-Semites should live this way, Sweet Father in Heaven, the way R' Berish'l *Badkhan* live, or as he was called R' Berish Marshalek.

R' Berish'l, a handsome Jew, with a combed out wide white and flattened beard, was a Torah scholar, well versed in minutiae, remembered many tales, homilies from the tradition, folklore, and ordinary tales.

He utilized this 'knowledge' in order to make a living, and was the village jester and storyteller at all weddings.

It was simply a pleasure to gaze upon the handsome R' Berish'l when he stood on the wedding table, and sang to the bride and groom before the wedding ceremony under the canopy.

Rivers of tears were shed by the womenfolk when R' Berish would cry out the traditional verse in a loud resonating and tearful voice:

> Dear Bride, dear bride
> So full of grace –
> To One Hundred and Twenty
> May you not be left alone.

The handsome R' Berish had even more beautiful daughters.

Fishl cast his eye on one of these daughters.

This girl was an 'assistant' to the wife of the town Rabbi, an '*Ozeret*,' as it is called in the Land of Israel.

[When] the girl told the *Rebbetzin* who it is that wants to take her to wife, she didn't think very long, and immediately presented an assessment of Fishl, who would transport her husband, the town Rabbi himself, in his wagon, that he was worthy to be Esther's – that was the girl's name – husband, and the father of her children.

[Page 89]

After such a ruling by the *Rebbetzin*, it was naturally forbidden to protest, and at the appropriately auspicious hour, Fishl found himself standing under the wedding canopy with his chosen Esther.

Things did not go badly for Fishl, he made a good living, when compared to the other wagon drivers in the town, he was something of a 'wealthy man,' and the locals didn't call him by any other name but 'Rothschild,' and that name stayed with him forever.

* * *

Chaim'l's first objective was to rebuilt all of their burned out houses.

Only with difficult and bitter effort was it possible for him to obtain three cubic meters of lumber, as a form of government support for his houses, not taking into account his past participation in the liberation of Poland.

At the time when Poles – Christians, were favored by the regime with a generous hand, and supported with large financial subsidies, and even larger amounts of materiel, Jews got next to nothing.

To his naive question put to the Polish authority for an explanation regarding this treatment concerning reconstruction, he received the clear reply that had no second meaning, '*Zydy – do Palestiny.*'

This reply penetrated deeply into Chaim'l's soul, and without giving it much thought, thoroughly discussed the realistic Jewish situation in the newly established Poland with his male and female comrades.

They organized themselves into a Zionist club, and gave thought to ridding themselves as quickly as possible of their new master, and to make *aliyah* to the Land of Israel.

In the meantime, a struggle began between the pious *Hasidic* parents, and their modern, Zionist children.

The struggle was conducted on all fronts.

The Zionist youth fought to take over the leadership of all the town institutions, which actually happened in a short time.

The first move by the young Zionists was to organize a synagogue for themselves in which all of the national holidays were observed, such as *Tu B'Shevat*, Hanukkah, Herzl's Yahrzeit on November 2, a *Keren Kayemet* evening, and so forth.

Chaim was one of the Zionist Jews in the *shtetl*, himself, as was known, a Torah scholar, he would hold forth a lecture in the Zionist Schul every Sabbath, with the teachings of the Sages woven into his speech, for the purpose of demonstrating the great mitzvah of settling the Land of Israel.

After his speech, they sat down to study the *Tanakh*, a page of the *Gemara*, or the weekly portion of the Pentateuch.

Chaim took this responsibility on himself as well, and apart from him, there were other young people who assisted in spreading Zionism with an admixture of Torah scholarship, especially, R' Asher Dieler, ז"ל.

[Page 90]

And, perhaps, Chaim'l thought, he is a complete ignoramus, and has no knowledge of Torah?

So I will ask him, let our Sages teach us – where are our modern day *Gaonim*?

What is the matter with: Koch, Wasserman, Weitzman, Einstein and thousands of others?

For a longer time, Chaim ceased to write in 'Heint,' until he had an encounter with two of his comrades, when the writer and Chaim'l campaigned for the same Zionist candidates for the Polish Sejm.

Juschzohn admitted that he had made an error, and asked for a pardon, and because of this Chaim rolled up his sleeves again and began again to express himself, and send in articles to 'Heint.'

Chaim'l was unable to build himself a house from all of his Zionist and community activities.

His girl, Sarah'leh justifiably argued with him. it is, she said, high time that you should give thought to yourself and your own future.

She, Sarah'leh a girl with all the virtues, beautiful, young with curly blond silken hair, very talented, with a pair of intelligent blue eyes, and a sharp mind as well, continuously demanded that Chaim'l lay aside what she referred to in her practical language, ass 'the community foolishness,' and in its place, be concerned with the renovation of the burned down house, and especially, with the question of how long will they carry on like this, being in love, but not having gotten married?

In the meantime, nothing came of the idea that Chaim'l and Sarah'leh were planning, that is, to make *aliyah* to the Land of Israel.

Sarah'leh argued that meanwhile, months and years were going by.

Chaim'l also became rapidly disgusted with the daily wrangling that went on with his anti-Semitic colleagues – the *Lavniks*, with whom he was compelled to sit in session together especially in the Municipal Council, and in addition, the struggle with the stubborn older generation was also burdensome, who fought him with all means at their disposal, against the Zionist youth and against the Yishuv in the Land of Israel.

Chaim took the words of his young lady to heart, whom he loved totally, with his entire ardent and innocent temperament.

He immediately resigned from community endeavors, and with a quick tempo, reconstructed his burned homes, set down the conditions for a marriage contract, and on an auspicious hour, began to plan for a forthcoming marriage together with his chosen Sarah'leh.

* * *

On a beautiful weekday of *Rosh Chodesh* Elul, Chaim'l stood under the wedding canopy with his Sarah'leh.

The wedding was conducted with great pomp and ceremony, Chaim and his bride shone with joy.

In the small town area where he found himself, through the boycott against everything that was Jewish, his

[Page 91]

entrepreneurial thrust was strongly interdicted and weakened.

The economic situation of our hero, like a fever in a sick person, immediately began to rise, and immediately fell, his businesses would rise, and then fall, and melt away, like snow on a summer's day.

His distress and sensitized feelings had a great influence on him, in the time when the political and economic crisis of Polish Jews became greater.

The frequent pogroms and daily boycott actions, put severe pressure on Chaim'l, and in between, they already had three little children.

Altogether, he was possessed by the thought and driven by the impulse to emigrate out of the Polish purgatory, and to flee wherever his eyes might take him.

They decided to settle in the big international port city of [Dan]zig, and from there, he thought, it will be easier for him to achieve his life's goal, that means, to make *aliyah* to the Land of Israel.

As the Jewish saying has it: 'Man plans, and God laughs,' Our Chaim'l lived waiting in [Dan]zig for this opportunity for a period of over ten years, and this opportunity never manifested itself.

In the first years, that is, until the Austrian house painter and adventurer Hitler ימ"ש , became visible to the obtuse Germans, the Jews were able to carry on a normal cultural life in [Dan]zig.

Also, Chaimchi did not feel himself to be in a bad situation, in keeping with his character and intellect, he was not suitable to do physical labor, and a particularly frightening and bad impression was made on him by the local so-called 'abzahlung' businesses, that the majority of the incoming Polish Jews took up.

People not qualified to do knowledge work would engage in this 'trade,' and these people, firstly, had to deaden any sense of their 'humanity,' and especially these were types who could step on dead bodies in order to be able to earn more money.

Chaim'l lacked both of these characteristics, which is the reason he did not take to this despicable line of work.

It was not only once, that such a young man was thrown down all the steps with the addition of a coarse anti-Semitic expletive for having provided the despicable German merchandise to be paid out over time.

After the unfortunate year, in which the brown-shirted Asmodeus took power in Germany, these sorts of occupations were exposed to much greater dangers.

The uncouth Germans, took merchandise from these young Jewish people to whatever extent they wanted, but practically cut off their payments, and when such a 'merchant' on the Sabbath, which was the day of settlement, came back to his wife and child with his limbs intact, he considered himself to be a fortunate man.

There was not only one instance where it occurred that these emboldened *Jaeckes* would break the bones of such a merchant, in order to rob the poor Jew of everything that he had, and add to it the well-known blessing –

[Page 92]

'*Judes – Verrücke*'[11] from his house.

Chaim could not orient himself to engage in this sort of living, he worked at a bank branch in the morning as a bookkeeper, and as a teacher in a community Jewish school in the afternoons, which had been established in all German-Jewish communities because of the political situation.

He made a good living, and after being alone for a half year, he brought his family down, and in time, became an important citizen in the old city of [Dan]zig.

He made a living, and hoped that the brown[-shirted] fire would stop and the good and tranquil old times would return.

As did all of the German Jews, he made an enormous mistake, the situation grew worse with each passing day in all of Germany, and especially in [Dan]zig.

Here, in this very international city, but having an almost one hundred percent German population, they wanted to show their 'Straying Führer' that they too are patriots of the so-called 'Reich,' and are also well-versed in the 'lore' of beating, robbing and abusing Jews, just like their brown[-shirted] brethren in Germany.

Like an unmoving black cloud, accompanied by a hating thunder and lightning that fills the skies, so did the brown[-shirted] plague grow ever nearer, and with every passing day, the air became more stifling for the Jews in all of Europe.

In the first period, it became a common occurrence to verbally assault Jews in the street through the use of coarse insults.

Later on, they were awarded beatings, and in the final days, literally with pogroms.

And it was in this fashion, with precise *Jaecke* calculation, that the great tragedy closed in on the German Jews, and in the end, almost on the entirety of European Jewry.

Chaim'l had a special good fortune, in that the brown[-shirted] bandits did not assault or insult him even once.

This was partly due to his not very Semitic features, or because he was involved almost exclusively with Jews, and was rarely around in the streets.

On this street, he could never give the right answer, and there were many instances when even such non-Semitic looking Jews were insulted and beaten by the Nazis.

During the early phases, many Jews did have the opportunity to gradually liquidate their assets, and send it over to the Land of Israel.

Our hero, Chaimchi did not have an insignificant part in such operations, because of his employment at the only Jewish bank, which engaged in this sort of a transfer, initially legal, but later on, illegal.

[Page 93]

Such fortunate Jews left the [Dan]zig purgatory immediately.

In the meantime, Chaimchi's family grew larger, and he was already the father of four sons and a daughter.

And he did everything that he could to obtain a certificate that would enable him to leave [Dan]zig along with the fortunate, but without success.

At the exact time of the greatest Jewish need, the English Mandate Authority, together with the well-known Anti-Semite, [Aneurin] Bevan, pushed down the so-called 'quota' to a minimum, not taking into account the increased demand for European Jewry, and especially the German [Jews] to be admitted to the Land of Israel.

In this manner, several years went by, hoping, and hoping for Bevan's just ways, but all of the hoping came to ruin, until on a somber Saturday at dusk, on the so-called '*Kristallnacht*' as it was called by the Hitler bandits, in [Dan]zig, with punctilious German efficiency, the great and familiar pogrom was also organized along with the burning of synagogues.

The Jews scented that something was going to happen.

[However], not a single person knew exactly what was going to occur.

But, at a time when Jews stand before large, sorrowful events, everyone, including the infant in a crib, knew.

As if by a signal, at exactly four in the afternoon, the march of the Hitler Youth began, led by the [Dan]zig police, and SS troops, through the Jewish businesses and private homes.

On the wall of each Jewish business, in red paint, they scrawled the word '*Jude*,' and stove in the large display windows.

Finishing this bit of work, they marched on, singing joyfully, the familiar song of murder: '*Und wenn das Judenblut von messer schpreizt*,' again smashing windows, and when they concluded this work, they gathered at the beautiful [Dan]zig Temple, throwing their lit torches at it from all sides, and carried on with glee until the Synagogue became a mountain of ash.

Chaimchi and his family sitting in their dwelling, in fear and terror, the small children who did not yet understand the real situation, played in the house, not understanding why they were compelled to spend the entire day locked in their house?

As to the older children, each was in a separate little corner.

Chaim'l along with his wife, Sarah'leh, were sitting apart, sadly, warming themselves at the coal stove, like on the day of *Tisha B'Av*.

In this situation, each individual was sitting, lost in their own thoughts and speculation.

Suddenly, through a crack – a frighteningly large stone came crashing through the shattered window, entering their home with violent force, flying between the oven and Chaim'l's head.

[Page 94]

From the impact on the coal stove, a piece of the stone went out through the nearby door, which stood not far from the oven.

This, for Chaim'l and his family, was the first harbinger of the approaching catastrophe.

Out of reaction to their woes, Jews cried, thought and laughed.

Many fled to distant places from this hell.

They crossed the border between [Dan]zig and Poland, getting out of the German Hell and entering the Polish Gdynia, which was not a small Hell, like German [Dan]zig.

The Jewish community of [Dan]zig quickly called together a secret meeting of the leadership of all the resident Jewish institutions, worked out a plan to immediately dispatch all of the young Jewish children to the Land of Israel of 10-15 years of age.

A prominent member of the community accompanied the children on their boat to Haifa.

Among these children who were sent away, were to be found Chaim'l's two older children, a boy of thirteen, and a girl of ten.

The rest of the family remained behind for the simple reason that the pseudo-socialist Bevan did not permit them entry into the Land of Israel.

The transfer of the two hundred children, or as they were called, the Exodus of [Dan]zig, took place shrouded in strict secrecy, so that even their parents were not permitted to see their own children off.

The joy of the community was without bounds on the day that news arrived advising that they [sic: the children] were outside the danger area.

On the Sunday after '*Kristallnacht*,' Chaim went to work at the bank as if nothing had happened.

The streets were quiet as if dead, except for the fact that shards of glass were scattered over all of the streets, the open window frames looked like the eye sockets of people from whom the eyes had been gouged out while they were alive.

Here and there, one could see a drunken SS trooper running by with his foul 'Gretchen' from a night of carousing.

The instinct found in every individual who finds himself in danger, is to keep himself strong and maintain a desire to live, also manifested itself as a delusion for the Jews of [Dan]zig.

After each anti-Semitic incident, they convinced themselves that this is all over, and nothing of this sort will ever happen again. And in addition to this, each individual talked himself into believing that he personally was not a target.

[Page 95]

Even the Chief Rabbi, Dr. Green, when initially he had an opportunity, as the representative of the Jewish community of [Dan]zig to speak on the radio, took such an opportunity to openly blame the '*Ostjuden*' and declared in full public view, no more and no less, that the '*Ostjuden sind unser umgluck.*'

Also, this 'Rabbi Ivan Green' really believed that not a hair would fall from his head, and the head of his ilk, that the entire anger was directed towards other [kinds of] Jews, but not against those of Germany, or so this light-minded 'Rabbi Ivan' convinced himself.

It was through this natural law, that Jews remained in their places, in subordinate positions, up to the last minute.

The majority, indeed, were exterminated.

On that same Sunday, sitting at his daily work in his bank, thinking, like all the other Jews, that from today on, everything will again be normal, a band of armed SS troops entered, went up to the safe, and robbed a sum of eighty thousand [Dan]zig Gulden, in addition to foreign specie.

The director, chief bookkeeper and treasurer were brutally thrown out of the bank.

In the street, a second gang waited for them, which pinned a sign that had previously been prepared on the breast of each of the Jews, with the writing on it of: '*Ich so-Jude bin ein verbrecher.*'

With jeering and mockery, they were led over the streets, and then incarcerated in jail.

After this incident, while still in the same day, Chaim packed together a few belongings, and in the middle of the night, together with his wife and children, crossed the border on the way back again, to his birthplace in the *shtetl* Cieszanow.

His comrades in the *shtetl* welcomed Chaimchi with open arms, they thought to themselves that they had retrieved their old general, who had abandoned them in the midst of their battle for more than ten years.

The battle between *Hasidism* and Zionism still was in existence.

The old crowd did not yet want to agree to the concept that to rescue the Jewish people, there was only one way, and that was to go to the Land of Israel.

In his old-new home, Chaim'l didn't have the time to even rest his wandering bones for a little while, after the difficult and complicated trip which he had just gone through to escape from the Hell in [Dan]zig.

When the idea of rebuilding a means to make a living finally ripened, and when he thought that surely the steps to carry out this initiative were just within his grasp, the reality of Poland arrived, along with the big disappointment.

Chaim had forgotten that in Poland too, in that time, the concept of exterminating the Jews reigned in a manner no less virulent than in Germany.

The hate between Poles and Germans had existed for hundreds of years, but when it came to the task of

[Page 96]

eradicating Jews, both of these eternal blood-enemies were prepared to shake hands, and present gleeful faces to one another.

The Pole, Beck, had invited the brown[-shirt] devil's representative Goering to visit in Polish Warsaw.

It appears that all they talked about was the Jews, and at that opportunity, worked out the now familiar plan, that Poland will become the slaughterhouse for all the Jews of Europe, and perhaps the entire world.

In the meantime, the brown[-shirted] plague continued to do its deeds.

Their work proceeded on two fronts.

[The first front was] a European one, such as the Czechoslovakian question, Danzig, Upper Silesia, Posen, former German colonies in Africa, which were divided up by the victors after the First World War.

The second front, and this was the central one to Hitler, ימ"ש, was the Jewish one.

* * *

In the year 1938, after the Hitlerist assault on the Czechs, the Jews began to understand that the global catastrophe waits for them behind the door.

However, by this time, it was too late to liquidate assets and transfer them to the Land of Israel, to settle there, and help to build a Jewish state.

The *Hasidic-Agudah* opposition to settlement in the Land of Israel reaped the fruit of what it had sown.

The Jewish people stood at the threshold of annihilation. The numbed opponents of the rising younger generation, as they demonstrated, did not have in themselves even so much as a spark of inspiration, in the way they persuaded their followers, on the contrary – they had blinkered eyes and dense minds.

From day to day, the European horizon grew more and more dark, especially that of the Jews.

The brown [-shirted] beast had successfully seen through almost all of its demands.

The familiar, English Minister, [Neville] Chamberlain, known for carrying an umbrella, conceded in satisfying all of Hitler's wishes, and in this manner, the German '*Mikhl*' came to understand that the world fears engaging in war, and because of this, he became increasingly bolder day by day.

He increased the scope of his demands at every opportunity, and in parallel, blocked and increased the destruction of the German Jews.

On a September day that was a dark day for the Jewish people, in that accursed year of 1939, the brown [-shirted] devil initiated the great and tragic world war of extermination, in spite of all the nations of the planet.

These events halted all of Chaim's planning, and he was left stuck in his *shtetl*, along with all the others, just like him.

[Page 97]

In the meantime, the Germans, in their Messerschmitts, sowed death and destruction over the burning Polish soil.

On the second day, after Poland was ablaze from end to end, from the west, her good friend Goering, with whom Poland had not long ago concluded a pact of friendship at the expense of the Jews, pressed with his heavily-armed army, and from the east, the Russian Bear fell on her, and suddenly, at three in the afternoon, Chaim'l's *shtetl* also tasted the flavor of German brutality.

Six airplanes bombarded the *shtetl*, and shot at the people with machine guns as if they were beasts in the field.

The Germans occupied Chaim'l's *shtetl* eight days before *Rosh Hashanah*.

The entered after the Soviet Army had vacated the *shtetl* pursuant to two weeks of occupation.

It became apparent that according to the agreement between the two anti-Semites, 'Ribbentrop and Molotov' the *shtetl* was to remain in German hands.

In the first days, they held themselves quietly, but despite this, the Jewish houses and businesses were locked up as tight as could be.

A Jew did not trust himself to go out into the day lit streets, and each person sat in their homes waiting for the Messiah to come.

The Jews of Cieszanow chose to deduce an *a priori* argument from this, reasoning that if after eight days of occupation, not a single Jew had been accosted in a bad way, this must be a sign that the devil is not as bad as he is made out to be.

And they chose to accept the simple extrapolation further, that since it was now the eve of *Rosh Hashanah*, it is necessary to give thought to how it would be possible to gather on the morrow for communal prayer, to blow *shofar*, and specifically in the synagogue;

A delegation, mostly of *balebatim*, managed, willy-nilly, to crawl out of their caves, and by a strenuous effort, using back alleys, gathered together at the domicile of one of their number, and decided that they would *en masse* make a request of Chaim'l to go to the German commandant as an emissary of the community, to request that he grant permission for the [celebration of] two days of *Rosh Hashanah*, that they be allowed to gather for communal worship in the synagogue.

The gaggle of *Hasidim* fell into Chaim'l's residence like orphans who were returning from the cemetery, after having interred their kin, with a sorrowful and low-voiced entreaty to present their request to him.

They based their request on the fact that he was practically the only one in the *shtetl* who had a good command of the German language, and it was [therefore] his obligation in the name of the Jewish populace to make the request of the German [officer] for the permission to assemble in the synagogue.

The idea did not appeal to Chaim right there on the spot, and he declared the following:

[Page 98]

It explicitly is written in the *Gemara*: one does not rely on the miracle, especially in a time like this, which is fraught with so much danger for Jews.

He declared further, that even if the commandant were to grant the permission, it is entirely not certain that everything will come off as desired.

Chaim'l's arguments did not help him, which were opposed, and he received admonitions that the entire town of Jews will think of him as being unfaithful, if he will not go as the community emissary to the commandant.

Being unable to get rid of them, he agreed, but on the condition that whatever the commandant will rule, must be adhered to without qualification.

Not thinking this through a great deal, the group agreed and expressed the view that this is the way it will be, and no different.

Unwillingly, Chaim girded his loins, put on his black [-rimmed] glasses for good luck, and with a heavy spirit, went off to the German commandant the town.

The streets, and the *Ringplatz* were black with tanks and other military machinery, and with a beating heart, and without paying attention, he passed through the way until he came to the place where the German was billeted.

The gentile did not receive Chaim'l badly.

He demanded of Chaim'l that he convey to the Jews, in his name, that he personally has no opposition, but as he further articulated, under the present situation, he cannot absolutely guarantee that the soldiers would not violate his orders, when the matter involves Jews, and he will then not be able to help, because they will think he is a protector of the Jews.

It appears to be decent and humane speech, and in addition, he argued why was it necessary to place one's self in danger, when each individual can beseech God in their own home, because, he says, God is to be found everywhere.

Literally a real human being, and not a German.

Chaim could not believe what he had heard with his own ears. He, the German extends his hand to Chaim'l, and once more requests that his message and intent be conveyed precisely to '*die arme Juden.*'

Chaim, a bit buoyed by the humane German, conveyed precisely what the *Jaecke* had said and they promised him that on this *Rosh Hashanah* they would not go to the synagogue, and that each individual would recite prayer in their own home, in order not to provide provocation to the Hitlerists.

After this assurance, Chaim'l was very satisfied, and was also proud that the great privilege had fallen to him to be the good emissary.

He calmed his wife down, who had opposed his acceptance of this mission by her husband.

[Page 99]

On the morrow, meaning *Rosh Hashanah*, very early, standing by his covered window, with an eye placed against a crack of the shutter, to see what was going on in God's little world, Chaim'l notes, to his great wonder, that Jews wearing *shtrymels*, with prayer shawls under their arms, women, with their thick *Tzena-U'Re'ena* prayer books are proceeding openly and freely to communal prayer, as if nothing had happened.

A fright fell on Chaim'l look at this going on, he thought to himself, and he was simultaneously afraid of two things; first, that no evil befall the Jews during their sojourn in the synagogue, especially – he was practically certain, that the Commandant will hold him personally responsible for what had happened, with the expression that he had not conveyed his words and warning with adequate conviction, and that Chaim'l had literally told them to go and attend worship.

He requested of his Sarah'leh that she prepare some clothing for him, along with miscellaneous foodstuffs for two days, and so forth.

He expected that they would come for him at any minute, and send him off to a place from where mostly one never comes back.

It happened otherwise, because Chaim'l was not in the least harmed, but everyone who found themselves in the synagogue were suddenly assaulted by a group of German soldiers, who beat them brutally, tearing out their beards along with skin, collecting all of the *shtrymels*, prayer shawls, and prayer books into a mound, lighting a fire under them, burning – beating everyone right and left.

A chaos and rampage seized the entire town, with everyone trying to save their own life, hiding in whatever hiding place one could find.

The sum total of today's attendance at synagogue, were thirty beaten Jews, the destruction of the synagogue, and in addition to this – all Jewish girls and women had to clean the *Ringplatz* with their bare hands, removing all the horse droppings that had accumulated since the time that the Germans marched into the town.

Also, our Chaim'l nearly became a victim of an accusation which seemed to be innocent.

Between Chaim'l's two houses was a large yard, and this yard served as a parking place for German tanks.

When the tank division left the parking area on one day, Chaim noted, to his great fright, that a large number of gun bullets lay in a corner of the yard, along with some guns, which belonged to those who had not long ago vacated the yard.

The accusation was lodged, as Chaim'l later became aware, by a Ukrainian living in the town, who held a grudge against Chaim'l for voting in the town council with the Polish representatives, and not with the Ukrainian representatives.

Chaim immediately oriented himself to the great danger that stalked him, and without care, tore through the streets that were filled with the military, entered into the town commandant, and described that the tank division had left a sizeable amount of ammunition behind in his yard by mistake, and that he makes a fervent request that the ammunition be removed from his yard.

Coming home, from the commandant, Chaim'l encountered two soldiers waiting for him.

[Page 100]

To the question of what they want of him, they succinctly declared that the ammunition located in his yard was stolen by him for use by Jewish youths would use it to attack the German military.

Hearing such a tale, Chaim'l immediately understood that his situation at that moment was not retrievable.

Interesting! Once again it was established, that when Chaim'l finds himself in a state of need, a salvation appears almost at the last possible minute, and he emerges whole from the danger that threatened him.

Not thinking too much, he says to the soldiers, that not only here does he have collected ammunition, he has, he says, another place, an assembled storage place with a variety of military equipment, a much larger one than the one they found on his yard.

He doesn't let the two soldiers utter a word, making a motion to exit, and asks them to accompany him to the second accumulated magazine, and he goes with them directly to the commandant, with a forced laughter, as if he is puzzled, he makes his way to the commandant, as if he doesn't understand what is going on here?

Who, he asks innocently, has the authority to designate ammunition in the strongest and most disciplined army in the world?

An officer, in this case he says – the town commandant, or two ordinary soldiers?

He doesn't understand, he says further to the officer, first, about an hour ago, I turned over to your disposition, the entire ammunition that the tank division had by error left in my yard, suddenly, these two ordinary soldiers demand that I should give them the ammunition, and at the same time they are threatening me with punishment if I do not obey their order.

He does not know what to do?

He beseeches that the commandant should rule as to what he, Chaim'l should do in this instance.

The two gentiles immediately became as white as lime.

He, the officer, noticed their pallor, did not utter a word, rang with his little bell, and a young officer immediately entered, gave them an order, '*kert auch, march.*'

The two lowlifes exited the commandant's room, Chaim'l was immediately released, and sent with an auto with soldiers to collect the ammunition left behind.

To this day, Chaim does not know what happened to the two soldiers, especially – in that instant, as he later proudly related to his Torah scholars, he came to understand the saying of the Ancient Sages: 'temerity, especially when a person finds himself in dire need, is helpful even before God himself.'

As soon as he saw, said Chaim'l that his situation was beyond retrieval, he took this daring and foolish step, and it was this temerity that indeed saved Chaim'l's life.

The Hitlerist-beasts went wild in the town for two weeks, with different disruptions every day, up to a certain day, when the Germans abandoned the tow for the second time, leaving this entire border strip for their

[Page 101]

partners, the Bolsheviks.

During the time when the Bolsheviks took over the *shtetl*, the Jews breathed easier after a two-week period of mortal fear under German control.

During the first day that they took over control, the Bolsheviks immediately organized a local leadership.

As the town elder, they appointed the illiterate Zissl'eh Bagruber, as Burgomaster, Beinish Fuster, and a Ukrainian shepherd as the commandant of police.

This coterie ruled in Chaim'l's *shtetl*, and over him personally, in the name of Karl Marx's 'ten commandments.'

When after two weeks of control, the Russians were compelled to surrender control of the town to the Germans, and this time permanently, the Jewish populace understood that they had been given the last chance to save themselves from the brown [-shirted] plague, to go along with the Bolsheviks, and in this manner, rid themselves of all the troubles.

On the day of the Bolshevik withdrawal, as a perverse consequence -- Chaim'l did not feel good, and he was beset with an intense rheumatic pain in the small of the back, and he simply could not move from his spot.

The Russians permitted anyone who was evacuated to ride along with them in their transport autos.

The allocation of such riding permits was found in the hands of the '*Starotsa*,' Zissl'eh Bagruber.

Chaim'l, led by two people, with great difficulty, and accompanied by much pain, clawed his way to the chancellery where this fellow, comrade Zissl'eh sat as the authority in charge, at Stalin's 'pleasure,' giving out the riding permits and blowing himself up like a strutting turkey.

As soon as he spotted Chaim'l, he proclaimed, with the voice of a ruler, generally into the surroundings, asked, as if he were the Emperor Nero, without looking at Chaim directly in the face: what does he want here?

Chaim told the censorious official about his illness, that he also wishes to leave the *shtetl*, and how he is unable to walk, and requests a riding permit so that he can ride.

Zissl'eh Bagruber said curtly to Chaim, that he will not be receiving a riding permit, that he, Zissl'eh, had been waiting for many years for the opportunity for Chaim and his ilk to feel the meaning of being under the control of others, and especially such persons as Zissl'eh Bagruber.

Not deterred, Chaim'l was compelled to hire a two-in-hand cart, for an exorbitant amount of money, in order to get him and his family transported over to the Russian zone, and he was able to get this done.

On the morrow, Chaim'l found himself in a place that was undoubtedly in the hands of the Bolsheviks.

It was in this fashion that, at the last minute, Chaim'l and his family saved themselves from Hitler's talons.

[Page 102]

He immediately took stock of the situation, and realized that there was no purpose to sit in the little *shtetl* of Nemirov, and thanks to his wife Sarah'leh, decided to move on to the east, wanting to be in the city of Lemberg.

As mentioned, in Lemberg at that time, there were already two hundred thousand Jewish refugees.

It was only with a great deal of effort that he was able to rent a small, damp room far outside of the city, for a very dear sum of money.

The first step of the Bolsheviks in Eastern Galicia was to confiscate all the large factories and businesses.

The second step, in order to find favor with the local populace, they established schools in all of the languages of the peoples that inhabited Galicia, that is, Polish, Ruthenian and Yiddish.

A Yiddish school appeared to be laughable in the eyes of the Intellectual Galician Jews, [because] they did not understand that Yiddish was a legitimate language, like all other languages, which also possessed a grammar, rules, construction, and a history.

At a Yiddish lecture in Lemberg, by a Soviet-Jewish teacher, our Chaim'l confronted the following type of spectacle.

The hall is filled with invited citizenry of both sexes, and from a variety of professions, doctors, engineers, teachers, professors, merchants and others.

On the podium, a young man stands with a not particularly intelligent expression on his face, next to him is a large blackboard, and he is teaching the gathering how to correctly say the following expression in Yiddish: placing the baggage trunk on the bench.

Everyone thought to themselves, this is not bad Yiddish.

After several declarations, he asks the 'students' to rise, and to signal with their hands in accordance with is command.

At the statement: Put the baggage trunk up, the 'crowd' should raise their hands, at the statement: Put the baggage trunk down, they should lower their hands, and it was in this manner that the hands of hundreds of students, teachers, doctors, professors and other intellects moved for several minutes, up and down.

Then he asks his students, what is to be raised?

All answer as if as one person – raise the baggage trunk, Good…

What is to be lowered?

To this question, all the men return the answer:

You must lower your trousers…. Bad, he shouts….

[Page 103]

The women blushed, lowered their eyes, and quickly left the Bolshevik school.

The little young man was left alone in the hall, and he straggled out as if he had been whipped, and vanished.

This so-called teacher later declared, that in the Soviet sphere, this is called 'sabotage,' and for this, one is sent for ten years to the White Bears.

* * *

In Lemberg, as was the case in the entire Soviet sphere, there reigned a shortage of everything that began with the letter 'A.'

Beginning with **A** shoe, **A** shirt, **A** dress, **A** loaf of bread, **A** needle, **A** watch, etc.

In the meantime, Chaim had made the acquaintance of the manager of the distillery in Lemberg, and he provided products for the workers, clothing and shoes, and he was not paid with money, but with a variety of alcoholic beverages.

Every month, Chaim obtained thousands of liters of liquor from the distillery, cognac, and primarily, eight-nine percent spirits.

The business got bigger and better for him every day, and he already had enough money to rent himself a large, beautiful residence.

Suddenly news spreads through the city that all male refugees, who have refused to abandon their Polish citizenship in favor of Soviet citizenship, are to be exiled to the White Bears, or to the *Taigas*.

Soon the truth is heard that on the previous night in the streets of a certain quarter of Lemberg many men were taken away, and nobody knows where their physical being is to be found.

It didn't take long before the N.K.V.D. appeared in Chaim'l's neighborhood, taking out a father here, a son, a brother, etc.

Immediately the expulsion was extended to include entire families.

One Friday night in the month of June, Chaim'l confided in his wife that his heart tells him that the kidnappers are going to show themselves in their streets on that night.

Without giving it much thought, his Sarah'leh agreed that he should sleep that night with a Jewish neighbor who was a citizen of Lemberg, who had become a Soviet, as he was certain that he would not be taken for exile.

Because that Friday night was so hot and humid, Chaim'l could in no way manage to sleep for the entire night.

At 3 AM, he was standing by the open window, in order to take a bit of fresh air.

Oh, my God! Darkness descends over his eyes at that moment.

[Page 104]

He does not know whether it is a dream or reality.

In front of his eyes, he sees them transporting his entire family in a wagon, with all of their belongings packed up, accompanied by a Tatar uniformed as an N.K.V.D. man.

He wants to scream, but nothing comes out, his voice had been taken away, and he is unable to get a single word out of his mouth.

Immediately, as in the case of all his exigencies, a good thought occurs to him, that whatever happens to his wife and children should also happen to him.

Like a wounded wolf, he leaps out onto the street, in his sleeping pajamas, runs after the wagon, his wife, sitting with her face to the rear, noted how he was running in their direction.

Out of great fear for having deceived the Tatar at the time he took her into custody, when he asked her, where is your husband to be found?

She told a lie, that he is visiting far away, and suddenly he is here in this place? Chasing after them, and who knows with what sort of angry thoughts?

This is what his Sarah'leh thought.

Sunk in her own thoughts, she indicates with her hands, despite this, that he should run back.

At that minute, Chaim'l grasped that he must be together with his wife and children, and with rapid steps, he reaches the wagon.

The idiotic Bolshevik asks him who he is, and what does he want?

To Chaim'l answer of; *eta maya semya* he received a clear reply: *davai!*[12]

Chaim was ensconced in the wagon.

They were brought to the train station, at which a large echelon of tens of cattle cars waited for them, in which men, women and children were driven together from all of Lemberg.

They were crammed into the echelon for a day and a night before it left the train station on the way to their new place of exile.

Until they finally lived to see the end and completion of the interminable ride, took over two weeks, in which day in and day out, they passed the time in misery, until they arrived at a place with the exotic foreign name of 'Cheboksary.'

We thought this was the end of the world.

[Page 105]

On the right side of the large river was the town, on the left side a desolate jungle of thick pine forests.

It appears that such forests had disappeared from Europe thousands of years ago.

An old ship was anchored at the edge of the river, into which they were driven like cattle.

To the question of why they were being treated with such brutality, they received the classic and familiar answer: *nichevo, priviknish ilyi zdekhnish – davai.*[13]

This river is the famous 'Volga.'

We sailed the length of the Volga for four days and four nights.

The only thing we saw was the sky and the forest.

After the four-day ride, Chaim'l and his fellow sufferers were invited over into a small open forest train, on the left side of the river edge, which made a sorry impression on them.

They dragged themselves on yet again for another day and a night, except this time into a deep forest.

At dusk of the following day, the contingent halted in a wooded area that was in the middle of a gigantic swamp.

The first 'welcome' they received was from the innumerable number of mosquitoes that fell upon their fresh faces, hands and feet.

The mosquitoes danced around them and buzzed about them with a wild glee. It appears that the fresh blood that they sucked from these new people smelled very good to them.

People, who were not well traveled, saw this kind of a world for the first time in their lives.

That world consists of two elements: trees and mosquitoes.

The controller of these two elements is the Soviet N.K.V.D. which reigns with unrestrained brutality over the million '*zakladchanehs*[14]' who find themselves to be free slave laborers in those *Taigas*.

It was to this sort of Hell that Chaim'l and his family were brought.

When the contingent suddenly remained standing in this God-forsaken place after having been brutally driven from the wagons by the militia men, they did not, in the first instance understand exactly what was being demanded of them.

It absolutely did not occur to them, that this dark forest had been designated as their new home by the great 'People's Guardian.'

[Page 106]

The N.K.V.D. immediately awakened them from their naivete, and they were informed categorically that it was here, in this forest, that they would remain forever, because this is the place which Comrade Stalin had designated for them, and added: *eta vsy.*

The commandant, Smirnov, a young, anti-Semitic gentile, by nature a sadist, vehemently ordered them to occupy the wooden barracks, which were hideously filthy, looked abandoned, with broken windows.

On the walls, there were written mostly the names of a variety of people, in a variety of languages, unfortunate people, like themselves, who had been housed here, worked in the forests, starved, and left their lives here, in this dark, God-forsaken jungle.

Chaim'l acquired a 'residence' for his five-member family, a small tarred dirty corridor, full of small itchy and biting forms of life all over the walls, against which a prison bunk could barely stand, on which all five later slept.

In order to reach their residence, one had to go through a room in the same filthy condition, which was allocated to three other families.

* * *

After the difficult journey, the people got a 'furlough' of a day.

On the second day, beginning at five o'clock in the morning, a militia man with piercing Mongolian eyes with a face of a person from the first stone age, drove the entire group of people – slaves, from the small to the older, men, women and children, healthy or sick, young or old, out of the barracks.

Near the barracks of the commandant Smirnov, there was a yard full of forest tools such as: saws, handsaws, arrows, axes, rope, a variety of wedges and other such tools.

Not far, was a second yard, with constraining devices such as: whips, crops, reins, a variety of nosebags, sacks, bells, wedges, iron horse shoes and other things.

People could choose between cutting trees or working as haulers, to transport the cut trees out of the forest.

There was a third group, the so-called '*gruzhchikehs*[15],' and to this distinguished group Smirnov appointed only young healthy men.

Our Chaim'l grabbed a saw, and enlisted in with the forest workers.

The men were divided up into brigades, and each brigade was accompanied by a militia man, and it was in this way, that these foreign citizens, who had no concept of what real communism entailed, began to get a taste of the communist paradise, for which tens of millions of people were compelled to offer their lives.

Work started at five o'clock in the morning, every two hours, the militia man permitted a break during which a cigarette could be smoked.

[Page 107]

The cigarette consisted of some black filling, or just simply from rubbed dry leaves, wrapped in newspaper.

Work ended at sundown.

Each brigade was given a quota, of so many cubic meters of lumber that it had to present for a day's work.

Usually, such a quota was beyond the strength of these foreign people to provide, I emphasize 'foreign,' because their own Russian '*zakladchanehs*' who were lazy, and worked in these same forests, were able to meet the quota, without any real input, but after doing this a couple of times, the person who set the quotas suddenly was found laid out in the forest swamp, and had given up the ghost.

Our people sought all manner of means to get themselves out of such a strenuous form of slave labor, and because of this a variety of conflicts erupted.

The men alternated the work every few days, from a forest worker, to a wagon driver, immediately to a water carrier, and again back to his first duty.

And it was in this way the struggle of the unfortunate went on, who had been driven away, as they referred to it in a bitter joke, to the land of the lucky.

Chaim'l also sought means to make his enslavement somewhat lighter, exchanging his bitter forest work for wagon-driving work, and to his good fortune, Chaim'l became a wagon driver.

Since he had been alive, his delicate hands had never touched a horse.

And now, when he presented himself to the stable master, a Pole, a certain Pan Hrabie Raczynski, a Pole who was in this camp along with Chaim'l, indicating that he should be allocated a horse and wagon in accordance with the order from Smirnov, this grand Pole didn't have any particular desire to place a horse in the hands of this one-time Yeshiva student.

To Chaim'l's question of why he doesn't want to give him a horse, he answers quite plainly, because he has pity on both of God's creatures.

He is afraid, lest the horse kill Chaim, or the opposite – that Chaim kill the horse.

Despite this, he took pity on him, and gave Chaim a horse, and told him to drive to the second camp which lay about ten kilometers deeper into the woods, and to bring back for himself a cargo of things that were missing from Raczynski's stable.

A fear and fright descended on Chaim'l.

As if he hasn't lost enough blood, but just for the thought alone, that here, he must touch the horse, and it is possible to imagine that at that first touch, the horse could bite off his fingers, or knock the guts out of his belly, and here he is asking him to ride, and deep into the forest, entirely alone, with such a large and wild animal, with which he doesn't even know how to begin to communicate.

Chaim reminded himself of the first Russian rule that he was taught, when arriving in the communist

[Page 108]

paradise: *priviknish ilyi...*

Chaim, placing his life at risk, drew close to the horse slowly, with uncertain steps, and reciting the familiar [prayer]: Lord of Rabbi Meir help me, stroked the horse with the reins for a long time, led the foolish horse out of the stall, stood up on a table, closed his eyes, went up onto the horse, stuck his feet into the stirrups, held onto the reins with both hands, and before he had a change to orient himself to his new situation, the stall master gave the horse a whack on the hindquarters with a rubber switch.

At this moment, the horse became terribly frightened, and reared up on its hind legs.

With eyes shut, pitifully, Chaim'l bent himself toward the hindquarters of the horse, and with all of his strength, pulled on the leather reins with a countervailing force, and again, like in the hospital, recalled the holy *BESH"T* and in such a 'Herculean' position, hung between heaven and earth for a couple of minutes which for Chaim'l seemed like an eternity.

God heard Chaim'l's prayers, and the horse righted itself once again, and took off with our hero at a trot for a couple of hundred paces.

The communist horse than remained standing, waiting for Chaim'l's next order, either from his pressure, or his riding crop.

Chaim stubbornly held on with all his might, and he did not fall off the horse, and a miracle occurred.

The delicate Chaim'l, in that instant, became welded to the horse, and in a rather short period of time, became to best wagon driver and the best rider in the entire camp.

The wagon driving Yeshiva student immediately became accustomed to his horse.

This communist horse became much more important in his eyes than the legendary horse of the Emperor Caligula which was appointed as a Consul in the senate of the Roman Empire.

The work of transporting the lumber out of the forest was equally as hard for Chaim'l as the forest work itself.

He thought to himself, giving up one's life for the communist prophet Stalin is for others, and that he, on no account, would engage in such foolishness.

He would never be one of those who sing the familiar song of the gladiators to their Emperor before they give up their lives for him: '*Ave Caesar, morituri tea salutamum,*' or '*Hail Caesar, we who are about to die, salute you.*'

He had no great desire to bless his comrade Stalin, and even less desire to give up his life for him.

Chaim'l got hot suddenly, and fell ill, and on that day did not show up for work.

He hadn't yet rehearsed a good excuse for why he had not come to work today, having not completed heating up his face next to the flaming oven, in order that he should appear to be flushed as if he were really sick and has a strong fever – and look who is here!

[Page 109]

Smirnov is here.

A tchto takoi? He asks Chaim.

The one feigning illness declares to him that he has suddenly gotten a fever, and a rather high fever at that, stomach cramps, and because of this, he cannot under any circumstance work today.

The first cure that the sick person got was Smirnov's order to the quartermaster to reduce the daily bread ration from eight hundred to four hundred grams.

The second cure a similar order in '*stalavni*[16]' the daily borsch which workers received after a hard day's work was no longer given to Chaim'l.

To Chaim'l's naive question of 'how an a person live without food?' He gets the clever, ingenious reply from Smirnov:

There is a statute in the Soviet area that the great compassionate father of the 'Работчй Иарод[17]' has promulgated:

'Кто не работит, не кушаит,' that is, 'One who does not work, does not eat.'

After this sort of rigorous diet, Chaim'l didn't go to work, but ran back to work.

The sick one, thanks to God returned to good health, before surrendering his strength, health, and for others, also their lives.

As punishment for being sick, he never got his horse back, and he again had to chop down the half-meter thick trees, and split each two meter part into quarters, in order to meet the daily quota volume, and basta.

This is the way Chaim spent his life in the camp. From early in the morning to late at night, with work, work, and more work.

Apart from the mosquitoes that sucked out the last bit of blood from him, that he had brought with him form home, he had not only one, stepped with is shoes made of rags on some snake, or other dangerous reptile, which could be found around his 'periphery' at very turn.

Only at one time did he attempt to pour out his heavy heart before the Master of the Universe, and that was at the Kol Nidre service for Yom Kippur.

Coming back from the forest, Chaim'l quickly organized two minyans of his suffering comrades, while still laden with their implements, they quickly set themselves to recite Kol Nidre.

As the only one literate in all of the details, his comrades designated Chaim'l to recite Kol Nidre as the leader

[Page 110]

of the service.

With a broken heart, the worshipers voiced their complaints to the One who sits in Heaven, with an empty stomach, blackened faces, bruised hands, and broken spirit, Chaim'l with hot tears intoned the verse, 'As clay in the hands of the potter…' and beseeched: Master of the Universe save us a quickly as you can from this dark Hell, so that we will cease to be 'clay in the hands of the potter' in the hands of Smirnov.

Praying, or carrying out other forms of religious observance, was from the first day on, strictly forbidden to the people in the camp.

Such prohibitions were observed all of the year, but at Kol Nidre time on Yom Kippur, the Jewish heart demanded its own need.

The people did not pay heed to the prohibition, and despite it, they assembled to pour out their bitter hearts before the Jewish God, who had, by the expression of the camp residents in bitter humor, since the accursed rise of the brown [-shirted] Satan, abandoned his people who were all over the world, whom he had taken to wed through the agency of the marriage maker Moses, on Mount Sinai.

As is known, it was not through love, but by force that His Jewish bride came to be wed, after he threatened her, that should she not agree to this union, He would: cover them with the mountain, and 'ere will be your burial place,' if the bride will not accept the Torah.

As a stroke of bad luck, at this precise, holy moment, a Polish Christian happened to be walking by the barracks of these latter-day *anusim*.[18]

This 'omen of trouble' lost no time in immediately conveying what his unclean eyes had seen.

It didn't take long, but three militia men, with Smirnov at their head, befell the room where prayers were being said, and brutally threw out the people who were there, confiscating the prayer shawls, prayer books and *makhzors*.

Chaim'l became very severely frightened, fright gripped him, and fearing that Smirnov will hold him responsible for this counter-revolutionary behavior, he jumped out of the window, and vanished into the dark forest.

On the following morning, it became known that the master of the room had been taken off with them.

On the fourth day he returned more dead than alive, he was a silent as a fish, and even had great fear in front of his own family, not telling them what had occurred to him.

It was only after the people, after a certain space of time, had left the camp, that they found out that during the three days and three nights, hie had been bound to a tree in the deep forest, every five hours, a militia man came to him, gave him a morsel of bread to chew on, and a half glass of water to drink.

[Page 111]

The end of this 'adventure' was that they did not recite Kol Nidre on the eve of Yom Kippur, but rather, two nights after Yom Kippur.

Chaim'l and his comrades literally lost track of the count of days, and took the count in a manner where they recited '*Al Khet*' on a regular weekday.

In the camp there was also a '*Zakladchaneh*' a Jew by the name of Zucker.

Formerly a tailor in a Galician *shtetl*, he was the only open communist, already for many years.

Not looking at his communist past affiliation, it appears that comrade Stalin did not have much loyalty to this 'sweet communist,' and bunched him together with all the rest, in this bright communist paradise.

Regarding instances of the sort posed by comrade Zucker, Our Sages had said: The wicked, even at the threshold of Hell do not repent.

Also, this comrade Zucker was in very bad circumstances, along with everyone else, yet despite this, he was the only one in the entire camp who taunted Chaim'l for organizing the Kol Nidre evening.

Chaim attempted to defend himself, and attempted to demonstrate to him that no single prayer has such an attractive power among us Jews, and such a powerful force, as this short prayer of Kol Nidre.

This is something of a rare religious attraction, a sacred folk-ritual that draws into the synagogue and brings there almost everyone, even those who have no cognizance of the Sabbath or the Festival Days, and do not want to know about other sacred things, and yet the prayer of Kol Nidre is sacred to them, very sacred.

The liturgical melody of Kol Nidre caresses and soothes their soul for as full year, until the next recitation of Kol Nidre.

You, comrade Zucker, with your equality, Chaim said further with heart, which you hold as a hyper-progressive indicator of tomorrow's day, in whose eyes, such foolishness will no longer be cultural or real.

In your eyes, this is old-fashioned and outmoded.

For you, only the teaching of Marx-Lenin-Stalin is cultural and real, and it is they who are guilty of, and responsible for, all of the ills that have befallen Jews and others in general, and also for your and my troubles right here in this camp.

For us from the days of past, every memory is dear and cherished, every image, even the smallest stirring or reflection of our ancient traditions.

See with what a rare language they speak to our heart and our memory, see with what a sweet expression they speak to us in the Aramaic of the Kol Nidre words, a language that in your eyes has died long ago.

And it is not only Kol Nidre, but every minor utterance of the mouth, of our past, sparkles yet in our recollection:

[Page 112]

Elijah's cup on the Seder night, the wax Yom Kippur candles of the Kol Nidre night, the silver border ornament on a grandfather's prayer shawl, the brass candlesticks on the table of the *Bet HaMedrash*, a grandmother's Turkish shawl, even the yellowed page in a mother's *Korban Mincha Siddur* speaks differently to us than it does to you, comrade Zucker, than the '*Das Kapital*' written by your leader Marx, who, by the way, has brought us to the travail that we must now endure in these jungles.

Comrade Zucker, do you know why this is so?

Chaim'l spoke on, because that yellowed little page speaks to us in the terms of our homes, warm, Jewish, it speaks to our soul with that sweet tongue that flows amicably, so familiarly, it gladdens us, warms us, making our heart and soul young and fresh.

That is the power, Chaim'l says further, of the Jewish reserve, 'old wine,' but the new bottle of vinegar from the factory: Chmielnicki-Stalin-Khrushchev, give the Jewish people a bellyache and troubles.

That is the reason, my dearly beloved comrade Zucker, why we find ourselves in these God-forsaken '*Taigas*.'

I am absolutely not an enemy of the communists, Chaim'l says further, but a Jew need not be anything more than a Frenchman, British, or Dutch, or something else.

Since each nation is proud of its own religion, culture, history and tradition, a Jew must be a watchman of a foreign vineyard, and therefore abandons his own Torah, history, tradition, and ethnic identity, so all of the 'isms' are OK for you comrade Zucker, except for your own nationalism.

We have to learn from what has happened to our German brethren.

They thought that they were already a part of the German people, and so the somber brown [-shirted] Asmodeus, Hitler מי״ש, arrived, and reminded them that they were, and would always remain Jews, the sons of Abraham, Isaac and Jacob.

As far back as Dr. Pinsker, in his famous [essay] 'Auto-Emancipation' he warned the Jews: a day will come when history will take vengeance for your verdict against your people, and your greatest offerings will be of no avail to you, they will always remind you that you are the children of Shem, and on one fine day, they will throw you out of the 'fatherland,' the rabble will escort you with the calling out of the familiar 'HEP-HEP[19]' and remind you that the laws of citizenship applies to everyone except you Jews.

Chaim'l ceased speaking, and he took note of the fact that tears were streaming from the eyes of the communist Zucker.

Suddenly, Chaim'l reminded himself that he must quickly run to help his Sarah'leh to heat the kettle in which Sarah'leh makes 'Kipiatak,' for the workers.

Sarah'leh received six hundred grams of bread for this work, a soup, or a borscht from thorny brenessel.

* * *

[Page 113]

Our great prophet Isaiah said: When The Master of the Universe wishes to punish the wise, he first deprives them of their common sense.

It was in this fashion that He took away the common sense from comrade Stalin in his pact with that second man of righteousness, the Polish General Sikorsky.

The slightest remark by Stalin מי״ש would have been sufficient for the Polish general, to exclude the Jewish Polish citizens, from this pact, and it seems, that deep in his filthy Polish heart, he would have enjoyed agreeing to having his Jews remain permanently in Russian hands,

But as previously said, God deprived these two non-Jews of their common sense, he took pity on his Jews in the steppes, and looked down from his heavenly heights, [seeing] how his children are being worked with mortar and bricks, as in days of old under Pharaoh in Egypt.

Therefore, he stopped up their heads, took away their reason, both, in the moment forgot to exclude the Jews from the pact, and literally, a miracle occurred, sent from heaven, and at the time of the rationalization of the 'Zakladshchanehs' out of the camps, the N.K.V.D. made no distinction between Christian and Jewish Poles, and all Polish citizens were liberated at once, directly, from these dark work camps.

Despite this, Smirnov attempted through terror, and all manner of possible threats, to influence the people not to leave the camps.

However, this was in vain!

The people, who in the space of a year and a half had been enslaved, locked away from the rest of the world, not knowing what was happening except in their part of the dark thick forest, under no circumstances wanted to agree to stay in this mosquito and snake-ridden place, crawling with other forms of life.

Smirnov immediately reckoned that all of his effort was going to the devil, and he assembled the camp inmates, and with a sweet cunning smile read the order to them, that from this day forward, they are free people. And each of them has the freedom to move on and settle anywhere in the entirety of Russia, except for Moscow and Leningrad.

There were no bounds to the joy, and migration immediately began a new.

Most of the camp inmates migrated to warmer climates, to Russian middle Asia, such as Kirghizstan, Uzbekistan, and so forth.

Logic dictates, that after twenty months of residing in a place where the cold dropped to forty-to-fifty degrees below zero, people lusted for a bit of sun, and a bit of warmth, in order to warm up their frozen bones.

Chaim'l and his family also took to the road.

They, along with an acquainted family whom they befriended in the camp, and were also burdened with the

[Page 114]

care of young children, on entry into the city of Ofo in the Urals, decided to seek their fortune in this large, but rather primitive industrial city.

The city of Ofo, like all large Russian cities, was divided into two parts. One part was called *Starygorod*, that is, the Old City, in existence for hundreds of years, remaining in the same medieval condition, with houses of an exotic style and appearance, with churches from the time of Ivan the Terrible.

The second part, is called *Novygorod* [i.e. the New City] and came into being after the revolution, with halfway modern houses.

With a very strenuous effort, Chaim'l was able to rent a room that was located on a high hill on the left side of the city.

To reach his dwelling, meaning, to pull one's self up the hill, it was necessary to crawl on all fours, because climbing, or other means for being able to go up the hill did not exist, as opposed to descending into the city, which one did by simple sliding down the snow and rolling down.

This was the most reliable and fastest means of transportation, there being no other means of communication for Chaim'l and his family.

True the Bashkirsh gentile had a small donkey with which he assisted himself to get up and down the hill – to and from his little dwelling, but he didn't permit Chaim'l to make use of the little donkey.

They went for an entire month this way, rolling down from the hill, when someone in the family needed something that needed to be obtained in the city, and they immediately regretted their leaving the camp.

In the end, they decided to leave the city of Ofo, and for a large sum of money, he bought an unused wagon from the station master, packed both families into it with whatever remained of their poor possessions, and took off for the warmer climates like all the other Jews who were former inmates of the camp.

Arriving in the large city of Tashkent in the middle of the night, they remained in the street until dawn, together with other thousands of people who fled from the various camps that were spread all over Russia.

The crowding, filth, thievery and outcry reached the heavens, nobody – not the authorities, and also not kin, took an interest in the homeless and confused, many fell sick from epidemic diseases, people fell like flies.

When the scandal became very large, the familiar beloved N.K.V.D. showed up again, took pity on the people, again packed them into wagons, and sent them off to collective farms throughout all of middle Asia.

Chaim'l and his family were settled in a collective farm in Uzbekistan, named 'Strelkov.' They were billeted in a small 'residence' that just before had been used to stable two small donkeys.

A hole in the side served as a window, a table covering, hung up by his wife, served as a door, the floor was sand, mixed with the dried out droppings of the previous four-footed occupants.

The fields of the collective farms were worked in return for a '*lepyushka*' and a bit of flour.

[Page 115]

The living conditions in the collective farm were a lot worse than that in the camp.

The difference was that in the camp, one starved, got sick and died on command, in the collective farm by contrast, it was permissible to make use of a measured means called '*skolko unadna*,' but under the oversight of the N.K.V.D.

In order to leave the collective farm, one needed only a couple of hundred rubles, to rent an '*arba*,' which is a higher wagon on two even higher wheels, spanned by a '*keel*.'

An Uzbek would do you a favor, for a dear sum of money, and transported you in the middle of the night to a small town that was not far away.

After a bout two months of wearing themselves out at the collective farm, Chaim'l concluded that they must leave this place as soon as possible if they were to remain alive.

But, man plans and God laughs, as the Yiddish expression goes, and standing out in the field of the collective farm at work with his wife Sarah'leh, thinking that they would leave this place in the morning, they see that two militia men were drawing near to them, with an officer at their head, not saying much, an order: take everything with you – and let's go.

* * *

A large '*arba*' stood in front of Chaim'l quarters, and everything was loaded on 'bistre.' – up on the wagon, off to the small train station, into the echelon, which arrived from somewhere else, full of other people.

The echelon began to move, and off in the direction of the Iranian border which according to the Russian estimates, was not very far, a sum total of about twelve hundred kilometers.

They traveled for a day and a night.

Suddenly, the echelon came to a halt in the middle of a field.

The people were not told what the journey meant, why, or when – no person knew where they were being taken.

Among themselves, the people conversed that they were being taken to Teheran, and from there, to the Land of Israel.

As later became evident, nothing came of this dream.

Stopped in the field for about three days, the locomotive was suddenly detached, it was re-attached in an opposite direction, the people were quickly driven into the wagons, there was a whistle from the locomotive, and about face, back to where they came from.

Ride back for something less than a day, the same procedure of dropping people off at collective farms begins again.

However, they were not taken to the same collective farms from which they came, but to new ones.

[Page 116]

It makes no difference, the officer of the transport declared to the people when they asked why they were being settled in new places.

'*Eto vsye nashi,*' he explained.

In reality, what difference was it for Chaim'l in the suffering he endured in the former collective farm named 'Strelkov,' which was found in the land of Uzbekistan, or in his present collective farm named 'Bolshevik,' found in the country of Kirghizstan, these are the same filthy, torn and, excuse me, barns – that is to say in simple language, it's the same old bag in different rags.

Life in the collective farm was hard, tragic and monotonous.

The principal activity was to crop and take the '*khlapak*' off the fields, that is 'cotton' which had been planted in that soil.

The compensation for this twelve-hour day of labor was a '*lepyushka,*' which is a sort of Arab pita, with four hundred grams of flour per person.

The trouble would not have been so bad, had this starvation ration been distributed honestly and in a timely fashion, but in reality, days would go by and nights, until you lived long enough to see a '*Lepyushka,*' or a bit of flour.

Hunger was intense through out, people became as brutal as animals in the wild.

One would steal a morsel of bread from the other, a bit of flour, salt, and a bit of ersatz tobacco, or a bit of newspaper with which to wrap the tobacco.

Chaim'l, his wife and twelve year-old son, worked from early in the morning until evening, and their accounting was simple.

For three workers, three '*lepyushkas,*' with a kilo and two hundred grams of flour a day, and from this, all five would somehow have to sustain their lives, but what was the decree when nothing was given?

Had Chaim'l not placed his life in danger for them, they would have certainly expired from hunger, and it would have been all over.

Two-three times a week, in the middle of the night, he would steal into the fields of the collective farm, and bring back a bit of onion, cucumbers, or another bit of vegetable.

Apart from his daily work, he had supplemental work.

Every evening, to sit hours on the officer's neck to extract his pay for the day's work, mostly without success.

Sitting one evening at the residence of the Kirghiz, waiting for a bit of flour, two unfamiliar men and a woman appear in his location.

[Page 117]

They introduce themselves as coming from the '*NaKrom*' in Tashkent (Narodny Komissariat) with an order that in the span of four weeks, our collective farm must construct a bath house.

Upon hearing this order, the Kirghiz, who was in charge of the collective farm, ran hot and cold.

Out of great fear, he approached Chaim'l with the following question: *Tovarishch* Chaim, is there a construction engineer to be found among you Polish people who can undertake to build this bath house?

There is a saying in the world Need can transform a shoemaker into a Rabbi, and a Rabbi into a wagon driver.

This very thing happened to Chaim'l at that moment.

Not thinking for very long, he replied to the Kirghiz that, indeed, he does know of such a person among his people, who is a construction engineer, an expert, who had constructed the largest houses and factories in Poland.

And this great expert, is to be found, right here, in our collective farm.

Hearing this good news, he regained his normal color, and it became lighter for him in his heart.

Chaim only asks if they had brought some sort of building plan with them?

At his wish, he receives the required plan, and after a few minutes, he says to them: *Tovarishch*i! I, myself, Chaim'l, am that great expert among experts, who has built up nearly half of Poland, and I take it upon myself to build this bath house in the course of four weeks, on condition that the four weeks will commence only when the officer in charge will have provided me with all of the needed material.

Hearing such words, the officer in charge, out of great inspiration and satisfaction gave Chaim'l such a slap on the back that he can feel it to this day…

He cemented this with a generous Russian blessing, and immediately agreed to turn over the work to Chaim'l.

The compensation for the work was set at seventy kilograms of wheat, so said, and so done.

* * *

At this opportunity, I also do not want to forget those of our brethren who live in these places.

My wish is to give a bit of an overview of the way of life of these children of Israel in a faraway place.

It is not my purpose here to give a [sic: complete] portrait of these Uzbek Jews, because I think this has already been done.

However, this does not deter me to underscore and reflect for my readers the character of this community.

I had acquainted myself thoroughly with their way of life, customs, and characteristics, which is the operative

[Page 118]

evidence of their innermost spiritual being.

The Soviet system impacted these Jews severely, and lowered them from the level of their standard of living that they occupied yet from the time of Tamerlane.

The revolution, as it had done to all other Jews in Russia, had permanently broken their economic status.

An entire community of Jews sit on the lounging chairs in streets, back alleys, on small benches, with shoe brushes in hand, and wait for a passer-by to have their shoes polished, in order to be able to sustain their impoverished lives with a 'pita and a tea.'

The entire physical and emotional focus is directed towards how to obtain, by all means, even if it is illegal, one more pita and one more teapot of tea.

This is the quintessence of the life of the community with a patriarchal past and a proud heritage.

The surroundings, ethnography, cultural-historical details and especially the regime, create the conditions that the intelligence of the entire community is occupied with only one thing, how to fill one's empty stomach [*kursak*], in their language, and through this, their thoughts and efforts and demands are attenuated to a minimum.

And when such an Uzbek Jew is enriched with a pita and a teapot full of '*Kipiatak*' his demands of that moment are fulfilled.

And it is, in this way, that the old folk saying is once again confirmed: 'when warmth comes only in the form of horseradish, one believes that there is nothing better.'

* * *

On the anniversary of the outbreak of the Bolshevik revolution, in my new location, a group of young people, of both sexes, encountered me with wild shouts of '*zdrastvuity tovarishch*[20]' sitting under heavy branches of nut trees, with pots of *Kipiatak* in their hands.

In the shade off to the side, sat the older companions, near them was a small music ensemble with a variety of different musical instruments, which were hard to even find inn the local areas, and which one of our people would not even dream that they were musical instruments, and despite this, the Kirghiz natives played their mournful and monotonic melodies on them.

My soul became a bit lighter, hearing this mournful music, but it was much more difficult to improve the mood of my wife and children.

Hunger in this place had reached its zenith, and our people fell like flies from starvation.

And when the knife truly lay against one's throat, suddenly a salvation arrived, we packed up our bit of

[Page 119]

impoverished possessions, and were sent back to our original home via an echelon.

Coming back to wartime Poland, our eyes, once again, were made dark, no sisters, no brothers, not a single relative, all had disappeared along with the Jewish houses, assets, and other belongings.

The ground literally burned under one's feet, and as if what the brown [-shirted] devil and his Polish accomplices had not done enough during the war years to the Jewish people, the Polish anti-Semites further murdered Jews on top of the Polish soil that was already soaked in Jewish blood.

It was under these circumstances that Chaimchi, with is wife and children abandon their 'fatherland' Poland, with the idea of realizing his old dream, meaning – to join up with his two older children in the Land of Israel.

Chaimchi sat in an American camp in Salzburg Austria with his family for about one and a quarter years, until his oldest son in the Land of Israel, who, in his role as an emissary of the Jewish settlement in the Land of Israel, facilitated the immigration of European survivors by illegal means.

On one fine day, using such a means of transport, he brought his parents and three younger little brothers to the Land of Israel.

* * *

During the days of September in the year 1947, a ship with a full complement sailed towards the direction of a shore that was still not visible, but one already heard about it, and talked of it, as if it was a visible parcel of land.

We sat in our cabin plastered with our satchels as if with large bricks from a building that had collapsed, with which one wants to rebuild the old, collapsed house.

The ship, on which Chaimchi and his family traveled, arrived in Haifa on the day of a *hamsin*.[21]

With the first welcome greeting, they were taken up an hour after their arrival.

A group of Jewish fighters had thrown a bomb into the English police station that happened to be right across the street from the hotel where Chaimchi and his family had been quartered.

Running out onto the veranda of the hotel out of great fear, Chaimchi saw body parts mixed in with chunks of wood and iron, with paper fluttering about, and a heavy black smoke which covered the entire vicinity.

A little at a time, the fear subsides, and Chaimchi manages to get himself onto the first bus that is bound for Tel-Aviv.

Arriving in Tel-Aviv, the war with the Arabs immediately broke out, and the fear of taking a bullet in the head starts anew.

[Page 120]

And as if the measure of travail did not appear yet to be full, all of Chaimchi's children without exception had to mobilize themselves into the Israeli Army, and it was in this fashion that all of the months and all of the time of the new war went by with a heart full of fear for the fate of his children who each separately found themselves at a different section of the front against the Arabs.

But God protected them from an Arab bullet, and all of Chaimchi's children returned healthy and well from the war, which gorged itself and spilled the young, pure Jewish blood of thousands of precious young boys and girls.

This was the fourth war that the former Yeshiva student Chaim had gone through and survived, starting anew, finally, to rebuild his life in the Land of Israel, and to rest his bones a bit, from dragging himself around for decades, from land to land, from city to city.

This is a short memoir, of how a Jewish life and suffering looked to be, in the time of The First World War, when the accursed clique of 'HiSta-Khrumika' began to dominate the world, with the two principal criminals Hitler and Stalin, may their names and memories be erased.

This desecrated era already spans three generations, and who is to know when the travails of the Jews will come to an end already?

Would that it were only now.

Translator's footnotes:

1.   '*Khakhmay Chelm,*' or 'The Sages of Chelm' are a series of fables surrounding the legendary foolishness and malapropisms of the Jews of that city.
2.   See Genesis 19:30-38.
3.   'Hi there, brothers!'
4.   Referring to Adam Mickiewicz, the national poet of Poland, and author of the epic poem, *Pan Tadeusz*, and Henryk Sienkiewicz, the 1905 Nobel Prize winner in Literature.
5.   The Polish National Anthem, beginning with the words, '*Jeszcze Polska nie ziegelna....*'
6.   The traditional riding crop of the Cossack cavalry.
7.   "The term, as it is used here, appears to be anachronistic, but appropriate. Here is a note on its origin, which appears to be with the Second World War:
After the invasion of Poland in 1939, the Red Army committed several horrifying war crimes in the city of Lviv (Lwow, Lvov, Lemberg, Leopolis). But Rockwell Kent, an American tourist and humanist, who was in the eastern Poland (western Ukraine) during the Soviet attack, greeted the Red Army.
The Soviet invaders who now liberated Ukraine from the yoke of Polish landlords installed their own Bolshevist dictatorship in the formerly Polish - occupied *ziemie*. To protect the Red Ukraine against the Ukrainian and Polish reactionaries, the Soviet commissars converted the old Catholic convent of the St. Brigide Order into one of the worst prisons in the eastern Europe, where thousands of Ukrainian and Polish patriots were tortured to death by NKVD-men. When the German army entered Lviv in June 29, 1941, they found in every cell of Brigidki jail a layer of a viscous mass. Dead bodies were stacked four or five deep on the cell floors. The Soviet policemen murdered about 3,500 prisoners before their retreat."
8.   A nomad's tent.
9.   The 16th Century brought forth the most influential Kabbalist in history: Rabbi Isaac Luria. A brilliant scholar by age 13, he was called "The Ari HaKadosh," which means "The Holy Lion."
10.   These Hebrew words are used in the sense of 'pro' and 'con,' to weigh the fate of the person in question.
11.   The epithet, 'Jewish Jerk!'
12.   Chaim'l says: '*This is my family,*' and the reply is to '*Come here!*'
13.   "Never mind, get used to it or croak – keep moving!"
14.   The Russian equivalent of an indentured servant, or a serf.
15.   From the Russian, '*groznyi*' meaning 'terrible' or 'awesome.'
16.   Daily diet
17.   Russian, for the laboring masses
18.   The Hebrew plural for describing those who underwent forced conversion under the threat of death.
19.   The acronym for the anti-Semitic taunt, '*Hierosolyma est Perdita*', (Jerusalem is Lost), used by Eastern Europeans to work themselves into a frenzy prior to inflicting a pogrom on the Jews.
20.   To your good heath, comrade!
21.   The hot, dry fifty-day dust storms of the Middle East, from which it derives its name in Arabic.

In the City of Killing

By Chaim Nachman Bialik

The editors have seen fit to reproduce this classic Hebrew poem, by one of the literary giants of his day. Written in 1904, it was inspired by the wave of pogroms that rippled through the Pale of Settlement, under the control of Czarist Russia, and is a threnody to the Jewish victims of senseless and brutal murder at the hands of anti-Semites.

We do not offer a translation here, since the interested reader may find such a translation in the general literature.

[Page 121]

Good Advice from a Friend....

by Dr. David Ravid

To our Cieszanow landsleit in America, England, and other English-speaking countries

The Second World War – the brand of the world which was impressed into the history of the Jewish people under the name of 'The Third Destruction,' -- ended in 1945, but we had to wait nearly a quarter of a century for the readers of a universal language such as English – and especially the Jews, who live in the spheres of the English speaking peoples -- for them to become familiar with the full extent of Jewish martyrdom, from the degree of the Sanctification of the Name endured by our people, of our heroism and resistance, beginning with the time that the Nazis began to carry out their objective of exterminating the Jews, up to the time of their downfall.

Our national-biological hygiene, so to speak, demanded that the upcoming generations of Jews should know why, and in what manner, the extermination of six million Jews was accomplished, and what Jews themselves did, in order not to allow the plans of the Nazis to be carried out to the fullest degree.

Finally, a work, designed for those Jews for whom English is their language of speech, reading, thinking, and feeling – has appeared.

I am referring to the 'Anthology of Holocaust Literature,' written by a variety of Jewish authors, published by the Jewish Publication Society in America.

In order that the reader should have a full grasp of the substance and content of this valuable anthology, it is worth pointing out that this collection contains translations of the memoirs and a variety of documents in a variety of languages, of which the principal one id Yiddish, because those who suffered the greatest from the German brutality were Jews from Eastern Europe, and because it is these Jews who were the principal fighters against the enemy.

We never need to forget the bitter truth, that the Germans had murderous accomplices among the degenerates of other peoples: Austrians, Slovaks, Poles, Ukrainians, Latvians, Byelorussians, etc.

Among the many documents of this 'Anthology' can also be found documents from those nations enumerated above, who took an active part in the annihilation of the Jewish people in the years 1940-1945.

It is insufficient for us to read about this martyrdom during the years of The Second World War in Yiddish, we have to see to it, that there will be many translations in all 'world' languages, and therefore, the anthology that has been brought out in the English language is a tool, to inform our brothers and sisters in the English-speaking world, about the great tragedy of murder and torture inflicted on the Jewish people by the nations enumerated above, during the time that the greatest enemy of the Jewish people reigned, the brown [-shirted] Asmodeus Hitler, ימ"ש.

We must be satisfied that such an anthology has been published in the English language, and as we hope that soon this work will appear in French, and also Spanish, such that our Jewish youth in those countries who do not understand Yiddish will familiarize themselves with the great heroes of their people, who with such heroic might stood up and defended their Jewish honor against a world of murderers, beasts with the faces of human beings.

[Page 122]

The First Explosion!

by Dr. David Ravid

The city was bombed by air assaults and incendiaries, and there was nothing with which to put out the flames, and they came serially one after another.

In one of the bombings, many houses were hit, destroyed and razed to their foundations, and the residents fled the city.

As I did not manage to escape, I went down into the cellar of my house that served me as a shelter from the bombing.

In the cellar, it was a dark as the Egyptian plague, windows shut, it was difficult to breathe, and fear gnawed and burrowed into my body.

When the eruptions subsided, I also fled from the city, and with great difficulty, I reached the nearby village, and I observed, that on a large flat space, men, women and children were lying, sitting and standing crowded together, and beside them were packages, suitcases, hand carts, babies. A din and pandemonium stood in the air, and from within this racket, there still pierced through calls of encouragement, strength of spirit, until they swelled and overcame the sounds of despair, which gave testimony to the oppression, weariness and lack of sleep.

The bridge that was beside this field had been sealed off by units of the retreating Polish army, and along with the remainder of the refugees, I managed to head off to the east, not using a real road.

Suddenly, I see an elderly Jew dressed in silken clothing standing beside me, with a had in the design of the Sanz [*Hasidim*] and a walking stick in hand. He looked straight into my face and said: Do not cry, you will be privileged to see the fall of Hitler, and you will build your house anew together with your entire family in the *Holy Land*.

I had barely heard what he had said to me, and grasp its meaning, and he disappeared, and was gone – I searched for him, however in vain.

When my consciousness returned, I became aware that I had received a concussion from the explosion of a bomb that fell not far from me.

[Page 123]

A Poem of Mourning to the Memory of Our Brothers and Sisters who were Killed by the Germans!

by Dr. David Ravid

Where did we learn to wipe away tears?
To bear the pain silently?
To entomb the complaint in the secret chamber of our hearts
The suffering and the weeping....

Hear the wind! Inhaled and open
As it roars through the valley and over the hills;
See the ocean in its anger and ire
As it dashes against the giant boulders.

All of nature roars and exclaims
Breaking through every gate and barrier,
The enemy draws near with '*Heil*'
And the martyrs respond with '*Shema Yisrael*.'

They turned their mouths against us, all our enemies
A fear and fright seized us,
Cascades of water will pour from my eyes
On the destruction that has befallen my people.

[Page 124]

A Hymnal of Praise for the Members of the Committee of the Organization

by Dr. David Ravid

"The righteous say little, but do much," the Gemara says (B"M 87).

When I proposed the idea to my comrades, who came from our town, that the time had arrived to commemorate those of our families that had fallen, and to erect a monument in their honor, they spoke up out of great astonishment.

From where are we to take literary material? -- they asked.

From where are we to take those means that such an undertaking demands?

Who, among us, will take upon himself all of the burdensome labors of publishing a *Yizkor Book,* the technical work, the literary work, and especially the assembly of the contributions for the contents of the book?

When I went on to explain that all we needed was one thing, that is: 'the right intention' because nothing can stand in the way of the will of man, especially if his objective is something for which he yearns with his entire soul, all of them were won over in a minute, from those with little faith to true believers, and they exclaimed the words made famous in ancient times, 'Na'aseh, V'Nishma,' without me having to put this on anyone like an unwanted burden.

After agreeing to my idea, each individual contributed what they could and undertook the actual work.

The members: Mr. Tepper, Mr. Lieberman, Mr. Glanzer, Mr. Langenthal, Mr. Schmid and Mr. Friedman, may they all live to ripe old ages, helped with all of their physical and emotional energies, in order to somewhat lighten the burden on me, of the yoke that up to that point had been placed solely on my shoulders.

Mr. Tepper was especially of assistance. I breathed a little easier when Mr. Tepper took control of the distribution of notices, etc. It was in similar manner that my burden was eased when Messrs. Lieberman, Friedman, Glanzer, Schmid, and especially Mr. Langenthal, advised me in constructive ways at the time that I was in need of it.

I am certain of this – that every person, whose heart aches and is filled with pain because of the terrible destruction that was visited on our people, will bless the members of this committee, for this work of memorializing the martyrs from our city, and may it be for them and myself, that in light of their endeavors, that we will soon see in the nearness of our days, the Comforting of Zion and Jerusalem, and peace for the People of Israel and the State of Israel.

———————

[Page 125]

A Birthday Celebration for Cieszanow Children in Danzig
Standing from right to left: Abraham Taubenblatt, son of Isaac, may they rest in peace, Feltzer, currently in N.Y.,
Ussi Shmukler, son of David, long life to him, currently ULSI Ravid, a lieutenant colonel in the IDF

The Jewish Youth Organization of Lubliniec, near Cieszanow, directed by Mr. Simcha Segal

R' David Michael Zurman ז"ל, a scion of Cieszanow – with his wife, Mrs. Bracha, the daughter of R' Mordechai Glanzer ע"ה from Cieszanow

His father, R' Michael died while still a young man, and was a respected man, regarded as one of the best of the *balebatim* of the city. He left a wife and five young children, with no basis on which to support them. They spread to all the corners of the world, in search for some form of economic sustenance, and after wandering through various countries, R' David designated his residence to be in the city of Antwerp in Belgium, and He who dwells on high granted him good fortune in this city.

His wife, Bracha, is a Woman of Valor, and garners praise for her good works.

[Page 126]

Nahum HaKohen Goldschmid
The Chief Rabbinate of Tel-Aviv
Rabbi of the Bitzaron Derekh HaShalom
Address: Yifrakh Street, 8, Bitzaron, Tel-Aviv
Tel: 36643

To my honored comrade, Dr. David Ravid,

I am responding to your request to participate in the documentation to memorialize the martyrs of the Holocaust in the book that will be published about the martyrs of the city of Cieszanow that you are putting together.

Even though much has already been produced with regard to this subject, the tongue will not relent from continuing the process of memorializing, even should the pen run out of ink, and the mind will not cease from contemplating those tens of thousands of holy and pure people, who sanctified the Name of Heaven with their lives and deaths, in the era when the beast in man manifested itself, under the name of 'Nazism.' During an era of world culture, and the advancement of technology to stratospheric heights, their high culture did not provide humanity the capacity to reveal a measure of morality. On the contrary, the technological accomplishments served as the means to implement genocide, tools and facilitators of mass murder, the extermination of a people, and the silencing of any echo of decency and morality.

Despite all this, the memory of the Jewish martyrs remains preserved for all time, in that, once again, the plan of the evil Son of Amalek to exterminate all of the people did not succeed, just as the plan of the first Amalekite – Laban the Aramean, 'who sought to uproot all.'

What then, is this eternal secret – of the descendants of that great patriarch, our Grandfather Jacob – the secret of survival? What is its source? – 'Eternal survival,' in which each word and syllable is full of little nuances and much quality, for these words have much broader connotation than their restricted literary meaning. These are words that contain abstract meaning with a very specific meaning that are unique to the Jewish people, the eternal people – that God, who is the One who makes Israel eternal, is the nation's Protector. The source of 'Eternal Israel' – as expressed by the greatest of the Jewish prophets, Samuel – is implied in the roots of our people, which are the roots of all humanity, as is explained in the *Kuzari:* 'Israel among the nations – is like a heart among the other parts of the body.' That is to say: Israel is the heart of the other nations of the world, and their refuge, the 'proving stone' for the spiritual elevation of the world. Despite the fact that the heart does not suffer the same maladies as the other parts of the body, it is the first to suffer if these other parts are injured, and vice versa. Just as there is no way for the body to sustain itself without a heart, humanity as a whole cannot sustain itself without the Jewish people.

If the physical existence of our people can be traced to our holy patriarchs, then the root of their spiritual existence reaches back to the beginnings of the human race itself – to Adam, the first man. Anyone who peruses the book of Genesis will be able to demonstrate that in all of the generations prior to the patriarchs, a single individual was selected in each generation that only through him, is the Torah narrated, and all others are subordinate to him, like leaves surrounding a fruit, or branches surrounding the main trunk. The wonder of this is that those very chosen individuals are not anonymous, but are specifically a direct descendant of the spiritual giant of the previous generation, and in this way, all the way back to Adam, and these individuals served as the mainstays to the humanity of their times. It is from here that the Jewish people obtain their designation as an 'Eternal People,' because its roots reach to eternity itself, that is to say: a

[Page 127]

creation that is itself completely eternal. Therefore, so long as humanity exists, this people will also continue to exist, because just like a body without a heart, without the Jewish people, all humanity dies, or reverts to the level of the beasts.

It is from here that we see that the continuity of the Jewish people is a law of nature that God imbedded in creation itself. 'The Eternity of Israel' is a metaphor for Divinity itself, and the intent here is not to say that God is eternal, but rather that the Name of God is attached to the people, that is, implying the eternal nature if Israel, on the permanent nature that God wrought in his creation, that it will not be betrayed, and it is not conceivable that this nation will be completely eradicated, because the Lord, Creator of the Universe carved a protecting law over Israel, to guard it throughout all generations, a protection that places responsibility on that aspect of the world that wants to be good and human. Therefore, there are no messages specifically directed towards the lives of Jews excepting that they are part of a greater whole. The Jew is a binding element, in the nation that has very specific missions to accomplish, that carries the international theme of the rectification of the [flaws of] the world [sic: *Tikkun Olam*]. Because of this, the Jew has been endowed with the unique spiritual strength that is the discriminating and purifying element, of the first generations, for the creation of a praiseworthy spiritual people, and this in addition to the gift bestowed by God that was given at the standing beside Mount Sinai – and that is the Holy Torah. It is from here that the great responsibility that was placed upon the Jewish people in fulfilling its mission can be understood, a mission aimed at the elevation of the spiritual level of the world in its entirety.

With all that has been said, the question still nags in the body of the world regarding the stunning silence that existed during the period of the Holocaust. We will dedicate a few lines to this from the teachings of R' Eliyahu D' Raba Chapter 30: On once occasion, R' Zadok entered the Holy Temple, and saw it in ruins, He said before the Holy One, Blessed be He: Master of the Universe, My Father in Heaven! Did you destroy your city and burn your sanctuary? R' Zadok immediately fell into a sleep, and he saw the Holy One, Blessed be He, how He stands in mourning and His attending angels mourn with Him, and they said: O, how lost is Jerusalem.... Before he fell asleep, R' Zadok would wonder, and aggravate himself without end, and cry out: You sat at rest and were silent? But once he was privileged to see, and viewed the great sorrow of how the Holy One Blessed be He grieved and wept, and how he was preparing for the redemption. This instant of being transported, the nullification of the senses in this world, the instant when eyes were closed to the experiences of this world, given to a human being the power to elevate himself to the revelation of secrets in the World to Come, to see how the Holy One Blessed be He, yearns and longs for compassion to spread itself over Israel, and to redeem them. To the ache in our hearts, the full measure of this law is interdicted and delayed, however, we do hope that the time will come when all barriers will fall, and the measure of compassion will cascade over the entire world, like a great light, and will reveal His honor, may it be blessed, in the fullness of its power and glory.

In order that we bring our redemption closer, and to fulfill our mission – the mission of *Tikkun Olam*, which is our international theme, because of which we have been privileged to be the 'heart' of the nations, we have been given the boon of being eternal -- it is incumbent upon us to make use of the tried and true means, that is – the education in fundamentals and essentials, the essentials of faith and the traditions of the purity of our Holy Torah, whose roots are in eternity itself. As the words of *Bereshit Raboh* tell us, 60' 21, Sub-Section 11 : 'The flame of the transforming sword' – it transforms the man and burns him from his head to his feet, and from his feet to his head. Man says: Who shall save my sons from such a consuming fire? etc... And the Sages reply: The sword is the Torah, as it is said: And they have a sword with points in their hands.

[Page 128] blank *[Page 129]*

It is here that the secret of the continuity of an eternal Jewish people can be found.

ב"ה
10 Heshvan 5730
To my friend the scholar and researcher,
Dr. David Ravid, peace unto you and blessings

From Lieutenant Colonel Rabbi Moshe Avital, Tel-Aviv
for the Members of the Committee of the Organization

With my respects!

I have heard that you are publishing one of the books from your writings, on the subject of the 'Holocaust,' – to be sure, a subject that has been explored extensively, but is it not the case that to the extent that we get further away from the period of the Holocaust, we see more and more its satanic scope, in its brutal intent and its implementation, that has no peer in a Jewish history that is distorted by blood, and it is hard to believe that human nature could have tolerated a Holocaust such as this.

Everyone who was there, that saw or heard what took place there, knows – that it is not possible to extract and codify what had taken place there in the course of one generation or two.

We, the Jews, who excel in invoking six remembrances daily, and one of them is 'remember what Amalek did to you,' how much more so the Amalek of our generation, who, by deed, descended below all of the Amaleks of all generations, this was a coalition of almost all the nations and states of Europe that the Amalek inspired, with the Nazi Germans ימ"ש at their head, a cabal of one hand in unison, to exterminate, kill, and annihilate God's people, the Nation of Israel, and because of this, everyone who engages in fulfilling the obligation of 'remember' and everyone who donates to assure that the people of Israel shall not forget, and not forgive – will be blessed, and more power to you on the publication of your book.

At this opportunity, it is my wish to raise some comments with regard to an issue from the period of the Holocaust, concerning the question that has been bruited about in conversations and discussions, with those who lost their dear ones in the Holocaust – that is, on the apparent absence of oversight from the Divine One during the Holocaust era.

There are those that ask this question, either in their hearts, or even vocally, but the question has not altered their faith and their way of life, and there are others who designate this question as a reason to abandon the path of faith and an observant way of life.

In my opinion, it is possible to respond to the former, but not to the latter, because the former are searching for the answer, and it possible to assume that [an answer] is acceptable, but the latter seek an excuse in that question for the justification of their inner desire to leave the path of faith and therefore, there is a basis on which to assume that they will reject any reasonable reply, because having made a decision – they are decided.

Therefore – to the former, one is able to reply by saying that this question did not first arise in our times, during difficult periods in Jewish history, the question also arose in the *Tanakh,* in the *Talmud* as well, and in later generations.

In Judges 6: When the angel appeared to Gideon, and tells him: 'God is with you, hero of the host.' Gideon answers him: 'Pardon, my Lord, if God is to be found among us, why have all these travails befallen us, and where are his miracles that our fathers told us about, to say, for was it not that He took us out of Egypt, and

[Page 130]

now we are abandoned and given into the hands of Midian.' However, this was not a question posed in the form of a challenge or criticism, but rather in the form of a prayer, that beseeches God to help us in the hour of our need, as he helped our fathers when they left Egypt, and because of this, he was answered as follows: 'Go, and with this might you shall save Israel.'

In a like manner, we find the following: Jeremiah and Daniel did not describe God in the form of a mighty and terrible force, as he was described by Moses Our Teacher, ע"ה, in response to the apparent absence of Divine oversight during their difficult times, rather, tradition teaches us that the 'Great Assembly' returned the metaphor to its original glorious form, to designate God as Great, Might, and Terrible,' as Moses ע"ה said, here, here, his awesomeness, here, here, his power, because were this not the case, how could the people survive in the face of several other nations. The fact is, that from an historical perspective, we have endured and seen the downfall of those nations that have assaulted us, and this is the most cutting proof, that this is *only* an absence of Divine oversight, and a day of retribution and settlement will arrive.

Regarding the phrase in Psalms 4: ' You have gladdened my heart by giving them grain and wine in plenty,' I am certain that to those who anger him, and to those who do his will, even more so, that in the future to come, is the day in which they will receive their just desserts.

Also familiar is the legend of our Ancient Sages, about Rabbi Akiva and his companions, who were walking the Temple Mount, and saw foxes roaming there, and the companions of Rabbi Akiva wept when they saw he was happy, and they asked him why are you happy? He said – after having seen that all the prophecies of reproof have come to pass, I am certain that the prophecies of consolation will also come true.

And so, even we can say here, now that we have seen all of the trials of the era of the Holocaust come to fruition, were are also certain in the fact that this will only have been a temporary Divine oversight, and now, all of the consolations will come to pass, and God will shine his countenance upon us. And in this regard, we have been privileged, and have seen the fulfillment of the first of the prophetic visions, the establishment of the State of Israel, the capture of the Land of Israel in its entirety, a united Jerusalem, with the High Place in our hands, and because of this, we are certain that if , along we are faithful to the covenant that we have with Him, He will be faithful to fulfill his covenant with his Chosen People – Israel, and he can be counted on to reward those who love Him and who guard his covenant, and that they will be privileged to partake in a complete redemption, and the fulfillment pf the vision of the prophets, and our prayer is that this be in our day.

[Page 131]

Polish Jewry

by Rabbi Mordechai Fogelman
Chief Rabbi, Kiryat Motzkin

In the European Diaspora, which was destroyed by the Nazis in the Second World War, the destruction of the Jews of Poland, and Polish Jewry, stands out sharply. There is nothing with which to compare it to in all of the decrees and exterminations that were perpetrated against the Jews at any other time. Polish Jewry existed for hundreds of years, at the head of the living, creative Judaism of the Hebrew people. The creative force and spiritual life of the Jewish people went over from Germany to Poland. The German Jews that settled in Poland during the fourteenth century received not only the German language, and they crafted the Yiddish language from it, but also the continuity and connectivity of the spiritual elevation of the Jews of France, Spain and Italy, who, in the Middle Ages, were the continuation of the Judaism of the Land of Israel and Babylon. And it was in this way that the Judaism of Poland advanced and evolved, into the fortress of strength and the spiritual bastion of the Jewish people. From there, rays of Torah light emanated, and the aura of its way of life, to all parts of the people and its far-flung elements. It was in her midst that the great intellects were raised and worked, cedars of Lebanon and exponents of Torah study, expert scholars in the *Mishnah, Gemara,* exponents of the interpretation of the *Talmud,* the interpreters of the *Halakha,* and great minds in Jewish thought, its interpretation and its explanation. Poland was the cradle in which the *Hasidism* of the BESH"T was born, the miraculous movement that revived the masses of despondent souls, that planted faith in their hearts in the Guardian of Israel, the power of patience, a pure faith and love. The *Hibat Tzion* movement grew in Poland, which was the foundation of the *Yishuv* in the Land of Israel in our times, of Zionism, the *Aliyah* of *halutzim*, and in the end, the establishment of the State of Israel.

It is not possible for us to describe the texture of the Jewish people of the last centuries, without Polish Jewry that strove and was creative, and in a like fashion, the texture of Polish Jewry without the Jews from the 'little Poland' that was called 'Galicia.' One credits the Jews of Galicia with a large and central role in all of the spiritual creativity and the revitalization movement for settling the Land of Israel in our times. We recall the communities of Cracow and Lvov who, for centuries, were 'mother cities' to Torah and scholarship, for accomplishment and learning, and along with them, thousands of sacred communities, large and small, among them centers for Torah study and *Hasidism*. All of these sacred communities that are destroyed and wiped out in Poland, have had the sound of Torah and the sound of Jewish life, with all of its nuances and expression, silenced. Along with the six million brothers and sisters who were incinerated in the extermination camps, the soul and the body of Polish Jewry were consumed in those same flames, the crowning glory of the Jewish people for hundreds of years.

In the schools of Israel, which is in existence for twenty-one and a half years, it is necessary to inculcate the youth using an explicit and recognized method, the facts pertaining to the Holocaust in general, and the destruction of Polish Jewry in particular. Israeli youth needs to know, that of all the destruction visited on the Jewish people, the destruction of our generation was the greatest and most frightening of all. It is up to us to remember glorious Polish Jewry that was razed to its foundation. The memorial to the destruction of Polish Jewry that was exterminated will be if we base our renewed lives in the renewed State of Israel, on the foundations of the legacy of the people, and the order of the continuity of the Jewish people.

[Page 132]

Cieszanow

by Dr. Lev Fishelzohn

There was a *shtetl*
One of many others,
Far-flung between forests and fields,
With small streets, and tiny plazas,
A place for the Wandering Jew.

* * *

Children grew up here
And played under trees,
Young people married here
Built a future, looked for happiness,
And weaving like perpetual dreamers.

* * *

Cieszanow – was what the *shtetl* was called
Built and wrought by Jews,
Until the night came,
Blood was spilled
And happiness was buried in the deep.

* * *

In the place of laughter – graves,
On the place f the streets – death,
The ovens swallowed everything,
The flames flickered high above
Need was brought to an end.

* * *

A small remnant remained
Having gone far away by chance,
Spreading itself the world over,
Approaching their new life energetically –
Becoming great and proud once again.

* * *

But, in memory, there will always remain
The *shtetl, shtibl*, house, and *Schul*,
Grandfather, grandmother, Holy Ark –
The precious graves –
As it once was.

———

[Page 133]

The Holocaust

by Michal Ravid, Age 10

From Ramat Sharon, granddaughter of the editor

Then – twenty-five years ago,
Then – when t Holocaust was occurring,
Then – Six Million Jews
Fell heroically, fathers and sons,
Hapless mothers, tender infants.
Ach! The murdering Germans have no heart,
Then – in the Holocaust – thousands were killed:
Fathers, mothers, families and children,
Then, all who were pursued, cried out
Let the Messiah come to the Jews!...
Even when the were already seated in the trains,
They still prayed for miracles and wondrous deeds...
Then – twenty-five years ago
In the time when the Holocaust was occurring.

[Page 134]

A Poem
From the Pinkas of the *Shtetl*

by Melekh Ravitch

I have taken this poem from the book, 'At the Pinkas of Lublin.' The Editor is Moshe Shulstein – one of the Yiddish poets of our generation.

Gates of Mercy, open your selves graciously,
Guardian gates of our book,
Guardian gates of our Mother City,
Blood on the sacred pages of the *Pinkas* –
Sealing wax on the little victory of generations.
Take, scion of the city, and with desire and passion,
Drink it like a hemlock, with eyes shut, drink it,
And sense in its burning taste, the conflagration
That consumed the bed and the cradle,
How it burned up the prayer stand, and book rest
Wedding canopy posts, and the first sleeping place of man-and wife
Angry, crooked roofs, and difficult stairs.
Make rust of chains from old gates(??)
Let us bang on them three times, like we did in times past --
As the *shames* once did against the gate of the Schul,
So that all the dead be frightened off and disappear,
Because the rooster has already crowed to call us to morning prayer –
The desecrated are exposed in the graves!
Come out from under your fragments of grave stones,
Torn out, where now dogs wander about,
And on whom steps the Unspeakable One
And the Tyrant and the instigator of false accusations.
It is only in stone that the letters of your name, the essence,
Which cannot be compelled [to be altered] by any effort:
Which have not been rendered null and void,
Erased by the scuffing of boots and the passage of years:
Strewn and scattered over all the desolate fields –
Roll hither and yon like rings
From our ancient beautiful lineage,
Its distant, distant ancestors become evident,
Great and famous scholars and leaders appear
From the dream, from imagination and thought,
And its duelists, perpetual protagonists with want
For the little spoon of warm food, and the tranquility of a roof [over one's head]:
Her studious ones, sunk in a sea of casuistic discourse up to their heads,
Those who burned and disgraced in the *Tak"h* Decrees,
Those who dissolved from fear of death in cellars and caves,
Those hacked apart on the chopping blocks of blood libel.
Guardian gates of the old cemetery,
Gates neglected, desolated fence

[Page 135]

As if the place of death was also put to death…
Come out of there, you, our ancestors,
Where the hearse had once stopped in times gone by,
A guest house was constructed near the church
And resting at the Schlossbarg, after the long, distant journey.
Let us, now, cut through the years, as if with a saw
Until we reach our own dark days of slaughter.

R' Menachem Mendl Yaroslavitz, ז"ל,
Son of R' David of Lubliniec

A Torah scholar, and *Hasidic* Jew who was engaged with Torah and science for his whole life, skilled in languages, with a sharp mind that didn't lose so much as a drop, gifted with exceptional skills.

May his soul be bound up in the bond of life, under the wings of the Holy Spirit.

[Page 136]

The High Holy Days of the Past

by Shmuel Lieberman

The High Holy Days of 5639 (1939) began much earlier before the fresh slate of the new year 5700 began. The upcoming days heralded their coming in advance by several weeks, when Berlin violated its non-aggression pact with Poland. Hitler demonstrated that his appetite had not been sated with the ingestion of Austria and Sudeten Czechoslovakia. The focus now came down on Danzig. Will there be a war or not be a war – the fate of Europe hung in the balance. It was this way – until a Black and Red wedding canopy was erected in Moscow – the Molotov-Ribbentrop -- Treaty. There was no longer any doubt: The global conflagration stood to erupt at any minute, Hitler had covered himself – he had obtained Stalin's consent to start. Both world dictators set themselves on the same platform, the knowledge of this Stalin-Hitler Pact reached me when I found myself, as was the case, each summer, at my sister's in Lubliniec for some vacation.

Memories of the Outbreak of the War in 1939

On August 1, 1939, the situation was bad, and Hitler fired the first shot.

The burning erupted, and a shudder ran through all of our bones, chaos reigned. Those who were mobilized from the surrounding towns and villages pressed with stuffed bundles and valises, crying women and children who escorted their near ones, not knowing what tomorrow would bring. [There were] sirens and alarms, and mothers wrung their hands. Herschel'eh Kaufman must go to be married under the wedding canopy, his wedding date having been planned for some time in advance. The *mekhutonim* had limited the extent of the wedding to only the wedding ceremony, a *Kiddush*, and the recitation of the *Sheva Berachot*, but now what to do? And, indeed, right in the middle of the wedding ceremony, a call-up certificate is brought to the groom, Herschel'eh Kaufman, to report for duty immediately. A fear and a fright envelopes everyone, the bride faints, the *mekhutonim* are pale and frightened, the father of the groom, R' Yitzhak Kaufman, who is still alive today, living with us in Tel-Aviv, to a one hundred and twenty years, was full of a black fear. The groom's mother, Dina Kaufman, wrings her hands with resignation. Herschel'eh went off to military service. With every passing day of the war, the storm grows more fierce. Tens of thousands of refugees passed through our *shtetl* of Cieszanow. Those who flee ask us where they should run to. The Germans bombard our *shtetl*. We all flee to the surrounding villages, one to Lubliniec, another to Novisil, etc. The conflagration spread over all of Poland and we have not heard anything about the bride and groom to this day.

May God avenge their spilled blood.

[Page 137]

My *Shtetl* Cieszanow

by Shmuel Lieberman

I will remember my little *shtetl* forever, I will remember what was good about you, and also what was bad, in your flowering and in your destruction. Cieszanow – where I saw my first sunlight, and there, where my eyes were darkened, when for the first time, I heard the epithet, '*Zyd*.'

O, my little *Shtetl*!

As if it were just yesterday, I began to attend *Heder,* played with the *Heder* students, and in which I wove my youthful dreams, and during the period of the Holocaust, was compelled to abandon you.

I remember everything – I remember your burgeoning youth organizations, I remember the large synagogue with its enormous hose of prayer in which we would gather to hear the *Kol Nidre* prayer intoned by the great *Tzaddik,* Rabbi Yekhezkiel Schraga Halberstam ז"ל. who with is leonine voice literally punched holes in the heavens. A fear and fright seized us at the time when he poured out his soul at the prayer of '*Malkhuyot-Zichronot-Shofarot*' and I will never forget is *Hoshanna Raba* prayers or the great joy and happiness at the time of the *Hakafot* during *Simchat Torah,* it is these very sacred sentiments that lie deeply buried in my heart – forever.

As if in a dream, I see how R' Leibusz Melamed tears apples off of the Rabbi's *Sukkah*, throwing them to the little children, disguised with a fur coat turned inside out, like a bear, and crying out: 'sacred flock.'

I remind myself of the *Bet HaMedrash*, the Belzer house, the Husyatin house, in which almost all of the Jews of the town would gather day in and day out, in order to pour out their discourse before God.

I also want to recall, that when the *balebatim* of the *shtetl* would escort their children to the wedding canopy, stepping sprightly through the wide *Ringplatz* accompanied by musicians who played the familiar wedding march, all of this, I will not forget to my last breath.

I also wish to recollect our scholars, *balebatim* and *Hasidim*, the precious youth movement, the spiritually rich committed community activists who, in their most difficult days, never lost sight of the fact that they were wrought in the image of God.

I recall how we gathered in the evenings at the home of our important comrade Shmuel Z. Tepper, נ"י, and I will take this opportunity to wish him long life and great *nachas* from his children.

'Cieszanow- -- May your sons and daughters who were by some miracle saved from the Hitler beast be blessed, and may all of you who are found in our liberated Jewish Land be blessed, and everywhere where they may be found, because they defended Jewish honor in a loyal and decent manner.

[Page 138]

A Memorial to R' Aharon Paluh ז״ל

by Shmuel Lieberman

R' Aharon Paluh was known as a great philanthropist, there were times when, in his town of Lubliniec where he led with the extensive 'assets' of his Lemberger enterprise, almost all the paupers of the city and environs would gather. And R' Aharon had a good word, and foremost, an emolument for everyone, for one a wooden cart, for another a sack of flour, etc. In addition to all of his virtues, R' Aharon was also a nationalistic Jew, and additionally a very pious person who took note of avoiding religious transgressions both great and small.

ת.נ.צ.ב.ה.

To Everlasting Memory

by Shmuel Lieberman

It is these whom I wish to remember for good – a number of those who made *aliyah* from /the village of Lubliniec beside Cieszanow.

R' David Yaroslavitz, ז״ל was a Jew who was a Torah scholar and a teacher, a man of many qualities and exceptional expertise, a Torah reader of exceptional quality, who could split open the heavens when, on the High Holy Days he stood by his place to ask for mercy upon him, his household and for the entire people of Israel.

R' Chaim Sholom Yaroslavitz, ז״ל – One of the most important citizens of the town, a good-hearted, honest man, going about his affairs modestly and doing good deeds, an ardent *Hasid* and a God-fearing man.

R' David Lempel, ז״ל from Olozov, one of the most popular figures in the entire vicinity, intelligent, a formidable scholar; Whether summer or winter, he arose early for Torah study and prayer.

His son, **R' Moshe ז״ל** followed in his footsteps, who was a model to the entire area with is good talents.

And the last of this list, **R' Nachman Fogel זצ״ל**. R' Nachman was expert in both the revealed and the esoteric Torah, a righteous man and a *Hasid*. Thanks to his enormous dedication and talents – he became prominent on Torah study and its explication.

He was important and very respected in the eyes of Rabbi Simcha Issachar Ber ז״ל the Chief Rabbi of Cieszanow, and no less that this, also in the eyes of the Chief Rabbi Issachar Dov ז״ל of Belz.

The great ones among the *Hasidim* offered the view that the soul of R' Nachman was in the hidden interstices of the High Heavens before it came down to the Lower World, hidden away – together with the souls of the AR"I ז״ל, and the BESH"T, ז״ל

May their souls be bound up in the bond of life under the wings of the Holy Spirit.

[Page 139]

A Few Words Dedicated to the Holocaust

by R' Shmuel Zeinvil Tepper,
Past Chairman of the Zionist Histadrut in Cieszanow

A holy shudder seizes me at the time I take up the pen in hand to write these few lines. The anger and pain has entered our body and soul since this great misfortune has befallen our people.

Our misfortune is as great and as deep as the ocean, and the wound is much larger and more searing that the sun in the month of Tammuz. The skilled artisan and writer has not yet been born, who is sufficiently skilled to describe even a part of the perverted misdeeds that the German Devil thought up for our brothers and sisters, whose last words were 'Shema Yisrael.' And' God will take vengeance for our blood, The blood of your brethren cries out from the earth.' Vengeance! Vengeance! Vengeance!

[Page 140]

The Accounting of Our Work to Publish the *Yizkor* Book

by Shmuel Z. Tepper

In this article, I wish to convey a short accounting of the start and finish of the sacred and difficult work in creating our Book.

The Organization of the Emigres of Cieszanow turned over the creation of this great work to its member, Dr. David Ravid, [this same] comrade Ravid who is also the Chair of the Organization, threw himself body and soul into the sacred work, and he also has the greatest investment in the grandiose work which our committee created.

The Chair of our Organization, Dr. David Ravid (Shmukler) was, as all in the old days, a Yeshiva boy, he studied Torah first, in Cieszanow with the well-known great scholar among the Jewish people, R' Israel Lehrer ז"ל, who taught altogether only 3-4 students, the scions of wealthy parents from which he, R' Zalman, made his living all year around.

It is to this R' Zalman ז"ל, indeed, this precious Jew, that I wish to dedicate a few words in our book – in his honor.

Tall, and with a broad build, with a handsome and long beard, with a *kolpak* on his head – he looked like the BESH"T personified.

He did not seek, or aspire, to the East Wall in the synagogue like other so-called high-class Jews, but rather on purpose, stood by the oven, and held onto it tightly, in order that he, R' Zalman, should not, God Forbid, fall down from weakness, whereas in the winter, by contrast, he simply held his hands to the oven – to warm up his scrawny bones, large and small held him in tremendous respect, and he was regarded as the most accomplished scholar not only in Cieszanow, but also in the entire vicinity.

The Old Rabbi constantly took counsel with R' Zalman on a variety of points of law and tradition, and this was the view of the teacher of David Ravid (Shmukler), certainly – from such a teacher, one can expect that much knowledge of the Torah will remain in the mind of the pupil.

In the moment that the sun of the revival of the people began to shine in our *shtetl*, our David threw himself into the Zionist concept with his entire youthful fire. We had a very difficult struggle with our parents who did not want to depart so much as an iota from their old, primitive habits, but after a difficult struggle, they capitulated in our favor, and our comrade David was elected as the *Dozor* in the municipal government, and other comrades of ours took over the power in the other Jewish and municipal institutions. We also took over the house of worship called the 'Padah-Schul' in which R' Asher Dieler ל"ז and our comrade Dr. Ravid, long life to him, were the lecturers on *Tanakh* and *Gēmara*. Among other languages, our comrade Dr. David has command of Polish and German, he had studied in Vienna, and completed the Teachers Seminary of Rabbi Prof. Hayot in Vienna. He also received his Doctorate in Philosophy and Jewish Studies from this same university.

[Page 141]

Now to the Issue!

At the beginning of the year 5729 (1969), our Chair and comrade Dr. David Ravid began to write various articles whose subject was the past history of our *shtetl*, Cieszanow. In his articles, the life of the Jewish populace is described from top to bottom, their origins, education, occupations, political orientation, and so forth, and his material makes up about 80% of this book, and it was for this reason he was privileged to be the editor and the publisher of our book, which presents itself as a substantive and precious work and a jewel in everyone of the our Cieszanow survivors.

In the month of Nissan 5729 (April 1969) comrade Ravid suddenly notified us that in his opinion, the time had arrived to publish a *Yizkor Book* for the Emigres of Cieszanow, and without giving it much thought, the committee, despite its sense of being so overwhelmed, agreed on the spot, and indeed, turned the work over to him.

Comrade Ravid took to this work with his entire energy, and as you can now see, with God's help, the book was created. To tell the truth – we were awed by the scope of his project, because he had secretly prepared everything and we, his friends, didn't have a clue that the product was real, and so close to being actualized.

After we had made a review of the prepared material, at a meeting that actually took place in Dr. Ravid's home, we immediately decided that the book is to be published.

With trembling and dread we took on the sacred, difficult work in order to prepare a permanent spiritual memorial to our dear fathers, mothers, brothers, sisters and children who were exterminated by the German anti-Semite aided by his Polish, Ukrainian, and murderous accomplices from other nations.

In Israel, there are close to 200 families from our *shtetl* that went under. We approached the, as we did our *landsleit* in the Diaspora, and almost immediately, the first donations arrived with hearty blessings for the committee, such as, 'may the hands who do this holy work be blessed.'

Along with funds, pictures were also sent, and on the second day of *Hol HaMoed Sukkot* 5730, the committee turned over the material to the printer, at a fortuitous hour, to have the book printed. The book will be an eternal memorial in honor of the precious, pure souls of our community that was brought down, which was once called the community of Cieszanow.

[Page 142]

The Extinguished Star

By Shmuel Zeinvil Tepper, Tel-Aviv

In this small article, I will pause beside the sorrowful occurrence that took place with the outbreak of the war of 1939, and the extermination of European Jewry with its 6 million martyrs.

On that fateful Friday, when Hitler ש"מי broadcast his declaration of war against Poland on the radio, at that same moment, his Messerschmitts penetrated deep into Polish territory, Cracow, and other western Polish cities had already been bombed.

On the third day after the assault, the first refugees from that area came traveling through Cieszanow.

A terrifying fear enveloped us all, naturally, thinking – who knows, perhaps the same fate awaits us too? Sadly, the instinct of that fear did not mislead us, and in only several short days, that occurred to us which we had feared, and the Germans broke into our *shtetl*.

We, residents of Cieszanow were more fortunate than our neighboring towns of Oleszyce and Lubaczow.

Our good luck consisted of the fact that the Russians had gone too far, because according to the treaty with the Germans, they had to pull back to Lubaczow, but after eight days, the Russians let it be known that they were abandoning Cieszanow and the Germans were to occupy the *shtetl*, and whoever wants to, can evacuate together with them, and equally placed for everyone the means of transportation, so that people could save themselves from the hands of the Germans.

At three o'clock afternoon, the *shtetl* became *Judenrein* down to several families, including Abraham Ber Starkman with his wife, Dwora Alter and Abel'eh Drucker the tailor, who for a variety of reasons, remained behind in the *shtetl*.

We went off in wagons, autos, and mostly on foot.

It is hard to forget the picture of 'and they traveled – and they decamped.' We dragged ourselves day in and day out, like gypsies, with the German Messerschmitts on our heads, with their murderous shooting of the people, the road from Cieszanow to Lubaczow was black, a wailing shuddering cry of children and women, the entire *shtetl* goes and goes… not knowing where to, and what sort of new and unanticipated surprises the morning will bring.

One had only a single objective, to protect one's self from the German bullets, and whether or not they are pursuing us.

When, people said to one another, will we ever see our dear little *shtetl* again?

At that moment, the star that was named Cieszanow was extinguished.

Into every corner, the new spirit penetrated that dominated the new Jewish youth, and Jewish life.

The young people were organized, the largest part having Zionist sympathies, also the *Bund* had its

[Page 143]

adherents, despite this, the struggle against the young people by the older, more primitive and backward facing generation, was partly so successful, and their success let to the fact that a quarter of our Jewish townspeople were killed by the Germans, and also through hunger and cold, and various diseases in the Russian steppes and jungles.

A limited number of people came out alive from the hands of the Red and the Brown [-shirted] Asmodeus. Among them – Moshe Mikhl Tepper who today lives in Brazil, and the two Singer brothers that live in Canada.

I was told that in the *shtetl* near Lemberg, in which our Rabbi, R' Yekhezkiel Schraga ז"ל was hidden with his family, people begged him to travel with them to Russia, he rejected the offer, arguing primarily – Russia is an unclean land, that is what I was told by Feivel Rosenstock – that one must by whatever means, distance one's self from this uncleanliness in order not to be compromised with *trayf* foods, and so forth.

In my next article, I will address the way of life and the cultural area.

A Zionist life bubbled in the *shtetl*, the young people, who were Zionist, committed itself to *Keren Kayemet* and *Keren HaYesod*, the Hebrew University, etc. with public assemblies.

We had a Hebrew School in which the presently known Argentine journalist, Mordechai Kaufman was the teacher and at the same time, the youth director. We also had our own library, and as the President of the Zionist Organization, I had the honor of helping to nurture the nationalist concept both with material and with my time.

As is known, the *Bund* was our political opponent, but when it came to defending Jewish honor, we stood together like a single piece of steel, united against our community foes. The *Bund* was blessed with good leaders, such as Tz. B. Berish Schuster ז"ל, Abraham Futsher, Leibusz Goldberg, his brother, the brothers Zusha and Shammai Goldberg, Hirsch Shmukler, may all of their memories be for a blessing, these were people of culture, despite opposing political points of view we respected and regarded each other well. The annual winter assistance for the poor was always carried out on a community basis, and theater presentations were always carried out in partnership.

Naturally, at election time to the community or municipal council, contests developed and despite all of the efforts, we Zionists managed to get our comrade, and the publisher of this '*Yizkor Book*,' David Shmukler (today Dr. David Ravid) elected to the municipal council.

We also wrote a Torah scroll, and despite all the difficulties, we put on an event celebration for this mitzvah by escorting our Torah scroll into our own house of worship where Asher Dieler ז"ל, a Torah sage was the *Gabbai* and who tragically, along with his wife and several children, was killed in the Red Paradise under Stalin ימ"ש.

In the name of everyone, I will take this opportunity to call out that we should hold their memory for a blessing forever.

[Page 144]

Yizkor!

by The Grandchildren

In Memory of Our Grandmother, Alteh, ז״ל
The Wife of Our Grandfather R' Shmuel Zeinvil Tepper, to long life

ת.נ.צ.ב.ה

Remember days gone by,
Remember days that have passed,
Days, not to be forgotten,
Days, to be always remembered.

Days, on which she came to visit,
Full of joy and radiating light;
Raising the spirits of the grown ups,
Shielding the souls of the small.
Forever, but she will never vanish from us

Until a malignant disease attacked her,
Lingering for a day and a year.
Until the day she fell silent forever,
But from us, she will never disappear.

We will feel her absence forever,
We will live in her shadow forever.
We will not be consoled for the bad time
That arrived with her departure.

Yizkor!

by Shmuel Zeinvil Tepper, Israel

This memorial is placed in lieu of a grave stone in memory of my parents and the members of my family, may God avenge their blood, who were murdered by the Nazi German murderers and their accomplices, and whose final resting place is unknown.

Sitting in the middle: My father, R' Naphtali and my mother Rachel, ז"ל
From the right: The grandchildren Motkeh and Chaim, sons of Sholom and my sister Tauva Gershtenfeld ז"ל
From the left: The grandchildren Michael and Chaya, the son and daughter of Beryl, my brother, and his wife Frieda Tepper, ז"ל
And Separated for a Long Life, sitting, my daughters, from the right: Tonya, Sala, and Lyuba

[Page 145]

I Remember: Sheva and her daughters Gartl and Faleh ז"ל, the wife and daughters of my brother Moshe Michael Tepper, to long life, and Fradl and her daughter, ז"ל, the wife and daughter of my brother Leibusz Ber Tepper, to long life.

I Remember: My brother Chaim and his wife Yehudit Tepper ז"ל, who died in Harbin in the year 5716-1956.

Woe to them who lose and do not remember. May their memory be for a blessing.

Yizkor!

Sholom and Tauva Gershtenfeld and their sons, ז"ל

This page is dedicated, by us, to the memory of our parents and the members of our family, may God avenge their blood, who were killed in the Holocaust by the Nazi Amalek.

Grandmother: Bina Gershtenfeld ז"ל of the Rosenfeld family.

Parents: Abraham and Frimet Zeitler ז"ל.

Our Brother: Yehuda and our sisters: Dwora and Rachel Zeitler, ז"ל.

Our Uncle and Aunt: Sholom and Tauva Gershtenfeld and their sons, Motkeh and Chaim ז"ל.

Yehoshua Zeitler – England
Sonya Rabfogel and Chava Fiksler of the Zeitler family – Israel

Mrs. Dwora Lempel ה"ע
Mother of Benjamin ל"ז who fell in the Sinai Campaign

ת.נ.צ.ב.ה.

[Page 146]

R' Zelig Wartzel and his wife Nechi ה"ע
A family known for its good deeds, from a Hasidic family and Torah scholars.
May their souls be bound up in the bond of life.

R' Menachem Wartzel and his wife ע"ה
The entire family was exterminated in the Cracow Ghetto. May God avenge their blood.

R' Baruch Aryeh Kalechman, הי"ד

by Shlomo Zinger, his grandson

Our Sages have said, concerning "Blessed are you in arriving, and in your departing." (Deuteronomy 28:5), may your departure be like your coming, if your arrival in the world was without sin, may your departure be without sin.

A blessing of this nature, to leave this world without the blemish of sin, is not easily accomplished, because "There is no righteous man in the land who can do good but not transgress (Ecclesiastes 7:20), and in order to purify a person so as to facilitate his departure from this world without sin, death was decreed on all human beings, even on the righteous and the pious. Death, and the agonies that accompany it, purify the human being of his sins, an a priori argument can be made, that if the tooth and eye which are working parts are liberated, how much more so then all of the limbs of the human, it is therefore appropriate to say that the entire human being is liberated of all sin and transgression (Berachot 5).

How appropriate and relevant are the words of our Sages, referred to above, to my Grandfather R' Baruch Aryeh, ז"ל! It was possible to encounter him morning and evening, treading with measured strides – in his traditional direction – upon rising, to the central *Bet HaMedrash* in our town, so that he would not miss out, God forbid, on communal prayer, since it was his custom to be among the early risers, who poured their hearts out to our Father in Heaven. This dear man, was modest and chaste, among the most chaste. For his entire life, he earned a living by the work of his own hands, doing whatever it was within his ability to do. By nature, he was careful in the way he dressed, a simple form of garb – but he was never extravagant about his clothing.

He took everything lovingly, and never complained about acts of the Almighty, and he was privileged to see his progeny continue in the ways of tradition during his lifetime, and also was privileged to reach a formidable old age – the age of 96 years.

[Page 147]

With the outbreak of The Second World War, he went together with his family to Nemirov, and lived there with my brother David, הי"ד.

My grandfather Baruch Sholom ז"ל, came into this world without sin, and he left this world as he came into it, without sin. He passed away on 19 Av 5700 [1940] in Nemirov – and there is his honored resting place.

[Page 148]

Memories

by Moshe Mikhl Tepper, נ"י

Moshe Mikhl Tepper from Rio De Janeiro

I was born in a village near Cieszanow, and lived in Lemberg.

In the year 1941, when Hitler ימ"ש ordered his wild bands to march into Lemberg, the lives of the Jews of Lemberg were immediately transformed, the process of dragging Jews out of their houses was initiated, and the unfortunate ones never again returned.

It happened to me, when very early in the morning, I had gone out on foot to go to work (it was forbidden for Jews to ride on the trams), and Jewish 'Kapos' captured me, and presented me to a gathering point, had me tossed into a cattle car, and taken away to a work camp in Zloczow.

There were already many unfortunate of our brothers and sisters, I lay in a barracks which was surrounded by barbed wire, half dead from hunger and cold.

We worked on the roads, doing such work as breaking stones and digging the earth. In a very short time, very many became completely exhausted and fell dead of hunger, cold and hard labor.

Thousands of Jews who became ill with Typhus were shot under the order that they were taking the place of others.

I, personally, was rescued by coincidence, since I also became ill with typhus, only my good fortune was that the commandant happened to be on leave, and his substitute was a bit more lenient, so he didn't have me shot, and God helped me so that by the time the tyrant returned, I had in the meantime returned to health; that is why I am currently alive ע"ה.

And when the defeats of the Germans became more severe, they began to liquidate the camps en masse. Also, in our camp, hundreds of innocent Jewish souls were shot every day.

Seeing that I had nothing to lose, I attempted an escape and ended up wandering about in the surrounding forests for a while.

Words fail me to describe the struggle for life and the suffering I endured in the forest.

On a beautiful clear day, the Russians arrived and liberated us, this was in the month of May 1944.

After exhausting myself for an additional 4 years, I was saved from Hitler's Hell as the only survivor of my entire family.

My wife and children ז"ל were exterminated in the year 1942 in the well-known 'Janowska' camp in Lemberg[1].

Wandering about in the Hell of Europe for a while, I settled in Brazil, where I started everything over anew.

Translator's footnote:

1.   In September 1941, the Germans set up a factory at 134 Janowska Street in the suburbs of Lviv (Lwow / Lemberg) to service the needs of the German Army. Soon after, they expanded it into a network of factories as part of the *Deutsche Ausrüüstungwerke* (DAW — German Armament Works), a division of the SS. From inception, Jews from Lwow were utilized as forced labor in these factories; by the end of October, 600 Jews were working there. At that point, the character of the factories changed. A forced Jewish labor camp (*Juden-Zwangsarbeitslager*) was established. The area became a restricted camp, enclosed by barbed wire, which the Jews were not permitted to leave.

[Page 149]

From the Older Generation
– To the Younger Generation of Cieszanow Descendants in Israel

by Dr. David Ravid

You – our sons and daughters, you succeeded in fleeing from the European Valley of Death bare and without anything.

You reached the enchanted land at a tender age – the Land of our Forefathers,

We raised you and educated you to a new life – a life of Torah and tradition together with practical day-to-day living, and we thank God who kept us alive, sustained us, and enabled us to arrive at the point where we can see the sweet fruit from the tree that we planted.

You are the younger generation, who are almost entirely intellectuals, there are among you engineers, artisans, certified accountants, lawyers, lecturers, technologists, zoologists, generals, Rabbis, ritual slaughterers and meat inspectors, and ordinary learned people, and you have become the pride of our clan, and we the ones who are growing old – feel blessed and take pride in you and consider that we are fortunate to be the fathers to sons and daughters that are like you, and we are fortunate in our progeny that has not brought shame to our old age.

However, to each healthy fruit, there sometimes is such a blemish, and consequently there are those, beyond the pale, who lack enlightenment among you –

> Like Korah in his time of great and heated anger
> When a fire seethed in his nostrils
> And who called out what is it that the elders are doing
> Who are publishing a *Yizkor Book*?
> 'Yet another book'
> And before they even set eyes on it – said,
> That 'Half the material of the book'
> Was as if tucked away in his breast –
> Hidden in his gut, which rises arrogantly between his teeth
> And no one knows when he lies down or rises up.
> It is not we who are to blame that you have selected the name for yourself of a 'scholar'
> A scholar – not that his stories can be found on the shelves…
> Rather – what is written can be found in his head.
> Well, show your power, and don't be a contentious man, bring us your book and receive your recompense.
> God in heaven! How long will the Korahs continue to revel?

[Page 150]

Chaya Angerst-Berger

My eyes, my eyes cascade tears over the tragedy that has occurred to the daughter of our town, Chaya Angerst-Berger, daughter of Yekhiel and Leah, who died after a difficult delivery on 8 Heshvan 5730 at the age of 40, leaving her husband, three of her children, her saddened brothers and sisters – bereaved and left alone.

May her soul be bound up in the bond of eternal life under the wings of the Holy Spirit.

Chaya Angerst-Berger

In memory of a sister that is no longer here,
We have been left aching and it is difficult to accept –
That she has gone not to return,
That little light and joy
Was granted her during her short life,
Suffering illness and the sorrow of rearing children
We will not forget ever.

The Bereaved Families
Weinstein, Rubel, Berger and Angerst

Also the Members of the Committee and the entire Community of Cieszanow Emigres
Join in Sharing Your Sorrow.

[Page 151]

R' Schraga Feivel Lehrer

R' Schraga Feivel Lehrer

Mr. Lehrer in destroyed Warsaw

R' Schraga Yitzhak Feivel Lehrer, ל"ז a scion of our town, is a descendant of the Waxman family. After wanderings and nomadic peregrination in the hinterlands of Russia, and after his relatives were exterminated in sacred martyrdom, and his younger brother died in exile, Lehrer appeared in Warsaw. He was not overwhelmed by the tides of despair that assaulted many of members of the younger Jewish generation, but rather, he was seized by the cultural sector that remained as a residue and began to organize himself in the capitol of Poland for a renewal and the restoration of a Jewish spiritual life. These were days of the collection of the remnants of books that remained, spread all over between the ghettoes of Warsaw and in towns that were abandoned by Jews in the midst of the maelstrom of the Holocaust and extermination. The committee of the sacred congregations in Poland, together with the Central Committee of Jews in Poland, enabled this effort to go ahead, in order that these books be saved and sent to The Land. Lehrer enlisted in this work immediately, and out of his love for the Hebrew book, he turned nights into days, and he did not spare any effort in the collection and organization of the books that were in part sent to the Hebrew University in Jerusalem, and part of them to synagogues and Yeshivas in The Land. With this, Lehrer made himself available to hear learning from sages during the day, and at night, he worked diligently on the books in the central Jewish library that had been established in Warsaw.

He also dedicated himself to the work of aliyah, and in the preservation of the memory of the martyrs of the Holocaust, he saw the purpose of his life; such was the case when he was in Poland, and such was also the case when he arrived in The Land. Here, he set himself up in business, raised a family, but in the end, he continuously returned to the mission that he had taken upon himself, continues to work, to stimulate himself and others, to address the responsibility of this generation, and that is the mitzvah of remembrance!

Great is the doer and the deed.

Schraga-Yitzhak Feivel Lehrer, Haifa – Israel

My addendum here is the fruit of an emotional effort.

While I [personally] did not remain under the Nazis ש"מי for more than two weeks, you must understand that despite this, what sort of ardor and how much love, and how much spiritual agony and searing pain is involved in order to be the one who must renew this era and to tell about it in memoirs. I refer to these chapters as memories, because they happen to be stories drawn from memory, enveloped in flames of love and hate. An unbounded love to our oppressed people, that was tortured in its weariness, and an immense hatred toward its unclean murderers, the scum of the human race.

*Yizkor book*s are in general a collection of threnodies and beseeching, in which every Jew, even if he is not a scion of the city, to find a faithful echo of the great human tragedy and because of this, to intensify strength and unify himself with the memory of all the pure souls of those who were slaughtered and exterminated, also of those members of generations gone by, and of all of these, who by their lives and death saddened our spirits and our souls.

[Page 152]

It is understood that everything depends on the mood and the creative capacity of the designated publisher. All of the tribulations to reduce these things to writing coalesce into a memorial that speaks to our proud and distinguished past.

[Page 153]

Chapters of Memories

By Schraga-Feivel Lehrer

When the Second World War broke out in the year 1939, I was Bar Mitzvah, and precisely on that day, I became a full thirteen years of age. I do not remember a great deal from my childhood. Despite this, something does bruit about in my memory. I remember my little town, populated by Jews living in great crowdedness, the town of my birth, Cieszanow. I remember my parents' house very well. Because of my father's occupation of being a grain merchant, we lived in the core of the town, at a bit of a distance from the center. My father was busy with his work all day, and during the twilight hours, he would go hurriedly to the synagogue of the Husyatin *Hasidim* as if someone were chasing him, or as if he suspected that he would be somewhat late there, and it was his responsibility to hurry along....

On the outside, he had a Jewish bearing that was a little difficult: he would speak differently, smile differently, and react differently to specific developments: I used to say, that he would restrain himself in his joy, and similarly in his sorrow. His relationship to the public was as if he constantly suspected that he was threatened by The Evil Eye. Personally, he probably didn't [sic: consciously] know that he did this because of the Eye that peers at him from the side.

However, he felt entirely different when he was in his own home, in the *Bet HaMedrash*, and in his *kloyz*. His behavior was different in his relationship to other people, to matters pertaining to one person to another. He became transformed, he became more intimate, gentle and closer, natural and more from the heart. Among brethren, the Jew feels as if the cables that constrain his steps have suddenly been cut away. His attitude towards a friend or a neighbor, to a relative, and other kin becomes more emotional without ulterior motive.

I remember the secular discussions in the *kloyz* in the intermissions between the afternoon and evening prayers. The subjects of these discussions dwelt largely on the condition of the nation, the world, the new generation, the young people growing up, who in part were going off in alien directions, distancing themselves from the way of life of their grandparents, that the generation is prodigal, some a little, and some a lot, in deserting the ways of *Yiddishkeit*.

My childhood way of life in the town was no bed of roses, for we lived in the Diaspora. In the end, it was an ambience that was sown with hatred, unfounded hatred... the young gentiles schemed against us – but for the sake of truth, we did not keep our hands out of the cookie jar, and didn't behave like good kids. They too, when the situation arose for them to pass through the Jewish neighborhoods, looked around very carefully as they proceeded... however, despite the hatred that was spread among us by implementation, the Jewish children did feel themselves in their own town as if they were in their own homes and their own country...this is more or less how the matter looked up to the outbreak of the war: the years of *Heder*, and their glow, the days of Hanukkah and the joy they brought, the days of Purim and their din. The noise of the *groggers*, and the whistles that deafened the ears, and cohorts, cohorts in masquerade, filling the streets of the Jewish district with a racket and tumult. All of this made a deep impression on the soul of a child. The eve of the Passover holidays, with the boiling of the dishes and the burning of the leaven, and the smoke that rose form the yards, were a source of joy to children. The Sabbaths and Festivals in the synagogues and houses of study, the courtyard of the Rebbe, and even the meeting places for the youth movements, all of this was genuinely Jewish to the core, have a Jewish flavor and redolence.

I am reminded of the large yard, the deciduous tree beside the house and the stand of pines nearby, where

[Page 154]

we spent our Sabbath days playing games and engaging in conversation and in all the other things that young people do while they are growing up. How great was the joy that we derived from all of this!.... In the Festivals and on the Sabbath in the afternoon, we would read in the shade of the trees that were in the thicket, stories of events...and newspapers. Out of great exhaustion, we would grab a nap in the embrace of the clean air. We fell asleep quickly after our play. During the summer, we would go out to the grove beside the river, or to the green fields, or we stretched out on the freshly cut bales of hay; during the brightly clear winter days, we would go out onto the fields that were wrapped in pure snow, and establish a base for our amusement, we would make snowballs, and throw them at our friends, our cousins, male and female alike, who returned the assault measure for measure, amid groans and cries of pleasure. We would slip and slide, and fall, in order to hug and kiss one another, and even…bite one another from the ever increasing sense of hilarity. And what was the wonder? The burden of making a living had not yet descended upon our shoulders.

Quickly, the childhood years flew by. The war put an end to them abruptly. My town, Cieszanow, with its beautiful ambience, the *Hasidic* Jewish *shtetl* – the malevolent and purposefully murderous hands of the evil ones has destroyed you, and transformed everything into a wasteland. To where have your young people vanished, and the entrepreneurial *balebatim*? Where are your Jews, with the shining faces, to be found, the scholars, the scribes, and ordinary learned folk, those, who evening in and evening out, after a hard day of burdensome work, who in trade, and who with his manual labor, would sit in the houses of study, in the *kloyz* of the *Hasidim* of Belz, or in the *kloyz* of the Husyatin *Hasidim*, or in the *Bet HaMedrash* of the Rabbi and study with such great focus and seriousness.

Even the young people would sit and learn. Even if the larger part of them preferred to spend their time in the offices of the various Zionist organizations, or non-Zionist ones, everything had the stamp of the truth on it. These, these are the words of The Living God. They sought some meaningful result in every undertaking. A meaningful result for the sake of the Jewish people, a meaningful result for humanity, the specific and at hand, as well as for the world in general. Everything was done with a Jewish dedication for the sake of the essence of the issue, to implement it properly. Everything was genuinely Jewish, and its flavor and its redolence were Jewish.

The towns adjacent to Cieszanow were: Narol-Lipsko. These were twin cities with only a small river separating them, and a narrow bridge connected them. It is from here that the double name Narol-Lipsko is derived. This was the birthplace of my father. It was a magnificent area, as if it had been dipped in a great greenness of forest and pasture. These added an escort of charm to the towns, and this is the way they lived in this little gorgeous gem in the center of Galicia. It's populace, even though it resembled the surrounding populace in its way of life, had its own special charm. The young people were more energetic, they were more joyful, but woe, there was only one single fate, and one bitter end that cut both of them down.

To the north was the Polish border. To the east, could be found Rawa Ruska, Lemberg (Lvov), and to the west could be found Oleszyce, Jaroslaw, Rzeszow[1], Lubaczow, etc.

The town of Belzec is not a great distance form Narol-Lipsko. In times past, before the First World War – it was a border point between the Austrian Empire and Czarist Russia. During the time of the Second World War, there was an extermination camp in Belzec well known for its barbarity and cruelty. In the period between

[Page 155]

the two wars, this entire district belonged to Lvov, and now, with no Jews, to the Resza District.

As said above, the War found me at the end of childhood, but nevertheless, I remember a number of the older people in town. I remember the Jewish craftsmen of my town – in our town, forward-thinking people, but people with a real Jewish feel to them. Before my eyes stand *Hasidim*, young married men, who would inject life and vigor into the town. There was a genuine *Hasidic* ardor in them, when they would literally besiege the courtyard of the Rebbe. I see the groups of the various professional unions, the various organizations, each to its own kind, in whom warm Jewish blood coursed, and a pure Jewish spirit reigned.

In passing from the general to the specific, the spirits of different people stand before my eyes, each man, standing distinctly by himself. First and foremost is my grandfather Meir. He was called Meir *Nossn's*, that is to say, the son of Nathan. During the days of summer, my father would take me to the home of my grandfather and grandmother in Narol-Lipsko. I would spend the long vacation there. My grandfather took me on a daily basis to pray at the synagogue, and after a generous breakfast would send me to study in the *Heder*, in order that I not sit idle and away from Torah study all these days. And my grandmother Rivka! Oh, how she spoiled me, fulfilling my every wish! And Aunt Mindl, and Aunt Gitla and Uncle Shmuel-Zeinvil? All of them strove on my behalf, to amuse me and make my stay pleasant in this Jewish home blessed with everything that was good, suffused with genuine love and patience. My grandfather was a renown host. Merchants that came from Lvov to transact their business, would arrive and depart from my grandfather's place. To spend time in Narol-Lipsko and not to stop off at R' Meir? To partake of a glass of tea from the pot, and to have a taste of grandmother's baking? It was not conceivable to skip this. And even the conversation in the house was not idle. The words of Torah and wisdom were always to be heard, or just plain news of the world. At Meir *Nossn's*, everyone felt as if they were in their own home. All his doings were from the heart. And all of this without any show of emotion, except for tranquility and modesty. And his attitude toward matters of spirit is best demonstrated by the fact that he turned over one of his rooms to be used as a Zionist Library not for the purpose of receiving a prize.

And it was this quiet heartiness, and atmosphere of love, of good deeds and elevated intentions these are among the attributes that were bequeathed to us by my father's grandfather, R' Nathan.

Regarding my grandfather Nathan Lehrer, a baker of fine breads, he was a Jew wise in the was of life, with an acute sense of perception, a doer of good deeds, and a whole person about whom many stories circulated in the family. I will recall one of them here: after The First World War, he stood at the head of an organization to provide assistance to the needy which dealt with providing aid for the reconstruction of homes that were burned, having gone up in flames during the war. (Narol-Lipsko was known for its fires even during peacetime, not to mention wartime). His sons and daughters, whose houses were also destroyed. turned to him with a request for periodic help, they being as innocent as others who had been burned out. Grandfather refused them and his reasoning was as follows: "This assistance has not been allocated for you. It has been allocated for the elderly and weak, the ill and the maimed, who do not have the strength to build everything from anew. You, my children, are young and healthy, capable to do all manner of work, so work and do commerce on the land, and with God's help, you will build and be built...."

Also, the conflagration did not skip over the house of grandfather Nathan, and he too, was among those who was burned out. My father told me, that most of all, the old man was saddened by the books that had become fodder for the flames. These were his personal precious treasure. He was a scholar, one of the people close to the Rabbi of the town, and it was his practice to engage in Torah discourse with him, and to analyze matters pertaining to religious law.

[Page 156]

I remember my uncles and aunts and remaining relatives very well, and I will add and tell about them. Let me recall a number of them: My Uncle Moshe Joseph Segal, a wondrous teacher, who sat day and night immersed in Torah study, and he was a perfectionist, being zealous and observant down to the tip of a *yud* in everything that touched upon tradition. Yet, in matters pertaining to the education of his sons, he showed a brought heart and tolerance, and did not interfere with them if they began to take an interest in secular subjects, and read a secular book or as it was then called 'the enlightened literature.' His sons proved faithful to him, in that they did not pursue a malign cultural path.

Uncle Abraham Yitzhak Lehrer was a totally different type of person. He, personally, did not depart from the tents of the Torah, practically a resident of the Belz *kloyz*, he sat hunched over the *Gemara*. He sanctions for his sons, in addition to the Shas, to partake of secular knowledge. In contrast to other zealous Jews, who are even suspicious if their sons even want to learn a chapter of the *Tanakh*, he would encourage his sons to imbibe all sources...let his sons grow up to be come well-informed people...that is what he would say constantly.

And additionally I recall Mordechai Waxman, and his wife Pearl, and their nine children: Moshe, David, Hirsch, Yeshaya, Eliyahu, Yaakov, Aharon, Esther and Faiga with their families הי"ד. And Abraham Feder ז"ל, an ardent, important Belz *Hasid*, and his wife Min'cheh ע"ה (of the Waxman family), and Yitzhak Waxman, a philanthropist and giver of charity, who never sought any thanks for all of his good works and his oneness with the world about him.

I remember Uncle Yaakov Waxman, his wife Eidel (of the Lehrer family) and their children. The young married couples, Yaakov Braker, a scribe of Torahs and Mezuzot, and Mottl Zambank and their families. Among the more prominent members of the community, it is worth recollecting: Leib Sternlicht ז״ל, R' Moshe Root, who exchanged responsa with the sages of the times. Additionally, I will recall Mordechai Glanzer, Meir Waxman, and his wife Elka, Joseph Waxman and his wife Tova, Hirsch Waxman, Gershon Lehrer, Chaim-Joseph Just, Benjamin Just, I would be in the habit of going to Chaim-Joseph's house on Saturdays for the purpose of being tested on the Torah portion of the week.

An here is the elementary level teacher, R' Itcheh, with whom I first learned my alphabet, my memory of him comes to me as if from out of a black cloud. And this is no wonder – I was then about three years old. Opposite him, R' Leibusz lives in my memory, a man from Narol, with whom I learned the Pentateuch with Rashi commentaries. I can even remember the special sing-song tune of the way we did our study. He loved his pupils with his soul, and we reciprocated in kind. The son of the Rabbi, R' Yekhezkiel Halberstam הי״ד, also studied in this *Heder*, and he was my classmate, Chaim Hirsch ה״יד. The Rabbi was in the habit of coming to our *Heder*, because it was adjacent to his study house, and during his visit on Friday, he would do so to test the children. It was only a few steps from the *Bet HaMedrash*, and the Rabbi would appear enveloped in his prayer shawl, and dressed in his phylacteries, immediately after prayers. For whatever reason, I was always among the first that he would question.

I remember well the parties that we had in *Heder*. Year in and year out, on the Sunday of the portion of *V'Ayleh P'kuday*, and if the portions were concatenated, then *Vayakhel-P'kuday*, a party would be arranged to mark the end of the period during which study would be conducted at night. This was because the days grew longer as we got closer to Passover, and we would learn only up to the time of the afternoon prayers, and not as was the custom during the long winter nights, in which we continued to study even after the evening prayers. (It is understood – before noon we were in secular school). Also, the following maxim was well inculcated: "When we reach *Vayakhel-Pkuday*, we have a party.' And the party was arranged under the

[Page 157]

supervision and direction of the *Rebbetzin*, that is, the Rabbi's wife, and in her kitchen, but it is self-understood that it was at our expense. For months in advance, we would insert money into a sealed box, made of clay, pennies from the Sabbath money that we received from our parents. In praise of this pleasant custom, it is possible to add that no accounting was taken of the monies that were put into the box, 'in order that a blessing reign there,' as the Rabbi said, but also in order that we would not know what each individual puts in, in order that the children of the poor not be shamed because they didn't have the means to contribute in a measure that was equivalent to the others.

The custom was, that when one of the children drew near to the box to make a contribution, that the others averted their faces, in order that they not see their comrade's gift. The box was well sealed on all sides, and only a tiny slit, like a crack was in it, through which it was possible to insert a coin. To take out the money was only possible if the box was broken open. At the time the box was broken, and on the occasion that the money was counted, the Rabbi also participated. We awaited this event impatiently for the entire winter.

Our *Gemara* teacher was R' Avigdor, who was stricter by far with us, even though he also was committed and faithful in his mission and to his students. He pressed down the full weight of the yoke on us, along with the cascade of *mitzvot* that we were obliged to observe. Nevertheless, everything that he did – he did for our own good, in order that we be good Jews when we grow up.

The memory of the Sabbaths in the town are especially deeply etched into my memory. The sanctity of the day was palpable in the entire area. Even the gentiles refrained from traversing the Jewish streets in their heavily-laden wagons, in order not to disturb the rest of the Sabbath Day.

The elevated spiritual state that the Sabbath brought could literally be felt with the hands. The burning candles, the bathed children, carefully combed, the cleanliness that stands out from every nook and cranny of the room, this atmosphere could be felt as early as Friday morning. Father comes rushing from town: get up, today is the eve of the Sabbath, and he would rush out to pray. Mother rushes off to the market to buy the last of her Sabbath provisions, that she had not managed to buy the day before. All of this creates a pleasant rush of sound in the heart of a young child. The difference in this day can be felt well: it is a weekday, but not like the rest of the days.

From the noon hour on, a flood of hurried activity commences in a race with time. Father runs to the bath house and on his return, he reviews the Torah portion of the week, twice in the original Hebrew text, and once in the Aramaic translation. Mother is occupied and busy in the kitchen, to finish her work on time, and not, God forbid, after the time of candle-lighting. Even I am taken up in this mood, and I hurry to get myself ready for the Sabbath. And my heart is full of anticipation. With the descent of night, after the final preparations, my mother's custom, Chava, long life to her (of the Waxman family) to rest a bit, after she had managed to change clothing in honor of the Sabbath, and awaits the appointed hour to bless the candles. With a glance at the clock in the kitchen, she squeezes in a look at the *Sefer HaTekhinot* that is ready in front of her, and she opens it to the page where the specific supplication is found to be recited along with the lighting of the candles. She prays for good health, and a living for the members of her household, and also offers a supplication on behalf of all Jewry, for the sake of the Holy Sabbath. And as it happens, tears fall from her eyes , as if by themselves, hot tears of gratitude for the week that has gone by, peaceably, and without any disabling obstacles, and she pleads for God's blessing for the coming week. After lighting the candles, we leave, my Father and I, for synagogue. The little daughters go outside to play with their girlfriends. Mother remains in the house alone, and she returns to her [*Sefer*] *HaTekhinot*, or to *Tzena U'Re'ena*, reading there what is said about the weekly Torah portion, and she closes the book with a kiss only when she hears our

[Page 158]

footfall outside. The door opens to its full width, and Father noisily blesses her with a gleeful '*Shabbat Shalom*,' and burst into an ardent rendition of "*Shalom Aleichem Mal'achei HaSharet*.' My mother's face radiates holiness, and like a secret shining, her tears reflect the Sabbath candle light like sparks, in the silver candlesticks on the set table. The Holy Spirit hovers in the house. and the spirit of holiness from other worlds stirs the heart…

On the morrow, with the conclusion of the Sabbath during the Third Feast, the sensitive should of the Jewish child fills with a longing that seems to threaten one's life. Slowly, slowly, the sun sets, and it is as if the Sabbath Queen is weighing in her mind if it isn't too early to return the evil ones to their purgatory. And the young heart spasms from pain and compassion for the evil ones.

I rush with my father to the Husyatin *kloyz*. From there, one hears the voices and melodies of the Third Feast burst forth and rise upwards, which is still being celebrated in accordance with ritual. And here, we are accosted by the familiar traditional melody, and the carrier of longing, '*B'nai Hilka Dikhsiffin*'… The Jews of the town come to take their leave of the Sabbath, and the sorrow of this parting becomes almost like an ache. They sit, crowded together, around a table in the atmosphere of the twilight. The singing is especially soulful, full of enchantment and weavings. A few run about the *kloyz* hither and thither. The holy fervor is intense, and it is difficult to sit in one place. Even I run about with them, with my eyes shut…in the recitation of 'May your servant run like a ram' that is now intoned sung by the singers. And with the singing, all boundaries fall away. All borders are erased between heaven and earth, between dream and reality, between illusion and what is truth. The *kloyz* is suddenly filled with shadows, as if all the souls of the generations past have gathered within its walls to escort the Sabbath Queen.

And it is odd: There is a co-mingling that reigns everywhere, among the shadows there are also the outlines of women. How is it that women have come to the Husyatin *kloyz*?

Apart from those whose passing was natural, in the manner of one generation following another, I also see families, each family according to its generation, also from among those who were exterminated much later by the Nazi Scourge ימ"ש, and not only them, but also entire generations of Jews, men, women and children, that are filling up the confines of the *kloyz*.

As the first one, I saw my paternal great-grandfather R' Nathan Lehrer, and with him, my grandmother Charna and their nine children: – Meir, Abraham-Yitzhak, Leib, Beryl, Ozer, Azriel, Sarah, Zelda, and Eidel. Except for the one, Azriel, who died naturally, all the rest of the sons and daughters and the families that they brought into the world, were all killed by the unclean Nazi murderers ימ"ש.

And here they are in front of me: Bran'chi, Miriam, Mottl, Mordechai, Simcha, Moshe, Charna, Chana-Esther, Shlomo, Baylah, Rivka, Chaya, Malka, Asher, Leah, Nathan, Shmuel, Peshka, Rocheh'cheh, Dwora, Tzeitl, Leib, Yitzhak, Shayndl, Hirsch-David, Chaim, Chana, David, Melekh, Khala, Michael, Malka, Zelda, and others, ה"יד.

And after this, I see my other great-grandfather, R' Schraga-Feivel Yitzhak Segal[2], נ"י, a Jew who occupied the tent of Torah study, and beside him is my great-grandmother Sarah-Tova; and with them are Sholom

[Page 159]

Waxman and his wife , grandmother Faiga, and here is my grandfather (beside my mother) R' Leib Uri Waxman, and my grandmother Shayndl of the Segal family of Cieszanow. And here is Uncle Yehuda Segal, from Rawa Ruska, with Aunt Mindl (of the Lehrer family), and their three year old son Asher, הי"ד, and beside them I see my uncle, Moshe-Joseph Segal and Aunt Pearl with their son, Chaim-Simcha of Cieszanow. And here they are in front of me: My grandfather (on my father's side) Meir Lehrer, whom I remembered above, and my grandmother Rivka (of the Just family) from Narol-Lipsko. And Aunt Bran'chi, Uncle Abraham-Yitzhak Lehrer, and Aunt Leah, Mordechai Segal from Pshebursk, Alter Meir and his wife Dwora, Moshe Reiss, Feivel Gruar. I add further, and I look, and here are the two sisters of my mother: Esther and her husband, their children Abraham and Faiga'leh, Min'cheh and her husband Yaakov Sternlicht and their sons, Joseph and Lipa, and also my mother's brother Joseph, and his talented sons Leib-Uri and Sholom, and others as closely related family members, from Cieszanow, Narol-Lipsko, Rawa [Ruska], Lvov, Rzeszow and others.

In the darkness of twilight, as the congregation sings '*El mistater b'shafrir khevyon…*[3]' I am borne aloft on the wings of my imagination to faraway worlds. I imagine that here I am, in the Seventh Heaven, in the company of my ancestors, and among generations of the righteous and holy, and for my pleasure, I walk among the great figures of the world. And this is not a simple optical illusion, because here is the Vilna *Gaon*, the BESH"T, and here, closest to us, the Chofetz Chaim, and there is one of us, a Galitzianer like me, and is this not R' Moshe Leib of Stov, who is also the closest in spirit and soul, the Cieszanow *Tzaddik* in with his coterie from Belz and Zanz..

And suddenly…in all his glory….King David himself! He is not strumming his lyre, because it is still Shabbat…but he is preparing himself for the feast, the *Melave-Malka* feast, the feast of the reigning of the Messiah…

And here is an intense light, and from the ordinary, the light of the Havdalah brings me back to the real world and its tumult, to the gloom of reality. I open my eyes, and think: where am I? Yes, the era is an era of murder and much death, that is what the Nazis sow with their advance, and I was then all of thirteen years of age. The recruits of Hitler tread on, and stream over, all of the land, and reached our town as well. Dark guests to celebrate the occasion of my Bar Mitzvah. With fire and sword, steel and lance, with chariot and cavalry, they reach everywhere. With an arrogant march in steel-toed boots they trample everything that is beautiful, sacred and lofty, every living thing that blooms and is developing, and among this the thirteen years of my life and childhood. In one move, I grow up and become an adult, and suddenly feel that I have been transported on the wings of tender youth to the age of seventy or so. From that day forward, I will see every minute of life, every breath, and every heartbeat, as a generous gift, as if given by God. A heavy sense of oppression descends on me, and a dark, black terror, and a heavy Jewish moan is torn from my heart when I observe the bitter resignation in the eyes of my parents, as I also saw in the eyes of our neighbors and in the eyes of the entire area populace.

My father, Aryeh-Leib Lehrer, was a man at the prime of his life at the time, full of the lust for life, happy and radiant, a man of initiative with creative capacity, and here, surprisingly, it was as if the lights of his soul were extinguished. He walked about muttering all day, and the echo of his sighs could be heard, along with his calls that lacked any vigor: What shall we do now? Where shall we go, and to where will we come? His words penetrated into my soul, they ate holes in my breast, and silenced my will. They tied heavy stones to

[Page 160]

my young spirit. Together with him, with my father, I would walk about oppressed and in despair.

As I recalled above, we resided at the outskirts of the town, at the crossroads. The roads to Lubliniec and Kosobudy met there. Our house was open to people leaving and arriving, it was an oasis of sort and a sitting place for the local residents, and neighbors would come in when they had a free moment, some to simply snatch a bit of conversation with my parents, some to drink a glass of tea, or ask for advice from my father with regard to business matters, or to hear news from the larger world. We had a standing sort of an 'inn' for merchants and transients, who would be traveling to the towns and villages of the area. And there were those who passed through who would inquire as to the welfare of different Jewish families in the town, or for directions to one of the nearby villages. In short, the house was something of a center of activity.

And now, even before the Germans attacked the town, and only the staccato of machine guns could be heard in the distance, and the deafening noise of the steel airplanes fills the air, and heavy tanks and cannon make the earth tremble, and the tramp of hobnailed boots arouses a dark terror, already the neighbors from the adjacent houses were thrown into a flight of panic. They abandon their possessions, for which they had worked hard for years, and forsake everything in order to increase their distance from the enemy. Even we fled, by way of the road to Kosobudy to the nearby village. Because of the panic and fleeing, an individual was left stuck at the place he was standing: Oh, my heart…. and his hand is clutched to his chest. and he cannot even finish his call for help, falls, and is splayed out on the ground for his full length.

My father, who had managed to get ahead for some distance, looked back when he heard the cry, and the fall, and he recognized that the falling man was the elderly and weak Moshe Koenig. He retraced his steps amid a hail of bullets, stooped over the fainted man, and succeeded in reviving him, and threw him over his back, and in less than an hour brought him the nearby village, which was our short term objective.

That night, we spent in a silo of a farmer whom we knew.

On the following morning, when the din of the invaders subsided, we returned home.

A silence pervaded the town, like the silence in a cemetery. Not a man from the local residents had the nerve to open a door or window. During the short while that the Germans had control of the place, the Germans managed to rack up for their account not only robbery and plunder, but also tens of deaths. The victims were from the Jews and non-Jews. There were no lack of reasons given for the killings, and they also were not obligated to explain. They brought ready-made excuses from the 'Nazi School of Murder' in Germany, just as they had brought ammunition with them, tanks, cannons, and other implements of destruction. Here, they would argue, someone shot and hit a German, there, someone opened their door, which was prohibited. Jews were killed without explanation. Jews, to begin with, were designated as targets for German fire. Jews were shot like geese in the field or like partridges…

After a few days had gone by, an incident occurred, that a satchel was lost from the inside of an auto, which contained very important documents. The matter took place in the courtyard of the Novoslya Palace. Tens of Jews were immediately arrested as spies, and they were threatened with capital punishment, and that the entire town and its residents was threatened with being put to the torch, if the lost satchel would not be found.

An outcry and a shriek went up that reached the heart of heaven, especially from the women and children. As if insane, they ran about to look for the satchel. The town Jewish elders, accompanied by the town priest, as well as Christian dignitaries came to testify that the Jews most certainly did not take the satchel, and it

[Page 161]

is certain that no one took it by mistake, because otherwise, it would have been returned immediately. The priest took it upon himself to travel and pay a visit among the local farmers, and called upon them to participate in this undertaking, and to try and help find the lost item and therefore deny a certain death to the residents of the town.

In the end, a miracle occurred. the satchel was found in the possession of one of the farmers. He had found it lying on the road, and did not know what to do with it.

And here, Rosh Hashanah drew near... Our editor, Dr. David Ravid tells us about this Rosh Hashana at the beginning of his memoir.

The Germans don't give us a chance to breathe. On the First Day of Rosh Hashana, they took out the worshipers from our synagogue, that is to say, the minyan of the Husyatin *Hasidim*, and sent them to work. The area is populated by Jews crowded together, and in its confines is found the Great Synagogue, the *Bet HaMedrash*, the *kloyz* of the Belz *Hasidim* and other various houses of worship. The worshipers in the other prayer houses, upon seeing how the men of our prayer house were being pushed about and shoved, abandoned their prayer houses and attempted to escape by way of yards to reach a secret hiding place in their homes. The Germans caught many of them and sent them to work. And understandably, this was a nightmare occurring specifically on the Holy Day of this festival, to have to go and work for the Germans.... and again a pandemonium ensued. A few Jews made an attempt to hide themselves in one of the nearby houses and to wait there until the fury passed over...until the Nazis withdraw, but they sensed something there, and burst into the house and took out all those who fled there. In the street, they ordered the Jews to stand up against the wall of the very same house, to receive their punishment, for having violated the German order not to show themselves in the street. And the punishment – the death penalty by firing squad. The Jews did not have any idea that such an order had even been issues (not to appear in the streets).

Those who were sentenced stood dumb and resigned. A few attempted to arouse the sympathy of the Germans... they asked for mercy for the sake of their children.

And then a senior officer passed by and among the sentenced men, he saw one who just yesterday had helped him in regards to a matter. He stopped and asked the head of the guard detail: what is going on here? (*Was kommt hier vor?*).

The Nazi responded that the Jews had violated the German order not to appear in public.

Hurry away from her (*Weg von hier*) the officer shouted to the Jews.

The Nazis arched their eyes in wonder. They did not grasp from where the officer had the courage to offer protection to the Jews.... even the Jews weren't certain if perhaps the officer was toying with them, or this was a ruse of some sort.

One of the Nazis repeated what he had said: –

'These people violated a German law.'....

The officer paid no attention to him, and did not turn his head, as if he didn't hear anything that he had said. For a second time, he turned to the Jews and shouted in a loud voice: –

[Page 161]

'Get out of here! Get to your homes with you!'

For the moment, the Jews were saved, and to this day, no one knows who this officer was.

At this time we know and understand what lay in store for the Jews of Cieszanow and its surroundings. Tuvia Friedman, the Director of the Documentation Institute, author of the book, 'I Pursued Eichmann for Fifteen Years,' told me, that the courtyard of the Rabbi of Belz and also the courtyard of the Rabbi of Cieszanow and other houses of prayer and study in the area, were converted into camps of labor and suffering as early as the summer of 1940.

But now, let us move to Warsaw after the Great Destruction. In postwar Warsaw, in the year 1946, I am working at the Central Jewish Library on Tlomacki Street. Here, I have the opportunity to see up close. the extent of the devastation of Warsaw, the crown of Polish Jewry, the center of its creative energy, the largest Jewish community in

Europe. The building in which I work, Von Verein (currently the Jewish History Institute) that was on the Tlomacki Street, as erected on the property of the great and magnificent synagogue , that the executioner of the Warsaw Ghetto, General [Jürgen] Stroop[4], ordered to be blown up on May 16, 1943 as a symbol of the final destruction of European Jewry.

Adjacent to the room in which I work there are still piles of bricks, mounds of wreckage, the residue of the collapse and the remnants of the magnificent synagogue that was no more. At a distance, only a few steps from there, a desert of rock and sand, a wasteland that remained after the destruction of Jewish Warsaw, a trace of a people that just yesterday was alive and in existence, alert, vibrant and creatively productive.

I work under the supervision of the aristocratic lady Batya Berman ז"ל, and the gifted scholar Yehuda Leib Bialer ז"ל, both experts in literature, both of them with their hearts and souls immersed in their work, to erect a memorial to the Library of Jewish Knowledge that was wrecked, and of its buildings, the Jewish Historical Institute had been saved since the war. As part of our work, we are occupied in transferring a portion of the books to the Hebrew University in Jerusalem, and to other similar institutions in the *Holy Land*.

It was here that I could see palpably that the sobriquet of 'People of the Book' was not just a metaphor. but rather that there is real substance to it. Here the name was transformed into substance. The two experts referred to above, Batya Berman, the author of the book, 'A Diary in the Underground' and Yehuda Leib Bialer, author of the book 'Days of Ashdod,' spill tears and blood over each page, and over each piece of crumpled paper, that fell victim to the burnings, and were saved by a miracle, even though they were half-burned. They treated these books like one treated Jewish children, that were found wandering half frozen in the forests, and with compassion for their sake, camps were established to gather them up. here was an urgent need to save them by all human means possible, for the sake of the future of their people.

The work with the books, and the attitude of awed respect to the written word on the part of these people had a tremendous influence on me. It was my great good fortune to be part of the redemption, in the final details, of Hebrew or Yiddish books from the hands of strangers.

By being so close to the destruction, I was troubled by frequent dreams and hallucinations, even while awake. I envisioned the large Jewish community of Poland, of Galicia, of my home town, Cieszanow, of Narol-Lipsko and its surroundings, of Rawa Ruska, Lvov, Rzeszow and other places…

[Page 162]

Here, opposite the windows of my work room, in the diminished Warsaw – a Mother City to the Jews in times gone bay, I see my family as well, along with my other kin both near and distant, among the millions that were exterminated by the malevolent Nazis.

And here, they too, are before me: those who were privileged enough to die a natural death and were given a proper Jewish burial before the outbreak of hostilities. The Scourge smashed their gravestones and eradicated all trace of them, and they are beseeching that we remember them for the good. To my sorrow, I am not particularly good at remembering the names of all the relatives, friends known to me, and all the townsfolk who have departed this world, after all of the experiences that I went through, during the days of the war and destruction, and I beg the forgiveness of their sacred memory. I will also beg forgiveness from all of those who were exterminated by The Scourge in the variety of ways involving torture after the war, and the names are also not recorded of those who fought among the allied armies, the partisans, and the underground, each in his proper place.

Our family, that is, my parents, my sisters Shayndl'eh and Sarah'leh and I, remained in German occupied territory, and of these, I remained for only two weeks. During their occupation of the large border between Germany and Russia, at the generous offer of the Soviets, we crossed over to Rawa Ruska, which at the time was under their control. The experience of spending about a half month under the oppressive lash of the 'Master Race' ימ"ש was enough for us to ease the decision to abandon our spacious home, on a foundation of plenty, and to go out on the long road of the wanderer, whose end we did not know, and brought us to the edges of Siberia.

And our way was not a bed of roses, for these were days of war, and the tribulations and suffering of the Russian people grew large and intense. And we were among the tens of thousands of refugees that moved to the east. There, along the way, we lost our youngest child, my brother Moshe-Joseph ל"ז, who was barely a year when he died. His fragile life could not stand up to the harsh, brutal conditions of those days. Even may adults were unable to survive, and perished along the way. It was on this trek that the pure soul of the Rabbi of Tomaszow-Lubelski gave out, Rabbi Leibusz Rubin. And there were deeds of cruelty by the officers in charge, but occasionally the act of mentioning the name of the Soviet Union would suffice…in order to cause the speaker to lower his voice, and change his attitude and manner of speech towards us.

So, this was a difficult journey, and the fact that we were exiled and uprooted from the roots of our sustenance proved to be an obstacle in every direction that we turned. We were thrown thousands of miles from our homes, into a world that had living conditions that were more difficult than we were used to bear on our backs, a brutal climate, cruel people, and in addition to all this, we were required to engage in labor that we had never been engaged in our entire lives. This work was not in line with our physical capacity, and not to our frame of mind. It was work that Jews had never engaged in at all: to clear forests, to cut trees, to lay new railroad track, and other such work. It was enough to become transformed into a source of bitterness and disappointment.

However, there were also incidents that were pleasant and encouraging: I keep hold of details that literally touch the heart. bearing witness to the generous heart of the plain Russian people. After the meeting with General Sikorsky[5], when we were released from the Taigas, we were taken to the city of Guryavsk in

[Page 164]

Siberia. When we arrived there, we were allocated a place to live in the home of the citizen Nikita Kowalczyk, who was the person appointed to look after security at the local factory: Drovilnaya Fabrika K.M.K. As we were subsequently able to deduce, this Siberian man was a rare person of high cultural intellect with a marvelous disposition. His considerably generous help to an exiled family, with day-to-day problems was of great value. He tried to help with the long-faced and sad appearance of the Jewish boy from faraway, trying to master the alien environment. Among his other good deeds on my behalf, and for the sake of my education, I will record here that he helped me get accepted in the above-mentioned factory, as an apprentice in its technical class, and there I was taught to be an independent locksmith technician, and much later the principles and practice of electrical machinery and train engines. And not only this.

This Siberian man had roots in the Ukraine. During his youth, he lived for a time with an elderly Jewish couple in a Jewish *shtetl*. From there, he brought with him the knowledge of the way of life of Jews and their customs. He encouraged my parents to bake matzos for Passover in his oven, and turned over his kitchen to us for exclusive use during the eight days of the holiday. He even reminded my father about the *mitzvah* of putting on *Tefillin*…. In order to elaborate on his words, he bared his left arm, and with his right arm, demonstrated the motion of putting on the *tefillin* and winding the straps around his arm. From that time, my father began to wrap himself in his prayer shawl, and put on his *tefillin* openly and in public, because up to that point he hid himself and did it secretly.

In this connection, I perceive a responsibility to myself to remember those dear personalities that I encountered along the way in my long journey, who taught me a chapter from the way people are supposed to relate to one another. One such person, who left such a deep and unforgettable impression on me was the engineer, Mikhail Savlovitz Igentov, and the second was the craftsman Fubronkin.

Igentov's approach to the workers in the business, he attitude to the general populace, all testified to an unusual personality, an a man of generous proportion. When he looked over the work of one of the workers, a craftsman, who was under stress, and was exhausting himself trying to get something done, he would go over to him, and approach him in a refined way, stop him, and tell him something or another, in the way of a joke. And then, when he had broken through the stress, and the two of them had a laugh, Igentov would ask casually, as part of the conversation: – what is your idea about trying to do this is a different way, for example, like this – and he would then show how it would be possible to overcome the dilemma, and he would add – wasn't that easy after all? – And this was the way the craftsman

Fubronkin also behaved. They did things only with pleasant remarks and considerate attitudes, and they had a great deal of success.

When we returned to Poland in 1946, we passed through many cities and towns. We found destruction and ruin in all of them. It was in this manner that the entire tragic scenario was revealed to our eyes, in its full measure. Like mourners, we walked about all the days. Regardless of where we turned, we saw total loss, and a heartbreaking complete destruction. The palpable result of German rule, the harvest of death of the brutal Nazi beast.

In one of the locations, a Jew told us the following: –

'Do you see that mound over there? After the extermination of a complete Jewish community by gunfire, and after they were covered up with the dirt in a mass grave, it

[Page 165]

became evident that one of the victims was still moving and still alive under the thin covering of the earth. Among those slain was also my brother's son, sixteen years old, and was unlike me, who possessed Aryan papers, and I was thought to be a Christian. I stood in silence, and looked on from afar. Immediately, a Ukrainian went over, with a axe in his hand, and struck the spastic body, and hacked it to pieces. Perhaps this was my brother's son, Berishl.'

Jews who survived Belzec told that the entire large expanse of the camp is covered with the killed and victims lie hidden under a very thin layer of soil. Later, when we reached Lower Silesia, to the village of Gshcfusta or Ludwigsdorf (we attended the seminary there), we saw a field, in which eighteen thousand Jews had been buried in one mass grave. These Jews held on to life until the last minute. They worked in the local German factory. hey were exterminated, literally on the night of the retreat. We divided up the field, and buried them in three separate graves.

In returning from Russia, we passed through Lublin, and we came to nearby Majdanek and we saw… in reality, we did not see, but rather we sensed everything and we passed through all seventy cauldrons of Hell. We stood opposite mountains of shoes, of brushes, of baby dolls, and all manner of children's toys, various items of clothing of the people who at one time existed, but were now no more. They brought us to the crematoria, that is, the rooms in which the corpses were incinerated. Up until we entered there, we maintained some sort of composure, but when we saw the six wall holes, through which the corpses were inserted for incineration, a terrifying scream burst forth from our throats, a scream of a breakdown and pain that simply cannot be described in words, that came from the depths of the heart, and spontaneously, the words came forth from all mouths: '*Yisgadal VeYiskadash Shmay Raboh.*'

So, our journey was a difficult one, through the Russian hinterlands. Today we understand very well that this was the only way to stay alive, with all other roads leading to torture and to death. Back then, in the first days after the outbreak of the war, in the period when the German Nazi beast had not yet gotten its talons dug in (I almost was going to say the 'Golden Age' of the days of conquest), the decision to abandon the warm ambience of our home appeared in the lives of aimless wanderers, into the heart of an unknown land as bad judgement… that is the way it looked to most of the people (who can be a seer?). In light of the findings afterwards, the terrifying Holocaust that overtook our people, it became clear that this was the only path to survival. At the time, the uprooting from those warm, solidly-based houses was difficult, it was difficult to become transformed into refugees, the ones who were leaving – fleeing their homes and the Nazi conquest to the districts that were in Soviet hands, but it was precisely the expulsion to those lands of perpetual snow and the shriveling permafrost of the Taigas, that saved the lives of many and kept them whole.

If their intent was to assure our welfare – we will never know, and who knows what is hidden behind the slings of their decisions and deeds? And who has the capacity to probe the inner secrets of high politics? We were exiled as refugees because of the Soviet rule, to faraway places and to conditions that were trying, but as it turns out, it saved the Jew during the darkest period in the history of our people.

It is a fact that because of this exile, we were saved – the exile was transformed into an act of rescue, the saving of lives…

With the completion of my work, in the gathering, and also in the library, and after literally sitting on the what was literally the wreckage of the people, that gave rise to such suffering in body and spirit, after having drunk from the cup of hemlock to its bitter dregs, I left Poland, the land in which in which our nation awoke

[Page 166]

to such a powerful spiritual existence, and upon which The Abrogator descended and exterminated its sons, with a merciless animal fury. Only a small remnant survived, traces, refugees from the sword, smoking embers pulled from the fire. And here we are, traveling to the Land that is going to be renewed, that was established again after two thousand years of assault, wanderings, murder and ruin. We are traveling to the Land of Israel, and who can imagine how high our spirits are lifted, the eagerness, the expectation?

Basha Batya Temkin Berman ע"ה, that good person, who looked after every concern, after each and every detail, in order to make things easier for us, to make the voyage pleasant. She accompanied my step like a dedicated mother. May her memory be for a blessing.

In the year 1948 we reached The Land of Israel. And the sequel to these memoirs, well – this is not the right place.

Epilogue

Our generation, that saw the Holocaust with its own eyes, and has felt the spiritual need deep within itself to raise its hand for purpose of memorializing those who were murdered by a malign hand, and to honor their spiritual legacy, seeks ways to pass on to future generations that which it received, and what was left to those that survived. We know that today's young people do not have their attention focused on the past, and all of their attention is focused on the future. And perhaps, there is a blessing in this situation, even though there is no meaning to the future without knowledge of the past, and without any feeling for the connection with past generations.

One of the traps that we fall into, and we are severely damaged by it, is the attitude of canceling out the Diaspora experience, but such an attempt at nullification is nothing more than proof of a lack of knowledge, of an absence of understanding in the events, and what took place. Many Diaspora generations found themselves in difficult circumstances, from many perspectives, whether in the political circumstances and in the absence of rights, or in economic circumstances, with a lack of a means of livelihood, all this had an influence on the somber image of the Jew and his spiritual condition; yet despite all of this, his spiritual life was vibrant even in the face of all these assaults, and many alternatives in economic and cultural life were opened up. The large, and glorious Jewish settlement in Poland and its environs was a notable exception in excellence in this respect (Congress [Poland], Galicia, Lithuania, Upper Silesia, and others). And a number of these lands and areas who with their spirit and culture enriched the people all over the world, served as a spiritual reservoir and source of inspiration, developed a large Jewish culture, and had an impact in every corner of Jewish life, and on every individual in them. It is possible to see in these developments a miracle in the deep and hidden power of creativity in this people. If, in fact, the Jews were able to achieve only limited goals in economic life, they did even greater in cultural accomplishments, creating in two languages (not to mention those of our people who gave of their energies to the non-Jewish world, and wrote in the national language, and how many there were who wrote in the languages of the countries in which they dwelled). Apart from the Eternal Tongue of the people, and this is the language of Hebrew – the Holy Tongue, they also wrote (most of what they wrote) in the spoken language of the common man, and that is the language of Yiddish (the language of the martyrs) that blossomed in their midst, guarded over us, and connected us to all the dispersed parts of the Diaspora (our spirit and our Jewishness). And it is a fact that history does repeat itself, because something like this had already taken place. It was not only in exile, but even when the people still occupied its homeland, it wrote in the Aramaic language, and the books of our Hagiographica [sic: *Ketuvim*] which are written in Aramaic bear witness to this, and in the Diaspora – the Babylonian *Talmud*, the pride of our people's creativity, and even the moving prayer, that soothes the soul

[Page 167]

of our people in difficult moments, even it is composed in Aramaic: '*Yisgadal VeYiskadash Shmay Raboh.*' In the distant past, and in the near past, a similar occurrence has reappeared, the poems of the people, love poetry, poems of work, poems of weariness, and poems of joy, all have been written in the Yiddish language, which many chose to see as a handmaiden to her mistress – Hebrew.

And there are among the great poets and writers who possessed the double talent and wrote their pieces both in Hebrew and in Yiddish. And who is greater among our nation's poets than Chaim Nachman Bialik? And how many of those poems that he wrote, which touch the heart were, indeed, written in Yiddish. And the great literary figures, such as Mendele Mokher-Sforim, Yitzhak Leib Peretz,[6] and Sholom Aleichem, and many others, who are famous the world over, wrote in both of our languages, Hebrew and Yiddish. And this causes the question to be asked: are we then relieved of the onus of taking an interest in this language and the pieces that were created using it, and are still being created with it, both in the remnant Diaspora of Eastern Europe, elsewhere n the world, and in faraway places? Is it up to us to terminate the connection with those of our people in faraway places? Accordingly, in adopting a nurturing, conserving posture, we see a way of honoring the cultural riches of our brethren who are there, and a sacred obligation especially to the enlightened members of the nation. After all, it is those who are learning in the schools today, who stand to inherit these riches in the future, and if we, the parents approach you, it is as if we are discharging the behest of those who are dear to us, the victims of the most terrifying Holocaust (in the history of humanity) and in our history [sic: as a people]. It is our wish to place in your hands the fidelity that we inherited ourselves, the essence of the spirit and culture of a nation that was tortured and killed.

There are several alternatives to achieve this goal: deepening the curriculum in binding together of the people, and integrating it by means of teaching history and literature from original sources, that is to say also in the Yiddish language, Yiddish clubs, initiative and preservation of communities, deepening research into their histories, customs, and especially in those communities from which the great people emerged, in all creative fields of endeavor, scholars, artists, scientists and entrepreneurs, people of idea and people capable of doing things, the teaching of creativity together with those that practiced it (folklore), sayings and words of wisdom.

The work of preserving the memory of the exterminated and the martyrs for all time, the establishment of cultural endeavors in their memory, translation of their works into Hebrew, compilation of an anthology of the best of the works of the poets and writers who were eradicated, in order to establish an institute in their memory, so their names are not forgotten and neither the fruits of their labor, it is up to us to imbibe from both sources Hebrew – Yiddish for the purpose of enriching out culture, our spirit and our unity.

There are ways of going about doing this, and we must attempt all means that bring us towards this positive, sacred goal.

It is up to us not to forget the self-organizing pioneering, the realization of the dream and the vision of the establishment of Israel. It was in the Diaspora that the better part of those of her sons that cam here to the Homeland of the Jewish People, to make the desert bloom, and to raise up what we [now] have here. Yes, in general, there is cause for us to memorialize all the Jewish organizations. In preserving their memory forever, we discharge an historic national responsibility, and a human responsibility of a higher sort, and may all those who engage in such works be blessed.

[Page 168]

Note: On page 256, there is a three page summary in Yiddish of the information contained in this memoir, which is not being repeated. The author provides the following final paragraph to explain why he did this added writing:

It was my desire to publicize my memoirs in Hebrew, because Hebrew is the language of the settlement of the nation in Zion, but being that almost all of the heroes and martyrs that appear in this book, spoke, wrote and suffered exclusively and only in Yiddish, I could do no other than write these words in their tongue.

After it became possible for me to assemble a part of my memories and I was privileged to do this as a free man in the Land of Israel, I raise my eyes to that place..and with the eyes of my soul – it is not only that I see them, I am also with them on their last journey.

Translator's footnotes:

1. Pronounces *Rayshe* by the Jews of the area. A principal city of Poland, about 40 miles west and south of Cieszanow. See, for example, *Poyln: Jewish Life in the Old Country*, by Alter Kacyzne, Owl Books, NY 2001, pp. 8,9.
2. The name is given in Hebrew acronym form,ל"גס, which stands for *sgan levi*, indicating someone of Levitic descent.
3. The beginnings of a hymn, whose words mean, '*Lord who conceals himself under a hidden canopy…*'
4. After the war, Stroop was tried and condemned by two different courts and subsequently hanged in Warsaw in 1951.
5. The Polish-Soviet declaration of Friendship and Mutual Assistance was signed by Prime Minister General Sikorsky and Prime Minister Stalin on the 4th of December 1941. It established the principles of full active military collaboration between them during the war and the existence of good neighborly collaboration and friendship and mutual observance of undertakings assumed-after the war.
6. The author incorrectly writes his first name as Yehuda.

[Page 169]

In the Cieszanow Ghetto

by Tuvia Friedman
Director of the Documentation Institute at Yad VaShem

Memories

In the summer of 1940, several thousand Jews were taken from the General Gouvernment [of Poland] which consisted of four provinces: Cracow, Warsaw, Radom and Lublin.

To this, the fifth, Galicia-Lemberg was added in the summer of 1941. Several thousand Jews were taken from these areas, in the age group of 16-30 years of age, for forced labor on the German-Russian border in the area of Belzec-Narol-Cieszanow-Zukow, a area of approximately 30 sq. km.

I wish to recollect that we were taken near to the Belzec station, on an open field near a large courtyard, and the Germans told us that the Rabbi of the *shtetl* had once lived there. There, we met up with about two thousand Jewish captives in the same condition as we were, uprooted, excluded, hungry and exhausted, not a shirt on one's back, with rags for pants, very filthy and infested with lice, because the evil Germans forbade us from washing ourselves.

We lived under the open skies, and in the middle of this large courtyard, there was a creek in which it was said that the Germans had drowned many Jews, and whoever allowed himself to drink from the dirty green water immediately contracted the disease, cholera.

A couple of hundred Gypsies were also to be found in this same courtyard, with their wives and children.

Many somber and exhausted older Jews told us that they are in this location already for a couple of months, and they come from Tomaszow-Lubelski and its environs, and they have to put up with a great deal of trouble from the Gypsies, being beaten by them, and being robbed of everything that they had.

We entered this Hell with a bit of meager foodstuffs, and our baggage, and these veterans immediately threw themselves on us with an outcry, that we should take pity on them, to give them a bite of bread which they hadn't seen with their own eyes in months, and our group unpacked the rucksacks and distributed whatever we had. We spent the night there, and in the morning we were stood out in rows, and after the order, 'March!' we were driven on foot to Narol.

Those who had been there, remained, and it appears that they had already been sentenced to death because they were like skeletons already, and incapable of doing even the lightest work. Their work in this courtyard consisted of a 12-hour day in which they had to carry large rocks back and forth, the intent of the evil ones was to exhaust the Jews to the point of death, so that they begged God that he should take them away sooner.

From Narol, we were driven on further to Cieszanow, a very pretty town which shone with green places of an artistic quality, flowers all over, redolent and enchanting, and we marched through the streets of Cieszanow, and the local Polish gentiles looked upon us with schadenfreude, with their shovels and other tools as well as litter poles in the instance that one of us should drop dead on the way, or the Germans shot someone, or similarly bayoneted someone because the person, out of weakness took a bit longer while marching, we were obliged to take the corpse and carry it to a specified place for burial, which was the purpose of the litter poles.

[Page 150]

SS Troops led us, together with the Ukrainian gentiles in their black uniforms, they led us into a place that was surrounded with barbed wire, the place was at one time the home and courtyard of the Rabbi of Cieszanow.

There, we encountered several hundred Jews with the same appearance as the Jews in Belzec. They were almost all from the Cieszanow area and province.

On the right side of our camp, stood the Great Synagogue of Cieszanow, which was already half wrecked, without a floor and windows, literally a ruin.

On that side was the bath and the mikva, behind the bath a toilet facility was created where the municipal one had been, and there was no handhold to prevent one from falling in, and no closet was created deliberately, and there were many instances when a person fell in, and this unfortunate was immediately shot by the bandits, because he could not [sic: was not permitted to] wash himself off, or change his soiled and smelly clothing.

To tell the truth, some of the time, the Christian Polish people threw over a bit of bread to us.

The Hunger was endless, we sold off everything that we had to the Ukrainian guards, for a dried out bit of bread, and we were there long enough to become naked and barefoot, just like our hapless comrades whom we encountered in Belzec, and we became the genuine veterans of troubles and torture.

We were led to work at six o'clock [sic: in the morning], two kilometers past the Rabbi's house we dug pits.

We were always required to march through the town singing, all the gentiles of the town looked at us but did not laugh at us, because, as it appears, they feared that the same could happen to them, and whoever among us sang too weakly received murderous blows, such that, because of this, we instituted an hour of singing, in order that all of us not be exposed to beatings for not singing along.

On a certain Friday evening, an SS trooper took the cap off of a Jew and sailed it towards the barbed wire fence, ordering the Jew that he should run and retrieve the cap, and in running this way, the Jew got a bullet in the head from that same German, and he told his officer that *Der Jude* wanted to go over the barbed wire, and because of that he was compelled to shoot him. We buried that Jewish man, and gathered to pray, despite the fact that it was strictly forbidden.

We poured our hearts out to He Who Sits in the Heavens, begging to be allowed to live long enough to see the downfall of the accursèd German nation along with their partners, the Ukrainian beasts.

When the opportunity presented itself, despite all of the difficulties, for one of us to escape to the Russian side, the Russians drove back these unfortunates, "Давай Назад!"[1] they would shout. and it appears that the two despots, Ribbentrop-Molotov had an agreement that the Jews that were to be found in German hands would be exterminated, otherwise, it is not understandable why the tyrant, Stalin the second worst murderer in humanity, would not have allowed the hapless escapees from the German Hell to remain on the other side

[Page 171]

of the border.

[2] An incident occurred when a young boy did something that did not please a German, and the German wanted to obtain a certain death sentence for the boy, and we – on no account – were willing to reveal the name of the boy, such that ten other young men paid for this, alas, with their lives, for the life of this one boy.

I absolutely cannot grasp how it is possible to withstand so much abuse and torture and still remain alive.

We dug pits from Cieszanow to Zukow Stara, for a period of six weeks.

After Rosh Hashanah many of us were dispersed to other forms of labor, and I escaped from the camp and after exerting a great deal of effort, and with difficulty, arrived to my home town of Radom.

This is a short description of the camp at Cieszanow where I spent some time, and it is deeply imbedded in my soul to this day, after 25 years.

Translator's footnotes:

1.   Go Back!
2.   History suggests that Tuvia Friedman may be giving the leadership in Germany and the Soviet Union entirely too much credit. It is difficult to imagine that the command and control system for the Red Army, which was in a shambles at this point, would have even been able to execute against such an order, much less internalize it.
A grimmer answer is more likely. The German-Soviet border near Belzec and Cieszanow was really with the Ukraine, not Russia proper. Accordingly, the Red Army troops there were likely Ukrainians. The antipathy of the Ukrainians for the Russians may have been second only to their hatred of Jews. Recollect that it was the Ukrainian Red Army General, Andrei Andreyevich Vlasov, who defected to fight with Hitler against Stalin, and had nearly a million men who followed him. It does not take much imagination to believe that Ukrainians would drive the Jews back into the hands of the Nazis, and their fellow countrymen serving in the *Waffen-SS* auxiliary units, in the black uniforms that Friedman refers to.

[Page 172]

Cieszanow, A Bastion of the Belz *Hasidim*

by Ben Zion Friedman

Cieszanow served as a bastion for the *Hasidim* of Belz. Almost every Jew of the Jews in the town, who confronted trouble, traveled to the Rabbi of Belz to enlist his prayers and supplications on his behalf, and when the *Rebbe* came to take rest in a town near ours, it was well known in our town that the *Rebbe* was in the area, and he spread his radiance and sanctity over it.

The extent to which the Belz following of *Hasidism* was spread throughout our town, can be appreciated from the following tale: The Rabbi of Cieszanow ז"ל, was sitting once with one of his intimates, and having a conversation on secular matters. In the middle of the dialogue about this and that, the intimate turned to him and said: Do you know, respected Rabbi, that a marvelous community has fallen under your aegis, a community of *Hasidim*, who are people of action (and indeed, Cieszanow was a town full of people of this type, so it was called "The Little Jerusalem"). The Rabbi answered him: And do you not know that I am the Rabbi here? You are surely mistaken, so you need to know immediately who the Rabbi of this place is.

Outside stood two boys aged 10-11. The Rabbi, ז"ל called to them, and turning to the older of them, he asked: Do you recognize the Rabbi, שליט"א? Certainly! The lad replied – And you, boy? – The Rabbi asked the second one. I – the boy said – do not know him yet, but my father promised me that on Rosh Hashana, God-willing, he will take me to Belz, to the Rabbi.

The Rabbi ז"ל laughed: And so, who is the Rabbi here, I, or the Rabbi of Belz? Because when a Cieszanow Jew said, "The Rabbi, long life to him," "The Rabbi" without any added modifier was intended to mean the Rabbi of Belz, and everyone knew the intent was to refer to the Rabbi of Belz.

The reputation of the *kloyz* of the Belz *Hasidim* was a glorious one in our town. The sound of Torah study never ceased there, not by day, and not by night.

From the dawn until the late hours of the night, Jews, scholars, and God-fearing people prayed there. Even anyone who entered the *kloyz* as late as 11 o'clock at night, could find R' Yaakov Weinig ז"ל and the young man R' Shabtai Frankel ז"ל who sat and were engaged in Torah study. On the severe winter nights, it was always possible to find an empty place on the benches of the *kloyz*.

It is my desire, here, to recollect a number of the dear Jews who were Belz *Hasidim*.

My father, and Teacher, R' Yaakov Friedman ז"ל – a Jewish man who was a scholar and God-fearing man, that almost never uttered a word having to do with secular matters, and every available minute that he was free of the yoke of earning his living, he would dedicate to Torah [study] and God's work. On each and every day, whether summer or winter, he was in the habit of getting up at about 5 before dawn, and after ritual ablutions in the *mikva*, he would head for the *kloyz*. Until the hour of 11, he engaged in prayer and study, and in the evening, immediately after he closed up the store, he returned to his work – God's work, until the late hours of the night.

R' Raphael Gutman ז"ל – a scholar who lead a *Gemara* study group at the *kloyz*, Additionally, he was also a good *Baal Tefila*, and he did marvelously when he led prayers in front of the ark on Yom Kippur – literally

[Page 173]

splitting open the heavenly firmament with his prayers. He was also one of the very few who were in the habit of reading a newspaper, and in the night, after study, he would communicate to those who participated in his lessons, all of the news, along with his own interpretations.

R' Chaim Edelman ז"ל – A formidable scholar, he was thoroughly familiar with the *Shas* and the *Poskim*, and would be in the habit of "surfing" the *Talmud* for several hours on the Sabbath.

R' Leib Sternlicht ז"ל – A scholar who participated in all of the study groups in the kloyz, and was also an accomplished Baal Tefila, who would lead prayers on the Sabbath and Festivals. He was privileged to come, and passed away in Our Land.

R' Leibusz Naroler – He was a teacher of the children in our town, and would teach them the Gemara, and the greatest satisfaction for him was to see one of his students – attain the level of being able to engage in independent study of a page of the *Gemara*.

Despite the fact that he was laden with troubles and worries, he was a rock of dependence, and always comported himself pleasurably and with a good heart. On Simchat Torah, he was in the habit of dressing up in a *kittl*, and went about with the Jewish children in the streets, singing and dancing, throwing apples about and making merry, and all of this in order to bring a bit of joy to the Jewish children, shouting 'The Sacred Flock' to the point where he just ran out of strength.

R' Isaac Katzbach שליט"א – A *Hasid* in all 248 parts of his body,[1] to whom each word of the *Rebbe* was as if it came from the Holy of Holies, id found with us today in Jerusalem, may he live to One Hundred and Twenty years.

I have recalled here only a few of the members of the aliyah, but there were tens of Jews like this in our town, in general, and in the Belz *kloyz* in particular.

Translator's footnote:

1.   This is the count of body parts in accordance with *Talmudic* tradition, and is used metaphorically.

[Page 174]

The "Bayt Yaakov" School in Cieszanow

by Ben Zion Friedman

A "*Bayt Yaakov*" school was in operation in the city for a number of years, where several tens of girls from all walks of life received instruction.

The writer of these lines was one of the founders of this school, along with the young ladies Bina Tikher הי"ד, and Faiga Alter ה"ע. Bina Tikher was a very refined, aristocratic young lady, the daughter of R' David Tikher ז"ל, the Rabbi of Tarnogrod that was close by to our town, who was a great scholar, and a granddaughter of R' Yitzhak Glanzer ז"ל, who also was a renown scholar and God-fearing man, known throughout the area.

Faiga Alter was in Cieszanow with her mother during the Holocaust period.

The skein will run short if we attempt to describe the immense amount of help that they gave to the Jews in the Cieszanow ghetto.

A Jew who was in the ghetto told me, that he owes his life to this mother and daughter of the house of Alter. They stole from the gentiles and distributed it along the road that the Jews went on their way to work; because of them, many Jews we saved from hunger and death.

The kind of personal commitment that they revealed themselves to be capable of, is hard to find.

The founders of the school worked, with rather constrained means, not for the purpose of receiving a prize, and they did not spare any effort in order that the school be able to exist.

May their souls be bound up in the bond of eternal life.

The Simple Cieszanow Jews

by Ben Zion Friedman

I am certain that such decent and good-hearted craftsmen and *balebatim,* such as we had in Cieszanow, were seldom encountered in other cities of Poland.

The majority of our craftsmen were observant Jews who did not miss out on praying three times a day with a proper quorum [sic: *minyan*].

The first minyan at daybreak in the *Bet HaMedrash*, was for the craftsmen, and if one went by the synagogue whether summer or winter before dawn, you could near the monotone, but sweet voice of the craftsmen who were reciting Psalms.

Our wagon drivers, during the time they were harnessing up their horses, were also not idle, but continuously kept reciting Psalms.

[Page 175]

The shoemaker, R' Joseph Eichler ל"ז, was literally a [true] *Hasid*. He was an observer of all 613 mitzvot with his entire heart and soul.

The three brothers who were tailors, R' Akiva, R' Yukl, R' Abraham, ז"ל were heartfelt and pious Jews. At this opportunity, I wish to tell a simple story about R' Akiva *Schneider*[1] regarding something that he once responded to the Rabbi of Cieszanow, ז"ל.

The Rabbi sends for him on Passover eve, and the Rabbi asks, is it possible, R' Akiva, that I gave you the material for a *kapote* before Purim, and you agreed to have the garment ready for me by Passover, and you have not kept your word? R' Akiva answers him – *Rebbe*! When you apply yourself to your work, the study of the Torah, that is, everyone's helps you in this – *Rashi, Tosafot, Maharsha, Rashi* asks and the *Maharsha* answers, and so forth, all of them help you, and no one of them ever gets sick, however, I have no one to help me, and I had a bit if an apprentice, and he got sick exactly before Passover, so tell me *Rebbe*! Seeing as I cannot complete all of my work before the Holiday, whose kapote should I not make for the Holiday, that of the poor man? A Jew who truly has no other garment for the Holiday, or yours, *Rebbe*, whose situation is not so dire, because, bless God, you have something to wear for the Holiday, and for certain, you will not be embarrassed for Passover by having to wear a torn *kapote*. The Rabbi smiled and said *"Halakha K'Rabi Akiva,"*[2] meaning that he was truly justified, and do have a Kosher and Happy Passover.

Translator's footnotes:

1.   The text is insufficiently clear on whether this trade name was also adopted as a family name by these individuals.
2.   The choice of phrasing here borrows from the *Talmud*, with an allusion to the great Rabbi Akiva, whose opinions were usually accepted as the governing ones.

How Fortunate is the Eye that Beheld a Sacred Community Moved by the Study of God's Torah

by Schraga-Feivel Lehrer

The Émigrés from Cieszanow at a Memorial Service
in Memory of the Martyrs of our Town, in Tel-Aviv in the Year 5722 [1962]

In the Husyatin *kloyz* in our town, there was a *Shas* study group, that met in the evenings whether summer or winter, who sat and studied diligently for several hours.

I had the privilege of participating in this group, and on frequent occasions to substitute as the leader of the study session in place of the regular leader of the study group.

In my time, they were already going through their fourth cycle of study of the *Shas.*

It is my desire to recall here, a number of people who participated in this *Shas* study group.

The regular leader of the study group was R' Moshe Ratah, ז"ל, who was a great scholar and very precise in his study, covering every minute detail of the *Gemara* and *Rashi*, and almost always leaning towards the

[Page 176]

analyses of the Rashash ז"ל, and because of this we were told that he had an essence in him of this great commentator on the *Shas*.

R' Yehoshua Ziegler ז"ל, was a *Shas* expert and host to guests without peer, his house being open to its full extent for every man. Every poor person turned directly to him, and R' Yehoshua Ziegler dis not rest or remain silent until he satisfied his needs, and in addition was completely fluent in the Polish language. He would write out all of the applications to the government agencies on behalf of nearly everyone in the town, without asking even a cent for compensation. He was prepared to dedicate hours of his time on behalf of the townspeople despite the fact that every minute of his time was valuable.

R' Jonah Kirschenfeld ז״ל, a great scholar and *Shas* expert, and was thoroughly versed in all four parts of the *Shulkhan Arukh*, knowing them by heart. He was not particularly engaged in matters of making a living, and was at the table of his father the ritual slaughterer and meat inspector, R' Yitzhak Meir ז״ל, and during all hours of the day he was engaged with Torah and God's work.

R' Jonah Berger ז״ל, was an aristocratic Jew, and was someone who was an advocate and activist on behalf of community needs.

I have recalled only a few members of the Shas study group, and there were many others like them.

May their memory be for a blessing.

[Page 177]

R' Leib Ber Geller

He shall deliver thee in six troubles: yea, in seven there shall no evil touch thee.
In famine he shall redeem thee from death: and in war from the power of the sword.

(Job 5: 19-20)

Already from the first steps in his life, the six troubles and seven evils began to dominate the world.

With the outbreak of the First World War, he was a young lad of 17, and was still at his studies in the *Bet HaMedrash*, in the early years of life, and he was known as a very ardent Zionist. At this age, he was drafted into the Austro-Hungarian Army, and fought there for about two years at the front and was seriously wounded.

At the end of the war, he returned as a young man to his birthplace – Przeworsk, and there he proved himself as an orator and community activist.

After he married, and took to wife, the daughter of R' Chaim Israel Schreiber ל"ז from Cieszanow, he established himself in his new home as the head of the "*Po'el Mizrahi*" Division, and after a short time was able to see the good fruits of the endeavors that he had planted.

His righteous wife, Mrs. Ethel ל"ז, good-hearted and known for her good deeds, passed away in the city of Szczecin in the year 5706 [1946], after a severe illness that she had contracted in the forests of Russia and a labor camp.

After he remained solitary as a widower, from the loss of his beloved wife, he wandered with his four orphaned children to Austria, on his way to the *Holy Land* to which he had dedicated all the years of his life, his energy, stamina and blood.

In making aliyah, he sunk his strength in the construction of a synagogue dedicated to the glory of his new home city – B'nai Brak.

He found the fulfilment of his life in the development of The Land. Every new home, every road, and every tree in Israel that was brought up to life, added to his sense of joy and his fortune.

R' Leib Ber ל"ז was a man dedicated to the outlook of his spiritual world, rational in matters of the secular world – in addition to his piousness in matters of faith.

He passed away in B'NAI Brak in the year 5726 [1966].

ת.נ.צ.ב.ה.

[Page 178]

Addendum

by Mina Yaroslavitz-Tanenbaum, his daughter

Thirty years have passed since we left our former home, Cieszanow.

I remind myself of my beautiful childhood years, and of the taste of the goodness that we felt from the care given to us children by our father and mother.

The natural setting in the *shtetl* was like it came from an artistic picture with its meadows, fields, forests and river.

The Sabbath, after noon – when we, a group of young boys and girls would stroll, sang national songs, and enjoyed ourselves and breathed in a full breath of fresh air and hope.

Many of us went for training in order to prepare ourselves to make aliyah to the Land of Israel.

Every one of us had our own problems, and also hopes for a better future, until the dark war broke out that cost our Jewish people six million pure and innocent victims.

In our "*Yizkor Book*," I wish to memorialize for all time the memory of my parents, sisters and brothers, who lost their precious lives at forced labor in the jungles of the Bolshevik forests.

Memories of Parents and Family

by Yaffa Weinstein-Berger

Because of our parents, and only because of them – who raised us in a spirit of good-heartedness and with boundless dedication, in the hopes that better times would come – only thanks to them, did we remain alive and continue to be able to live.

Our warm home, the straightness of heart, nobility of spirit of everyone who surrounded us, those who gave us the strength to resists and to remain alive.

Our father, that most precious of all men, R' Yekhiel Berger ד"ע who was always occupied with the matters of making a living, would turn to us, his children, only on the Sabbaths, and at that time he would regale us with wondrous tales about the BESH"T, R' Meir of Rawszic, and R' Nachman of Lubliniec ז"ל. According to his words, this R' Nachman dedicated literally his entire life to the poor, and was always prepared to provide assistance to the community, and he was an exalted role model for my father ז"ל.

Our mother – a dear soul, who inspired us greatly from her noble spirit.

I remember in the most difficult of times (and times like this were not missing during war), during hours of

[Page 179]

hunger, cold, deprivation and fear, she would sing us songs about the *Holy Land* that so enchanted her. She would tell us wondrous tales in her sweet voice, and thereby take off all worry and sorrow from us. Her strong belief was that we, her children, would reach the Land of Israel, and live a good life there, and she was such a powerful force, that we literally clung to her.

It was as if she instinctively felt that we would go on without her, and she would repeatedly say: remember that in all places, no matter what will be, always behave as if I am with you, so that it will not be necessary for me to, God forbid, be ashamed of you.

Accordingly, we forgot nothing, and we hope to raise the generation that we brought into the world to continue in this path, and that the benefit of your life stand in good stead for our children, and that they will endeavor to carry on the good works and your name with pride.

My grandfather, R' Jonah Berger and his wife Reizl, along with all of their children, and my maternal grandfather, R' Chaim Wolf and his wife Shayndl with their children all were exterminated during the Holocaust. May God avenge their blood.

[Page 181]

General Section

[Page 182]

A Memorial for All Time !

Come, and let us offer our good wishes and blessings to the great and dear man of enlightenment and good deeds, my exalted and respected friend and fellow *landsman*, R' Dov Koenig שליט"א of Antwerp, who together with his sister-in-law, that lady of so many good charitable deeds, Mrs. Leah Koenig, long life to her, who donated a sizeable gift that is well-known, for purpose of publishing this book.

This donation made it possible for us to realize the idea of creating a spiritual memorial marker to the memory of those of our townsfolk that fell as victims of the Holocaust.

The Committee of Cieszanow Émigrés in Israel and the Diaspora convey, in this place, our deep thanks, congratulations and blessings for good health and everything good.

May the Lord grant them a just reward in the present and the future.

Amen

[Page 183]

R' Aryeh Leibusz Koenig ז"ל

R' Aryeh Leibusz Koenig ז"ל

R' Avigdor Taubenblatt of New York

Let these stand to be blessed, who are the volunteers among the people who helped us.

The *Gemara* tells us: When Ravina passed away, the eulogist opened and said: If a brilliant flame fell among the cedars, what are the bereaved to do? Bar Avin responded by saying, God forbid – rather you should say: 'Mourn for the bereaved and not for he who is lost, for the deceased is at rest, and it is we who grieve.'

R' Aryeh was a familiar personality and figure among those who emigrated from our town. His roots are in a family of scholars and *Hasidim*, and the apple did not fall far from the tree, because he, too, was an enlightened man, in addition to being a man of good deeds, generous in charity – both discreetly and publicly.

After wanderings, and after terrible suffering that dogged him in the forests and deserts of the Evil Red Empire, he succeeded to establish his household anew in that Mother City to Jews in the Diaspora of Belgium – Antwerp, and precisely when he finally achieve greatness, he contracted a very severe illness full of suffering and exhaustion, which shortened his life in this world.

He left a very beloved wife behind, who looked after him, and assure him all that was good in life, dear children, well trained, who did not forsake their father's ways, who observe the Jewish traditional legacy.

After the passing of the Chief Rabbi R' Aharon Rokeach ז"ל in Tel-Aviv, R' Aryeh ז"ל was among those who held the view, was a striver, and founder of the Belz Yeshiva whose sun had set in Tel-Aviv, and with his charitable help and support was caused to shine anew in Jerusalem, the Capitol, and in this way, helped to safeguard the spiritual legacy of the Torah and its traditions among the youth of Israel.

The following is copied from a letter of the Yeshiva Institute in Jerusalem to R' Aryeh, ז"ל.

"With respect to our exalted friend, a great man among the giants in the measure of his generosity, the generous Grandee, whose name is praised greatly among all of us who are scattered to the ends of the world, our Teacher, R' Aryeh Leibusz Koenig שליט"א.

We have received news through our emissary the *Hasid* and *Gaon*, from the Devoted *Shames* of The Honorable, Holy, Our Teacher, the Chief Rabbi Zatzulka, that a pure spirit from the Lord has aroused the heart of your good self,

שליט"א, to build the *Bet HaMedrash* to God and his Law in the midst of the King's sanctuary in the center of the building of the place beside the institutes of the Belz *Hasidim* in the Holy City of Jerusalem, may it be rebuilt and reconstituted.

There is insufficient song and praise in our mouths to thank your good self, שליט"א, for this sacred idea, because from the day that *The Abrogator* descended on Belz, that shining ancient place in Galicia, no man has arisen since who would take upon himself a deed so great as this.

[Page 184]

Let the sake of our Holy Rebbes of Belz, may their memories be for eternity, and the sake of the Torah and its recitations, that will go up to the heavens in this holy house, guard over him and the members of his household, to fulfil all his heart's desire for good, and may he be privileged to participate joyfully in the dedication of the building of this institute to which he has dedicated his entire energy and fortune."

May the sake of his good deeds guard over his pure soul that rests under the wings of the Holy Spirit.

'Go to your end, rest and stand ready for your destiny to the end of time.'

Memories from the Last War

By Schraga Feivel Lehrer

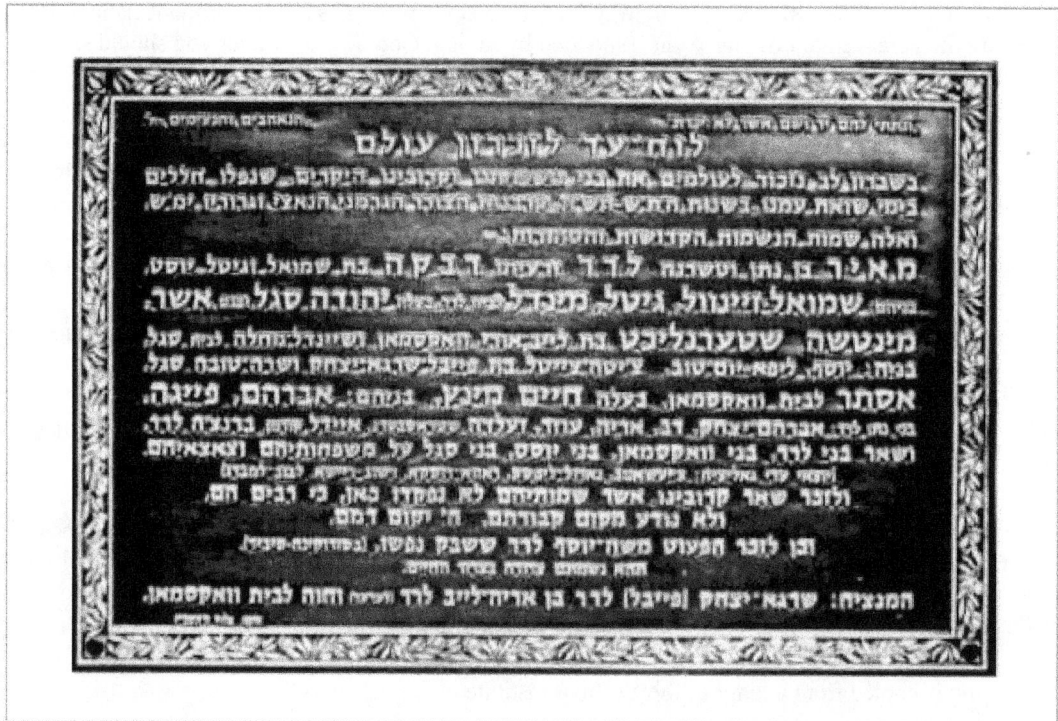

A Memorial Plaque Affixed in the Haifa Synagogue in Memory of the Holocaust Martyrs and Heroes (Lehrer and Waxman Families)

A Kickoff Meeting for the Memorialization of the Cieszanow Community in the Moriah School in Haifa, in the month of Adar 5729 [1969]

From right to left: Rabbi Dr. Mendel Frankel, Dr. David Ravid, Rabbi Yaakov Funk, Mr. Schraga Feivel Lehrer, Rabbi Dr. Mordechai Fogelman, and Mr. Nathan Lahav

[Page 185]

Yisgadal VeYiskadash Shmay Raboh...

By Schraga Feivel Lehrer

In Memory of All the martyrs of our people who were cut down and made to vanish,
At the hands of the accursed Nazis and all their accomplices and followers,
And who had no sin on their hands.

In Memory of All Six Million of Our People, and in memory of
One million, three hundred thousand babies,
And martyred children, pure and without blemish.

In Memory of All our heroes who showed strength in their souls,
By rising like lions against their exterminators,
Who risked their lives, and saved their honor
And the honor of all the Jewish people, may their names be preserved
And their memory, to the end of all generations.

In Memory of All members of our people, who fought in the forests and in the armies
Of all nations, in all places, against beasts
Of prey, in the form of human beings, and with their heroism, erected
A memorial and a model of wonder for all time.

In Memory of All the fighters in the Underground, in the fighting divisions
And the engagements of the people.

In Memory of All military dead in the Israeli Army, *Tzahal*, in all battles.

In Memory of All of our people, who died for liberation, independence
And defense, who fell in eternal heroism
On the altar of Our Land and Our People.

תהייה נשמתם צרורה בצרור החיים

[Page 186]

Our Cieszanow Community is Adopted in Haifa

By Schraga Feivel Lehrer

In the month of Nisan 5729 [1969], the government religious school 'Moriah' in Haifa adopted our destroyed community, thanks to the initiative of the writer of these lines. The adoption and memorialization ceremony of our community as well as the communities of Narol-Lipsko and Belzec, was initiated with a recitation of a chapter from the Psalms, recited by a cantor, the children of the school lit candles in memory of the Six Million martyrs and heroes, a student recited 'Yizkor' and the music professor, Shimon Mutman played dirge music from the Holocaust on his cello.

The initiator, a scion of Cieszanow, stressed the importance of the obligation to memorialize those of our people that had been cut down, in a variety of ways, and for all time:

"I wish to give a blessing and to greet this circle for Jewish cultural activity in our mameloshn, who has privileged us with putting on this evening. I also wish to add that between Yiddish and Hebrew, I have selected Yiddish, because Yiddish was the language of our martyrs that they uttered at the last, of our last martyrs, such that even in reciting 'Shema Yisrael' before death, they said this in Yiddish, and because of this, not only is this language dear to us, it is also holy. R' Akiva said: All is anticipated, permission has been given, and the world is destined for good. The entire human race, is measured only by its good and bad, with each human value being either good or bad, tragedy and comedy, life is drama, and the lives of the Jewish people are especially dramatic, and the mix of the two emotions is, indeed, the subject of this evening. We Jews, our entire history, is always at the extremes, either on the edge of comedy, or at the edge of tragedy, and it is always dramatic.

Even our music and drama, one would say at weddings, Nu – play for me either a *freilach* or something sad, because sad music is an artful form of weeping without the use of words. While I am recalling our Yiddish music, I permit myself to introduce the noteworthy professor, Mutman, who unites art and heart, with *Yiddishkeit* in one gifted virtuosity.

We are, indeed, a Chosen People, because only we have the greatest and most dramatic life story.

No other people has suffered as much for its nationhood, culture and religion, our suffering never let up despite the fact that we did not take them upon ourselves, nor made by ourselves, but it is other nations that inflicted themselves upon us.

Almost all the nations, all of them, all! We have a bloody reckoning with almost all of those so-called 'cultured' peoples – but the climax was the catastrophic destruction of the Holocaust Europe killed us off and disinherited us. Why? For what reason? What? My Lord, why? For nothing – only because the worst of the world, since the time the world was created, always murdered the best – because since Cain murdered his brother Abel, all peoples live as such antagonistic brothers!!! Simply stated – like Cain and Abel.

The clearest lesson to be learned from this latest tragedy, both today and for all time, is the following: The Diaspora doesn't work! Being rich doesn't work, being smart doesn't work, being foolish doesn't work, and refined does not work, educated doesn't work, patriotism doesn't work, and to be heroes on behalf of foreign nations and lands doesn't work, etc. A people can only be free and remain alive in its own land.

[Page 187]

The prophet says: The eternity of Israel is no lie! Jews will never succumb, so? 'Israel' does not, on the face of it, refer to 'The Sons of Israel,' but rather 'The Nation of Israel,' indeed, only: The Land of Israel. Today, our country is called 'Israel,' and 'Eternal Israel' refers specifically to the 'Nation' Israel in the Land 'Israel' which will never vanish, appearing to be the only meaning in substance for the prophetic pronouncement.

Because Israel among the gentiles…because Israel among European gentiles… because Israel in the Diaspora has been doomed.

We Jews have built all of those other countries.

When Kazimierz III the Great, in the 14th century[1] *invited* the Jews of Germany to come to Poland to develop commerce and industry, they came with their Yiddish language and with head and hand built up almost all of the centers of the Polish cities…. until they were killed out, spit out and swallowed up, when they thought we were no longer necessary.

All the nations (with the exception of those who were exceptional among the nations) paid us back with stones for bread, we had built up almost all of Warsaw, Lemberg, Lodz, Katowice, Rzeszow, Vilna, Kiev, etc., and even Vienna and Berlin, we are the myrmidons of history…we are the yeast in the dough of humanity, both materially and morally, and in the same way, in matters that are cultural and intellectual, because our Central and Eastern European brethren created monumental cultural works of everlasting value.

When we recall only a few of these, such as: BESH"T, the Berdichever, Salanter, Sandzer, Belzer, Ryuzhiner, Sholom Aleichem, Peretz, Asch, Manger, Dr. Tahn, Krochmal, Dubnow, Yavetz, Graetz, Schulman, Einstein, Zeitlin, Ringelbaum, Ziegelblum, Weitzman, Trotsky, Buber, Leivik, etc. And those, set apart, living, for long life: Agnon, Uri Zvi Ginsberg, Sh. Shalom, Shlonsky, Shazar, Greenbaum, Dr. Sneh, Gideon Hausner, Ben-Gurion, Professor Sadan, and many others, in the scientific, cultural, social and other fields, I have brought them here as examples of talent and of a prophetic superhuman capacity, and in order to observe the spiritual height and contemporary character of the branch of our people that has been cut down.

We Jews have a good memory, and for all time to come, we will not forget what the Germans, Poles, Ukrainians, Lithuanians, Latvians, and many peoples of other lands, did to us.

After 3500 years, we still continue to recite the *Haggadah,* as if the flight from Egypt and the miracles of the Exodus had taken place yesterday.

For it is this memory of ours, which is the one and only solace, and psychic reaction, to all the Pharaohs, Amaleks, Torquemada, Petluras, and Hitlers, may all their names and memories be erased.

The European Jews have vanished, but our free Land of Israel is, and will remain, forever.

The People of Israel Live – The Eternity of Israel is No Lie

Survivors [sic: of the Holocaust] have taken part in this ceremony, and also Dr. David Ravid, and Mr. Kurman as representatives of the communities mentioned.

[Page 188]

Dr. Ravid, in his remarks, mentioned that during the last Holocaust, certain leaders and representatives of the [Jewish] people were blinded by Divine oversight from seeing the tragic outcome, just like Our Sages (Gittin 56), are not ashamed to admit that 'because of the sins of R' Zechariah ben Avkalos, they destroyed our House, and burned our Hall, and exiled us from our land,' and the Gemara recalls for itself the familiar sentence: 'He sets back the wise, and addles their sense,' which we take to mean that 'if the Dweller in the Heavens, forbid it, wants to inflict something on His people Israel, first He deprives the so-called leaders of their common sense, and , forbid it, they become blinded from seeing the approaching evil, and so this statement supports what occurred in the last Holocaust'."

Rabbi Fogelman and Rabbi Funk have also spoken, as have others.

All recollect the communities that were cut down.

At the conclusion, the children recited and sang ghetto songs, and the cantor recited '*El Moleh Rachamim,*' for the fallen martyrs and fighters in the armies against the Nazis, and those who fought for *Tzaha"l.*

Translator's footnote:

1. The writer erroneously said 15ᵗʰ century. The reign of Kazimeierz III the Great was (1333-1346)

A Memorial Prayer

By Shlomo Zalman Baumel and his son, Jonah

Merciful God, who dwellest on high, above all that is high
Take vengeance for the shed blood of your servants, the vengeance for our offspring
Our frail newborn, who were murdered by accursèd evildoers
With terrifying brutality, to sanctify Your Name, May it be Blessed and Praised,
Mothers on top of their progeny were dispatched;

Remember:

My beloved, God-fearing wife, a prominent woman, may she be praised
Rachel daughter of Jonah Baumel ה"ע, and my children Sheva and Faiga ה"ע
These pure and holy souls that were brought to the altar of sacrifice
On 25 Heshvan 5703 [1943] in the Tarnow Ghetto.

We affix our signatures to memorialize them for all eternity.

ת.נ.צ.ב.ה.

[Page 189]

Children on the 'Aryan' Side Together With Their Families

By Ala Mahler

1. A General Overview of Life on the Aryan Side

Jews who fled from the ghettoes of Poland lived on the 'Aryan' side as gentiles, so long as their manner of speech, their accent, and appearance did not expose the secret of their Jewish identity, and as a consequence, if they were found in the hands of religious leaders, and the globally-minded members of the land, and were able to conceal themselves easily in the midst of the non-Jewish populace. Jewish who lacked such characteristics, were forced to conceal themselves as Jews. However in the two instances, and especially in the latter instance, they needed to resort to financial means in order to pave a way for themselves and to preserve themselves on the 'Aryan' side. And because of this, they had to be adept in the skill of being able to function in an atmosphere of constant fear. Those people who had Semitic features, and received a consideration from non-Jews not only had to be constantly afraid, a palpable fear that was very real, but they also had to bear the justifiable fear of their hosts.

Dangers without number confronted Jews on the 'Aryan' side. Furtive eyes, a posture that communicated insecurity, and the behavior of someone who is hiding something, were ultimately capable of easily betraying that person. If a Jewish woman and her daughter were living among Poles, she was accustomed to request of her daughter, that if she had the nerve to go out of doors: 'Close your eyes, Anya, they look so Jewish.'

A camouflaged Jew was inclined to reveal himself by a phrase that had a Jewish resonance to it, by means of behavior and Polish expressions a bit more indirect, and in the different manner in which he manifested concern and affection for his children, by the refusal to participate in any discussions that were anti-Semitic, an absence of friends and relatives, an abundance or a lack of money, etc. All these indicators potentially could reveal a Jew, as actually did happen many times.

Even a dream was capable of revealing a Jew's secret. A crippled Jew, who was lame in a leg, whose appearance was that of a respected Polish soldier wounded in the war, having an enchanting presence, a long moustache and blue eyes, mumbled a few words in Yiddish while asleep, while riding in a train. His traveling companions turned him over to the German police in the next train station. Seeing that his papers appeared to be in complete order, he was given a physical examination – and was shot at the rear of the station.

Apart from accidental meetings, such as letting down one's guard with people who knew the true identity of the Jew, and were likely to reveal his identity accidentally, hundreds of extortionists lay in ambush for him, who could smell a Jew from afar. They would engage in innovative techniques, to snare their prey in their traps. For example, they would publicize a room for rent, being certain that most of the interested parties were likely to be Jews without a roof over their heads; they would entice Jewish children to draw near to certain 'offerings' and whisper Yiddish words in their ears, looking for some form of a reaction in the frightened eyes of the victim. It is no wonder then, that many Jews would return to the ghetto, when their nerve failed, or their money ran out. The life of the Jew on the 'Aryan' side can be summed up in one word – fear.

Jewish children who were with their families and friends were exposed to the very same dangers that lay in wait for the grown ups. Solitary children, with their profound sense of imitation, and their childish fidelity,

[Page 190]

were forced to learn how to conceal and deny their Jewishness the hard way. they learned this very quickly.

To conceal one's self alone, in general was less complicated that concealing one's self in a group. Despite this, many Jews refused to part from their families and friends out of fear of having to go it alone, face-to-face with the dangers of life on the 'Aryan' side. It is understood that this was particularly so with regard to children.

Gisela M. (A dancer today, in Israeli Europe) was only five years old, when her despondent parents decided to send her, and her eight year-old brother to the 'Aryan' side. Gisela refused to go. In her own despair, she clung to her mother, holding onto her dress, took her in her arms, and covered her with endless kisses. When the little child was taken from the room, she held onto the door handle, and kissed it with emotion, just like she had previously kissed her mother. The door handle for her was a symbol of the house.

Mata Varubel was twelve years old when in the confusion and chaos of one night of the 'aktionen,' she became separated in the dark from her parents and brothers in a field. 'I remained alone in the world, in the darkness of the night' – Mata relates – 'I didn't know where to go... I crawled through the grass, and I remained there with bated breath...suddenly, shooting opened up. A woman with a baby in her arms were murdered not far from me.' Seized with fear and pressure, I thought: 'God knows if my mother is still alive. I don't know where to go... all about there were shots and outcries... I have nothing to eat. And there is no one to whom one can say so much as a single word.'

Her parents, and four of her six brothers were murdered. Mata hid out with one of the surviving brothers, and she remained alive only by a miracle. When she was again by herself among the grasses, she sensed wounded: 'My brother is no longer alive...my mother is no longer alive, and my father and four older brothers, even they are dead. For whom am I supposed to live? There is nothing to eat... what is the point of me remaining in the cold like this among the grasses? I will go and surrender myself to the Germans....'

Children who were hidden together with their parents and relatives, succeeded in guarding their mental and physical health for a more extended period of time than those children that remained alone. They developed a remarkably practical sense, a keen sense of observation and a bias to action. Their senses became sharpened and their emotional state was something miraculous.

The principal dilemma facing parents that had gone into hiding along with their children on the 'Aryan' side, was how to protect the lives of the children and their own lives. Children who were accustomed to a way of life with their families in villages and towns, were sleeping in forests and fields, begging for a piece of bread, etc., and were always busy, they were in danger every minute of their lives. But parents who hid their children in more conventional refuges, had an added dilemma – how to occupy the children for their own good, and for the good of everyone connected to them.

2. A Life of Wandering

Excerpts from the autobiography of a boy and a girl aged thirteen, written in a Displaced Persons Camp, portray a nomadic life in the shadow of death on the 'Aryan' side. The girl, Leah K. tells of the incidents in dramatic and encompassing lines, and even if the boy tends to details, and together with this, having a practical grasp of the total picture, a real picture unfolds in front of us of his nomadic life and that of his family, and he describes their struggle for survival.

[Page 191]

Here is what Leah tells:

"From that day, our tribulations began in earnest. Every day that went by was flush with miracles. We were living in that hospital. and afterwards, transferred to another ghetto. Once again, we were pushed into the pits to be shot – and we escaped. We came to a friend of our father's, a non-Jew. He kept us for a number of months. When it became necessary for him to flee in order to save his own life, we fled with him.

We were getting close to the front line. Not once did we encounter a Jew, and not once did we even hear of them. At frequent intervals, on a cold night, somewhere in the forests, hungry and shivering from the cold, I pressed myself up against my mother and beseeched her: 'Mama, I'm scared, speak to me, tell me, how you are going to bring me to the Land (of Israel).' And my mother would tell me that the entire world will welcome the surviving Jews, and we would travel to Israel, and I will study Hebrew along with other Jewish children.

Day by day, the hiking around the area grew more difficult, and we were vulnerable to falling into the hands of the Germans at any minute. For this reason, we found it necessary to hide during the day. But in that case, we had nothing to eat. My mother was very weak. She did not believe we would stay alive. She would plead to me: 'Leah'leh, let us go to the pond, and drown ourselves. Let us put an end to our issues.' I wept and pleaded with her: 'Make yourself strong, Mama, do this for my sake, I don't want to die. You will see, you will overcome all of this, I won't tell you I'm hungry anymore, but please don't take me to the pond.'...."

The Story of Yitzhak Sorovitz (excerpts of his autobiography have been cited in the previous chapter):

"We fled to the forests (at the height of a night time 'action'), myself, my aunt and sister…we blundered along the way, and in the course of three days, we wandered around the ghetto in an enfolding darkness, without food. But who thought about food? For we had become accustomed to hunger. At the same time, we did not hear anything about my mother. We were cast into bogs of such a nature that we didn't know how to extricate ourselves from them. When we heard the barking of dogs, we went along the trail of the sound of their barking. Almost naked, we and our feet were swollen from the cold… when we came out of the swamps, we came to a farmer…he was frightened about giving us any assistance; he gave us some torn rags, a loaf of bread, and ordered us to move on…

Afterwards, we came to another farmer, and we asked him, if he saw a woman with a baby, but he responded negatively. We begged him to let us lodge. But he was afraid to take us into his house, and told us to go to his grove and hide in a pile of hay. The night was cold, and the hay kept us warm.

That night, a woman and a baby came to the same farmer, and asked him if he had seen Jews who had fled from the ghetto…. when she saw us she screamed: Yitzhak, Lyuba! And we knew that this was my mother….

And this is how the wandering began, going from one farmer to another. We went at night, during the day we remained close to the forests, in order that no person be able to see us. We were – as the saying goes – like a serpent who slithers out of his hiding place (nocturnal) and going out onto the road… We would go about without any sort of food. Only at night would we go out to beg for charity by tapping on the windows. We would rummage through piles of garbage in order to find something to eat, like scavenging dogs. When a farmer didn't want to give us anything, he would holler at us: 'Get away from here, and if you don't, I'll call

[Page 192]

the police.'

We were alone in the forests, without a person to light a fire for us. We were compelled to cut branches of trees by hand and ignite something of a fire. Obtaining food from the farmers, grew more and more difficult day by day. The Germans proclaimed that whosoever gives assistance to the Jews in the form of clothing or food, will be taken out and executed along with his family, and his possessions will be burned. The farmers were seized with a fear that if a Jew were to approach them for food, they would drive him away like a dog. We reached a state of energy, such that we could barely walk. We were in the forests, and we ate acorns…

Snow began to fall, winter drew nigh. We were naked and barefoot. But to eat or be hungry – this was not important in any respect. What worried us, was that we could no longer remain in the forests. there was not another person with us: we were doomed to die from the cold.

We heard about a farmer who knew where several Jews were hiding. We walked to him all night, and we prevailed upon him to show us their hiding place. But he said: 'what is the point of hiding, the world is not a world any longer. Your place is by the river bed.' When we heard what he said, we thought in our hearts: He's right. But the spark of hope always flickers in the heart of man ('the man' at that time was seven years old). No man by nature gives up on his life. We went back at him so many times, that in the end, he showed us where the Jews could be found.

When we found the Jews, we finally knew what a real life meant. They had the skins of potatoes and pots. We were literally filled with wonder. In the entire period of our wandering, we never saw pots. In living with these Jews, we tasted what cooked food was like. When we had been alone, we didn't have a taste of anything cooked, and here utensils, potatoes, etc.

That winter was very cold. All these Jews joined the partisans, but we were destined to remain apart, because we had little children.

Once we were thrown onto a Baptist priest named Jakob, and we begged him to be permitted to remain in his woods. He could not refuse us, because he was a good-hearted man. Somehow or another, he took up an axe, and went with us into the forest. He made a sort of bunker for us… and we remained in it, until the great snow fell. Then, again, we went to him. When Jakob saw us, he began to tremble out of fear, but he said: 'Alright then. So we will all be killed. Come inside, somehow, and when our hour arrives, we will suffer together.' We didn't know how to thank him. Out of great joy, we fell to his feet and kissed them. He immediately gave us work to do, and in this way, we did not idle, and we earned our keep…"

Israel M. from the city of Buczacz describes several other aspects of life on the 'Aryan' side in his collected testimony. He looks back on his life under the Nazis. His approach is less emotional, even if it has the freshness and resonance of a child.

Israel, his parents, and his older brother fled the ghetto when Israel was seven years old, and the family split up…. the father took the older boy, and the two of them worked at the home of farmers, tailoring jackets from sheepskin. The mother wandered about with Israel.

" We scavenged around the villages. The young and healthy people joined the partisans, but this was denied to us. Those who wandered without any objective were distressed. We wandered from village to village, from house to house. Most of the time, we stayed close to the village of Wicikhowka. Good people lived there. They would warn us when the Germans

[Page 193]

drew nigh, we had a bit more ease during the summer. We would sit in the fields of corn and beans, in our clothing, and in the dark of night, I would walk to the village to beg for some bread and to fill the bottle with rainwater, in which small frogs bounded about. Because of the dark, I could not see clearly.

We remained in the midst of the corn days and nights, during rainy days and clear days, without knowing what day it was. There was a hiding place after the field near the village – grasses as tall as a house. and within – a hollowed out area. We would hide there also, and not only ourselves, but also other families, we agreed among ourselves on a few signals when the hiding place was occupied. But the curse of a terrible plague hovered over this hiding place – lice. We saw them crawling on the branches, and swarming about on the ground. We stepped on them as if we were stepping on a carpet.

My clothes became torn from the outset, and my mother sewed me trousers from a sack of jute. The farmers gave me shoes with wooden soles and straw sides. I did not have socks, and the straw scratched my bare legs. During the summer, I walked barefoot, but I could not do this in the winter. One time, my mother persuaded a farmer to take me to work. My mother helped out in the house, and I pastured the cattle. I was barefoot, and I was required to run over sheaves of wheat, and I rushed as if I was stepping on nails. I returned when my legs were covered in scratches and light bruises, and could not then walk at all. The farmer [then] gave me other work – to separate grains of corn for planting. I did this by rubbing ears of corn together. I was not particularly good at this wok either, and my hands became covered with scratches and bruises.

The farmer gave us food, and permitted us to sleep in his granary. We were very fortunate. We knew the meaning of having to sleep on the ground out in the field. We had only one sheet, and we didn't know how to conduct ourselves: to cover ourselves with it, or to put it under us. Not only once did we have to sleep with slime dripping down on us, and yet we were delighted that we were certain that they would not come chasing after us. The quarters that we had in this place appeared to us as if they were a boon from heaven.

We didn't always come out of the cornfield at our own will. It was pleasant there, except for rainy days and at night. However, we had to leave the place, not only because of the Germans, but because the farmers also chased us. We trampled their corn – the crop that they anticipated. Once, while we were sleeping in the cornfield, my mother and I hear the footfall of people, who were speaking in Ukrainian. A terrible fear seized us…we were certain that the end had arrived. We covered ourselves in the sheet, and remained silent. The people got closer, and shouted out: 'Jews, Come Out!' We acted as if we were deaf. And so they shouted louder: 'We are required to kill you' With that, we leapt up onto our feet, and pleaded in front of them not to hurt us, because the end of our suffering is so near. One farmer said, that he would turn us over to the Germans, a second farmer added that they will kill us. Only one said: 'Let them go, can't you see this is a wretched woman with an infant.' These words made an impression. They ordered us to leave the village within two hours.

…we located a poor farmer, aged eighty. A widower, he sometimes had, and sometimes did not have food. He agreed to permit us to live with him, on condition that we feed him. We remained in his hovel, hidden behind a large oven. However, it was not possible to rest even there, and also not to raise one's head. It was only possible to lie down prone. He was very lucky, because it had been a long time since he had eaten cooked food. It was my father who provided the food.

We did not stay with the old man for a long time. We knew that there was no point in trying to live with him, unless our father would be able to provide him with food. This, and other things. This was a Ukrainian village, and it was clear to us, that if we were caught, our

[Page 194]

sentence would be uniform – to be killed. We moved to the village of Polny-Ukrainy.

In the meantime, the summer returned, and we decided to hide ourselves in the corn until winter. Once again, I was compelled to go out each evening to beg for bread, and to fill the bottle with water. There were instances when I had to go out in the rain and storm. I was not frightened. On the opposite. The light was of help to me, because in the total darkness, I found it difficult to find my way back. I waiting for a lightning bolt to illuminate the road for me. I would run for a few steps, and again wait for lightning. My mother waited for me always in prayer that I would be spared any and all evil.

This was our life in the summer. In the winter, our worries doubled. We suffered from hunger and cold. There was no high corn to conceal us… the Polish houses in the village were at a distance. We scavenged in the rain, and sunk into the snow up to our knees. Sometimes our shoes remained stuck in the snow, and in general, there were times when I could not extricate myself from the snow, for after all, how tall was I altogether at that time?

Soaked to the bone, and covered with snow, we once came to the home of a farmer at the edge of the village. For this entire time, we had not changed clothes, because we had nothing with which to change them. We begged so profusely from this farmer, until he finally agreed to let us stay in his hovel. He gave us potatoes and buttermilk. We were lucky to find ourselves under a roof, because there was a snowstorm blowing up outside. We lay down in the straw and fell into a deep sleep. When we woke up in the morning, I couldn't move any limb. That night was cold, and my wet clothes froze to me…"

Many children like Yitzhak and Israel who lived a nomadic existence, adapted to their conditions to the extent that they viewed ordinary daily routines, such as eating cooked food, sleeping under a roof, clean warm clothing, as exceptional – as if it were a miracle and an exceptional joy.

3. Life in the More Permanent Refuges

Gabriel H. from the city of Czestochowa (today a geography teacher in Israel), and his parents, remained alive it the end of the war. They hid themselves in a residence that was prepared for them by a Pole. Here is his story:

"… Vaclav Milewski came and took us to our dwelling. This was on April 13, 1943. Milewski was a tall solidly built Pole. He rented a small residence – a room and kitchen – in a very old house in the center of Czestochowa behind a compost heap… The residence was on the level of the ground, and looked out over a yard. Under the floor in the center of the room, there was a cellar, as was usual in the home of farmers. Most of the time we spent in the residence, but in times of danger, went down into the cellar.

We could have remained on the east side of the cellar. However, after trying it, we discovered that if we have to remain there for an extended period of time, the air becomes asphyxiating to the point where it is unbearable.

The central issue lay in the fact that it was difficult to move in an unencumbered fashion, while at the same time assuring they could not see or hear us. We lived in this place for nearly two years. During this entire time, I didn't see so much as a sliver of the sky…. the huge compost heap was a barrier to the eye. I was also unable to see the sun, and I could not play in the yard….

[Page 195]

I invented all sorts of games for myself, and as it were, I fancied myself to be in a variety of places. I would scramble about beside the corner near the window, the one place where it was possible to mover around. My parents began to worry about my health. They saw me moving about and idle away the hours in this little corner, and the look on my face was as if I was standing in the garden, in the field, or in some other place.

The problem of trying to keep me occupied was a difficult one… in the beginning, my mother tried to teach me….but after this, the situation became tense, in that my parents did not have the patience to continue with the lessons. The dilemma was resolved by a recognized method, by which I found a book from Mr. Szynkowicz, 'In the Desert and in the Forest.' I read this book a countless number of times. I practically knew it by heart…. This book was spiritual fodder for me during long months… I was fortunate, that this was a good book, and suitable for my age. This book was a great help to me. I was in the company of two children (heroes of the book) in Africa, and in the thick of all the tribulations that they encountered.

Hunger was the dominant force in our lives. For the entire time, we ate only bread and potatoes. And even this, in amounts that were insufficient. My father ate the least of us. Most of the food was set aside for me. He made do with a slice of bread per day, and perhaps less than this. My parents imposed a fast on themselves of one day per week, and afterwards increased the fast to two days per week….

My tenth birthday drew near, and for the celebration of that day, my mother had saved a number of potatoes and some fat. On that day, my mother made pancakes, and I received a portion equal in number to my age in years. This was more than enough for a boy of my age, but I was very hungry. I achieved the goal of filling up my belly. This was the only day in which I was not hungry. I recall that my father fainted from hunger on the day of his fortieth birthday. If I remember correctly, this was exactly a month before my tenth birthday…"

We can see in the conditions under which Gabriel lived, circumstances somewhat more permissive than the places in which other Jewish families lived under the Nazi occupation. Faygl Platel-Meindzydzca describes in Yiddish in her book 'On Two Sides of the Wall' the hideaway and the life in which a Jewish mother and her ten year old son lived, in the following terms:

" I saw a hand stretched out between the branches of a dead tree, and I heard a choked voice that said quietly: 'Good Morning.' This same hand began to move the twigs on the branch of the tree. I opened the door to the stable a bit, and then I was able to discern a woman and a little boy laying down on the bare floor, clutched together, in order to occupy the least amount of space possible. Around them and above them were walls of dried branches. It was evident that it was not possible to make even the slightest movement there.

The faces of the mother and child were black, skin and bones, with eyes sunken deeply into their sockets, cracked lips, with the gate faded and full of sawdust. The first thing that they asked of me was to close the door, their eyes were unable to stand the light.

This is the way the two lived, shut away, and pressed together on the ground. It was in this state that they ate, slept, and guarded the door. Twice a day, the lady of the house brought them food. She was very careful, and never permitted them to leave their confines…. they did not bathe, they did not change their clothing or their underwear.

Occasionally at night, when the mother was no longer able to bear the suffering, and was afraid that her limbs would go numb, she would orient herself and crawl outside in order to straighten out her body. She could not reach her right arm, and this also caused her great pain….

[Page 196]

The boy looked at me from behind the pile of branches with burning eyes. Tears rolled from the mother's eyes. Were she alone, she could get by with the absolute minimum, but she feared for the fate of her child. Before long, the child caught a severe cold. He began to cough. In a matter of days, the mother began to hold him in her arms, day and night. He had a high fever. The mother did not know what worrier her more – the cough that was destined to reveal the secret of their hideout, or the fever that was destined to bring on death. The lady of the house was afraid to take in the child and put it in her bed.

It was necessary to be very careful not to arouse the anger of the lady of the house. Everything depended on her. Once, rumors were circulated that panicked the lady of the house, and she ordered them to leave the place. The mother and child wandered for a span of days in the nearby forest. They had no place to go. Somehow, the mother begged the lady of the house to take them back…"

Among the children who remained alive, were many who lost the ability to walk, many were struck blind, and many contracted skin disease, typhus, and other chronic diseases, as a consequence of life in the course of months in places that are indescribable for their inhuman conditions. The damage that was done to their emotional development after an extended period of time like this was immeasurable. However, the return of the health of these children in both body and spirit was something miraculous to behold.

[Page 197]

Cieszanow – My Second Home
(Memories and Assessments)

by Mordechai Kaufman

Eastern Galician Jewry – A Pillar of the Jewish People

The Jewish scholar, Prof. A. A. Roback unfolds a wonderful thought in one of his books, about the deathless nature of the Jewish people. He says:

"An ethnic body politic rarely dies, a people, a language, a culture is not in the domain of the individual. We know that an individual has a heart, a head, which if they cease to function, then the individual is gone. A people, however, is like a plant, which, if certain parts fall away, others grow in their place, so long as the taproot is not impaired, the plant is able to bloom further and further."

I cannot write about my fragmentary recollections of Jewish Cieszanow, a city that I rightfully think of as my second home, if I do not give proper recognition to the Jewry of Eastern Galicia, which lived so gloriously and was brought down so tragically at the Hands of Esau, woven into the murderous force of Nazis, Ukrainians, and Poles, may their names be eradicated.

Jewish Cieszanow was just a small part, but its Yiddishkeit and Zionism has remained historical, a great part of this Jewish people, which produced wise men, Gaonim, scholars and educated people, thinkers and writers, in prose and poetry, whose thoughts and ideas points of view and spiritual thoughts, enriched all of world Jewry with permanent fundamentals, with genuine endeavors of Zionist striving, with concrete pioneering implementations in the Land of Israel.

And while the "Cieszanow *Yizkor Book*," with the help of the letters of the Hebrew alphabet, and the facilitation of the lines of memorialization, lights an eternal light to the sacred memory of a Jewish community that was cut down, of a Jewish community that was destroyed, let my modest words in this article also be an addendum to the "Yizkor" and the Eternal Light, which the survivors from Cieszanow light in their hearts, in their minds, in order not to forget the dear Jews of Eastern Galicia in general, and of the community of Cieszanow in particular.

* * *

The spiritually rich Jewry of Eastern Galicia was a strong foundation on which World Jewry relied for centuries. During the course of many centuries Jewish communities in Galicia presented themselves as a comprehensive, internally rooted organizational creative strength of such scope, that it had the force to hold together all the parts and sectors of this Torah-loyal and culturally devoted Jewry, and I am of the opinion that whether in faith or religion, its scope was global.

The Jewish communities nourished the Galitzianer Jews with those energizing nutrients that were vital for their lives, from the inexhaustible well springs of Torah, as well as the redemption ideals of Zionism. The voice of Torah and education, rich in wisdom, could be heard the length and the breadth of Jewish Eastern

[Page 198]

Galicia. The *Heders* and Yeshivas, the "*kloyz*", and *Hasidic* "*shtibl*" the courtyards of the Tzadikkim, and the Belz, Sanz Sadigur, or Chartkov Rabbinic dynasties, altogether was a formidable and grandiosely fiery religious Jewish manifestation, a fortress of ardent *Hasidic Yiddishkeit*, which was assaulted by all kinds of anti-Semitic elements, as well as internal forces of assimilation, and traitors to the people, but all were smashed and eradicated against the rock-hard walls so well armored with Jewish lore, Torah and tradition – *Yiddishkeit*, which were so zealously guarded by the Galitzianer overseers of Jewry....

* * *

Up till the outbreak of the Second World War, Galician Jewry looked like a full-colored rainbow, whose shimmering colors of spirit and culture, of Torah and *Hasidism*, of ideas and principles, of Zionist differentiated ideas, directions in *Hasidic* dynasties, lit the heavens of the Jewish world with all its candles, which like lightning bolts from Sinai, showed the direction in all ways and paths of the many-sided Jewish life in Eastern Galicia.

With the invasion of the Soviet armies first, and the coming of the murdering Hitler Hordes later, the lives of our brothers and sisters were torn apart, the echo and reverberation of the voices of Torah were stilled, the Jewish spirit was destroyed, together with those who were the bearers of its religion and spirit, and those fresh well springs were stopped up, the Zionist movements were brought down along with the "Rabbinic courtyards" made desolate, the communities and everything attached to them were smashed, and gruesomely annihilated, the kloyz, the synagogues, and the houses of study, were wiped off of the face of the earth, and almost the entirety of Galician Jewry was martyred by extermination, together with all the other millions of Jews, pure and holy, by all manner of bizarre deaths. A wholesale slaughter for which there will never be any forgiveness or pardon forthcoming from Jews, the blood of innocent Jews cries out from the depths, from the earthen fields, wailing from the burnt ash on the fields for the Galician vale of tears, from all the gas ovens, from crematoria, murder factories of the gentile world, through whose portals, our unforgettable brothers and sisters gave up their lives through asphyxiation by gas and incineration. Their vibrant lives went up in smoke through blackened chimneys, going immediately up to the highest heavens, and perhaps reaching the Divine Throne...

The brutal feet of Esau trod on the wreckage of hundreds and thousands of Jewish communities in Galicia, during the time of the Holocaust and extermination of the Jews, and even today – free and publicly – these bloodthirsty hyenas in human form continue to go about in these sanctified places, but without any Divine Presence, in the hateful form of the sadistic Ukrainians, of hooligan Poles, of murderous Germans, despicable Hungarians, and in contemporary low and high officials in today's Soviet Ukrainian regime.

* * *

We mourn the annihilation of Galician Jewry, we bow our heads in deep sorrow with the pained sadness before the graves, not graves, but the mountains of ash and for the unburned bones of hundreds of thousands of exterminated Jews of Galicia. We, those who are the remnant of survivors of Galician Jewry, cry out a renewed "Pour Out Thy Wrath" on such gentiles that have laid waste Jacob's tents, destroyed our lives, and cut down our tree of Jewish Galicia to the taproot, along with almost all of its many-extended branches , leaving behind only a burned base, a Jewry cut down, and an unbearable sorrow for those left alive.

[Page 199]

The sorrowful words of Lamentations will never part from our lips:

Look around and see. Is any suffering like my suffering that was inflicted on me, (I:12)

Young and old lie together in the dust of the streets; my young men and maidens have fallen by the sword. (II:21)

The sorrow of the Jewish survivors from Galicia has been woven into the fabric of the great pain and heartrending sorrow of the entirety of World Jewry, which mourns the extermination, and the hot ash of six million brothers and sisters, among which the richly Jewish tribe of Galicia occupied an honored bench against the "Eastern Wall" of the Jewish people.

We recollect, with a trembling respect – through these pages of the Cieszanow *Yizkor Book* – the sacred memory of our holy and pure, the Jewish communities of Galicia that have been cut down, of brothers and sisters who were killed. They will forever remain engraved in our minds, in our souls, just as they will remain in the history of the Jewish nation, from its epoch-making avant garde in the Land of Israel before, and in the Jewish State today. Galician Jewry has already taken its historic place against the "Eastern Wall" of the Jewish people.

The fecund life of the Jewish settlement in Galicia as its tragic denouement, will serve as an enduring stimulus for the surviving remnant of Galician Jewry in the entire world, especially in the State of Israel, and most certainly to the scions of Cieszanow wherever they may be found, and they will find themselves in the front ranks everywhere, in the most demanding positions in the difficult struggle for the survival of the Jewish State, as well as for the continuity of the Jewish people.

Memories of Zionist Activities in Cieszanow

Very substantial memories remain with me, from the months and years that I spent in my second home, Cieszanow, thanks to which I am able to relive those happy times of great striving, of exalted missions, of important objectives, of invigorating activities, accompanied by attractive efforts and by dedicated Zionist realizations among the Jewish young people of the referenced city, as well as among all of the ranks of the local Jewish populace.

Memories, if they are substantive and worthwhile, especially if they are of the type that derive their sustenance from a happiness that one has lived through, from struggles for truth and serious ideals, from beauty in the heart, they do not ever leave the memory of their owner.... not even for one minute of his life. I therefore feel myself fortunate from the gladdening fact, that in the course of my days and nights in Cieszanow, I gathered up substantive impressions, unforgettable memories and hid them away in the most beautiful compartments of my heart, so that for my entire life, I may obtain a great satisfaction, in an ongoing manner, that I have accomplished something, that I filled my hours with specific accomplishments for the Zionist concept, for the not falsified education of the young, and at the core, before everything else, that I have united myself with the Jewish nation and its striving for redemption.

My terse sense is best summed up in the following saying:

"Live your days in a manner that you will be able to say that I have done something good on each and every day."

[Page 200]

In the entire time that I spent in my second home, Cieszanow, when I lived there, in all the days, months and years, when I found myself in her outstretched Jewish arms, whether as a teacher or as a youth leader, not to mention my activities in *Hitakhdut* and *Gordonia*, I came to love the local Jewish people, the Jewish youth and even the opponents of Zionism. I lived their happiness with them , and felt their sorrows with them. My educational work among the adults, the youth and children, based itself not only on educational methods alone, in that dark time of Polish anti-Semitism on the one hand, and the time of Jewish want, on the other, but I also focused on the joy that comes with fraternal community, which our gatherings, assemblies and trips to the forest, promoted among all those who participated. During such times, who thought of need, about crowded little rooms for dwelling, from an unsatisfied hunger, from sorrows at home, and parental aggravation? Hebrew song carried itself through the length and breadth of the town, the discussion about the end goals of Zionism drove a new hope for individual and collective redemption into the hearts of every participant. The Sabbath summer sky, even the midweek one, became that much more blue, even more beautiful than it was... and also on cloudy days, young and old Zionists alike from Cieszanow knew, that under the heavy, coal-black clouds, a warm bright sun is shining...

I recall a conversation, that at the time, I had with a local *Bund* leader about Zionism. Cieszanow was one of the Jewish towns of Eastern Galicia which had an active *Bund* organization. In a sarcastic tone, he asked whether I believed that the Zionist utopian ideal would someday be realized. I replied to him that much sooner, before communism, and its entire Marxist entourage become transformed into a single anti-Semitic horde against the Jewish people, an independent Jewish state will already be in existence. We were both standing up, leaning against the wall of Shmuel Tepper's "Delicatessen," store, and heaven and earth bore witness to the outburst of laughter that my conversation partner let out, when he heard my unusual reply....

This very same *Bundist* was also of the opinion that socialism will bring both the human and material means for the national liberation of the Jewish nation, on the "mighty wings" of "freedom, justice and righteousness. regrettably, these wings were broken by a frightening storm of blood and fire over large parts of the Jewish nation. If Hitlerism wanted to exterminate us, and indeed, excised a third of the Jewish people by the taproot, whether physically or spiritually, Communism carried out a spiritual genocide against more than three million Russian Jews, which also, in a different form, was a great catastrophe, and a severe annihilation...

It was not only once that I had to carry on such discussions with contentious Jewish people. and not always were the Zionist arguments understood, because to the degree that a Jew was willing to diminish his loyalty to Zionism, the more he could divide his soul into two parts: a larger part for "suffering humanity" [sic: in general] and only a bit of his heart – for the Jewish masses. In Cieszanow, there were also found such Jews, and it was not important if they agitated on behalf of the *Bund*, or believed in communism, or, separately, believers in assimilation, or in a Messiah from a faith point of view, or had their own hopes and did not believe in disappointments, they would often reject Zionist hopes openly. To our great sorrow and pain, they, too, were exterminated in a martyr's death together with all the others from Cieszanow and Eastern Galicia.

From my earliest youth, and I came to Cieszanow while I was very young, I promoted Zionist fantasies both in word and through teaching, and this was not exactly saleable merchandise in the Jewish market... Anyone who wanted to jeer at the peculiar fabulist, was certainly able to do this with pleasure in his heart, and whoever could not hold back his anger at the Zionist "buffoon" broke out into a pointed hysteria of words, but despite this, I was a believer in the Eternity of Israel.

This is not the place to recollect how I was brought to Cieszanow, and who among the local Zionist youth activists helped to make that possible. At that time, I was already a recognized leader of "*Gordonia*," not only

[Page 201]

in my birthplace of Nemirov, but in all the regions of Rawa Ruska and Jaworow. I had also taken my place in the ranks of the "*Hitakhdut*" movement and my place in Zionist party activity, with the recognition of the central committee in Lemberg. The important thing is, when I received the call from the comrades in Cieszanow to remain with them in their city, as a teacher and youth leader, I assumed that [burden] with affection. I knew, that it would be difficult for me to take leave of my family, with so many tens of loyal friends, with hundreds of Jewish homes, which were a refuge for me, from friendship gatherings and spiritual surroundings, but I overpowered many difficulties, overcame many stresses, and arrived in Cieszanow with a youthful ardor, with boundless Zionist fire, with an unbending will, to continue to remain with the mission of spreading the Zionist agenda, which others referred to as Zionist fantasies...

Individual Zionists, such as R' Shmuel Zeinvil Tepper and his family, uniting the *Hitakhdut* organization with its "*Gordonia*" received me with love and a full heart, and whose good feeling I can still feel today. After several middle level contacts with circles and youth groups, I earned everyone's trust, and I became surrounded by a full-hearted envelope, and despite the fact that I was rather young, in my heart, I sensed, and all my senses established for me, that I have loyal students, that I had achieved making life-long friends, possibly even someone I would marry, and ignoring age entirely, or at the age difference between them and myself, any doubt about the degree of the bond between us emotionally could be laid to rest by the vivid sign that the very personal connection between kin and close friends, the ongoing love and heartfelt sense of friendship, was not vulnerable to either time or forgetfulness.

Memories-Episodes

Education and Study in Cieszanow

Immediately upon my arrival in Cieszanow, I assumed the double yoke of study and education.

Every educated person clearly understands the difference between studying and education. It is possible to teach someone a great deal about reading and writing, but this does not influence the thoughts or the thinking of the "learner." One person can have a more beautiful penmanship, a second person, less attractive, but no ideas or fundamentals can be obtained this way...

When, upon my arrival in Cieszanow, I came into a direct contact with the unforgettable young Jewish people, with those Jewish children – engraved in my heart – with older young people, and those of middle years, I grasped it was not only the mastery of Hebrew as a language that was essential to them, but rather their life's goal, or their single striving, I felt their inner spiritual will to obtain instruction about our Zionist ideals, as if like by an electric shock, to dedicate themselves to loftier pursuits, consisting of serious Jewish-ethical principles, and to cherish lifelong, a grounding in the essentials of the Jewish struggle for redemption, which are based on the foundations of the Love of Israel and the love of the individual.

Our Hebrew school was located in the rooms of R' Pinchas Szpiergel, the owner of a large house, with a saloon in the front, and a large salon on the side for meetings. Day in and day out, the sound of learning could be heard, and the echo reached other cohorts of the more mature young people, organizations and groups, and all together, sought an appropriate time to study Hebrew, to listen to discussions, to carry out acts of greater ideological significance, and education and learning became united, each having an influence on the other, raising them, inspiring and rounding them out...

The study of Hebrew, accompanied by an earnest educational endeavor, led to the fact that I put on short but

[Page 202]

substantive scenarios with the unforgettable young boys and girls, a variety of celebrations, a choir – and oratorical presentations, substantial memorial meetings in memory of the creator of political Zionism, Dr. Benjamin-Ze'ev Herzl, and the national poet, Chaim Nachman Bialik, ז״ל, whose ideas and works were portrayed in images by the Jewish children who were pupils in our school.

Who of us, in Cieszanow, especially during the summer months, did not await the Sabbath afternoon? In the first row, my students and myself, joined by the tens and tens in "*Gordonia*," committed Zionist youth, who in regulated and disciplined ranks marched out in groups from the center of the city. Each section, group, was led by a director, wither male or female, and the entire host headed to enter the nearby woods, where according to a previously drawn plan, of discussions and communal singing, each group carried out a variety of activities. The energetic singing of Hebrew and Yiddish songs of hope wafted over the city, carried over the gentile fields, and reached the nearby villages.

At the time of such marches, I would always thing the line [sic: from the HaTikvah] "Our Hope is not yet Forlorn..." as if some special force, I thought, could be found within us, which life in exile has not been able to overpower, that all our enemies have been unable to break, or break us, or our faith in a better Jewish tomorrow, without fear of pogroms and their perpetrators. On such a Sabbath day, every one of us, knowingly, or unknowingly, thought of ourselves as a Prince of the Jewish people, and with our inspired eyes, we saw the Land of Israel during the time of our discussions, and who felt the physical presence?....

It was with this Sabbath-imbued spiritual Jewishness that we lived for the entire week, and spiritually influenced our weekday environment along with our study and educational objectives.

I Am Arrested by the Cieszanow Police

I do not know who among my beloved Cieszanow Jews remembers the episode, when I was taken down by the police from the dais, and was arrested for almost the entire night in the local "jail" under confinement. What my transgression was: it was – a story like this:

The First of May arrived, and the local *Bund* "celebrated" the "the Holiday of the Proletariat," in its own fashion, with a pre-planned international flavor, with the poor Jewish worker in Cieszanow required to be concerned, alas, with "suffering humanity" and I received my directions, notwithstanding my tender age, from the central *Hitakhdut* office in Lemberg, that this Zionist People's Party, which takes its spiritual nourishment from the teachings of A. D. Gordon, and draws its concepts from Marxism, as well as other prophets about justice and righteousness, about justice and compassion, should make a separate May 1 presentation, in order to permit me to bring out Zionist points of view, to portray the frightening condition of our people and to come to the same conclusions.... because there were deeper ideological differences between the genuine Jewish striving as opposed to the socialist justice in the original socialism.

In the middle of my speech, police broke in and arrested me. I remember a variety of details of the arrest, coming to the police station, the commandant had already "examined" me and took me for a "dangerous revolutionary." He took out thick volumes of statues, and showed me, how severe my punishment would be for my "May 1 transgressions," and at the same time, he portrayed me as a well-informed expert of all the ideological directions of the Jewish street. He enumerated Zionist and anti-Zionist parties with their programs, and began to "analyze" the ideological differences among these. My heart was a bitter as gall, but the "knowledge" of the police commandant impelled me to burst out into laughter, but I contained myself, in my situation, which required all my strength to do so.

[Page 203]

Quietly in my heart, I only wished that all haters of Jews should have so much physical strength, as this police commandant has intellectual prowess and understanding, of Jewish matters....

Today, I no longer remember exactly which of the Jewish city *balebatim* it was, who made the necessary intervention to get me released, but it was for many hours, on the night of the end of April to the first of May, that I felt the taste of what it meant to be a prisoner, which the Cieszanow police had apprehended and wanted to accuse of "fomenting revolutions," and calling on the masses to battle for a "new order" in Poland, as well as disseminating communist literature.

Indeed, I was released, however, during those days and nights, a feeling remained with me that in the eyes of gentiles, we were all communists, and for a long time, the feeling of pity did not vanish for the few Jews with whom I sat for those hours, in the local jail of the Cieszanow police.

A Regional Get-Together of *"Hitakhdut"* in Cieszanow

Two ideological directions took priority in the pulsating Jewish life in Cieszanow: *"Hitakhdut"* and the general Zionists. It needs to be said, for the entirety of truth's sake, that there never were any ideological discussions between the members of both organizations. If anywhere, one sought to find a common endeavor, a friendly form of expression, a heartfelt relationship among friends, and overall – cooperative activities in the local *Keren Kayemet L'Yisrael*, as in the general area of the clarification of Zionist ideas, the unification of schooling and educational objectives, especially for the Zionist youth organizations in the city, one could encounter this at ever turn in Jewish-Zionist Cieszanow.

Apart from my specific work as an educator and a director, having received a set position, I was also the representative and instructor for the *"Hitakhdut"* Party and its central offices in Lemberg, as for *"Gordonia."* On a certain day, I received a request from the central office to carry out a regional get-together in Cieszanow for the previously mentioned ideological movement and its branches in the surrounding towns and villages. After a consultation with my fellow comrades in Cieszanow, I obtained their agreement and everyone took themselves to the organizational activity. The preparations were intensive. Members, along with me, first visited Lubaczow, Oleszyce, Havenyiev, or as the city was properly called: Dachnow, in order to make certain of the participation of the larger delegations.

On a summer's Saturday night, the introductory session of the meeting was opened in a festive manner, with the participation of many delegates, and I, the junior, gave the opening speech and at that time, touched on all of the timely questions of the day, that were connected with this very movement, as well as those situations concerning the plight of all Polish Jewry. Also, the entire day of Sunday, bathed in sunlight, was taken up with serious discussions, conversations with many practical implications, which led to real decisions. Other speeches and debates were held in a fraternal context – happiness accompanied by song. To this day I can see the picture: gentiles are leaving the Orthodox church, and are getting ready to go to the saloons to grab a glass, and we are occupied with communal singing, and hours later, those who visited the Orthodox church will stagger around dead drunk in public through the streets of Cieszanow, and we, Jewish young people, will still remain occupied with the dissemination of Zionist lore and bringing into Jewish homes, the warmed up fantasies of the Jewish redemption, of a life in the Jewish homeland in the Land of Our Fathers.

The regional *"Hitakhdut"* conference elicited dissatisfaction among the more dilute ranks of the local *Bund*, but the theme that was undertaken, and the large number of participants in the gathering, the inspiration of the members, the stimulus that was received to assume even greater obligations, this by itself made a great impression on the Jewish populace of Cieszanow proper, as in the neighboring towns.

If I do not err, and my memory does not betray me, I believe that such a congress was literally unique in all of

[Page 204]

Eastern Galicia, where a Zionist-ideological force was actuated and made an impact. When such gatherings were carried out in those days, they were usually held in the really large cities, such as Stanislawow, Stary, in which I had the privilege of directing the *"Barzel"* training as a recording secretary, but never were regional conferences of this sort held in the smaller towns. Jewish Cieszanow, in this regard, was truly an exception, and in addition to this, not only did the regional congress receive a great deal of publicity in the central party organ *"Dos Freie Vort"*, but it also had a broad distribution in the *"Lemberger Tageblatt."*

The regional congress of the membership, and its agenda which was its constant companion, presented an inspirational, and Zionist-Jewish supplement to the drab and uninspiring daily work of a large number of the loyal Zionist membership. which Cieszanow had by the hundreds, for the ultimate benefit of the concept of the rebirth of the people and its Land.

A Petit-Journal, *"Der Baginen"* in Cieszanow

All these memories are crammed into a slice of time from the year 1930 to almost the end of the year 1933, with minor interruptions because of my travels to my birthplace in Nemirov and other places in connection with a variety of missions.

It is not possible to write and portray all the important, and possibly also interesting episodes from this –for me – unforgettable time, which supported me in Cieszanow. However, I cannot move onto the memories of other episodes, if I first do not recollect the defining fact that Jewish Cieszanow began to produce a small but substantive monthly periodical under the masthead of "*Der Baginen*."

I, the junior, sowed this thought among my dear friends, and also transferred it to the older Zionists, and inculcated this idea even into my students in school, and all of them gave their very enthusiastic conceptual support to the idea, and it became a reality.

It was far from easy to produce a periodical in that time, when there was no Jewish printing press in Cieszanow, and this could not be found even in other towns. Well, to write down and describe short essays and episodes from Jewish life in the city, the Zionist activities in the city, was not the most difficult task, so we were well-provided with content. The concern surrounded the Jewish printing press, which was the most difficult one to solve. At that time, a good idea came to me, to tie up with the members in Rawa Ruska, which already had a large Jewish community, with a Zionist as a community head. This city already had a printing house, and, indeed, it was from here that the first edition of *"Der Baginen"* was published, of which over two hundred copies were sent off to Cieszanow.

The appearance of such a local periodical was a bit of an event for everyone, for many a real to-do, for a few – a joke, but the essential fact was, that in Cieszanow, a small Jewish community, a monthly periodical had been published, printed in Hebrew font, with a quite respectable content, added a meaningful appearance and much significance to our cultural work.

Only two editions of the periodical *"Der Baginen"* appeared, and were in the public domain, but I was sent to Sokolov, near Stary, to conduct a seminar with *"Gordonia"* and I was compelled to disrupt all of my activities in Cieszanow and this brought an end to this periodical.

"Der Baginen" went down, literally at the very time of its "Beginning."

[Page 205]

But through these lines, a very glad fact is fixed. that a monthly Jewish periodical was published in Cieszanow, the only one of its kind in the region of Rawa Ruska, Lubaczow, and Jaroslaw.

My memories and portrayed episodes have the same value to me as a memorial candle that has been lit in the memory of the destroyed Jewish community, as was the organized Jewish congregation in Cieszanow.

[Page 206]

How Many Traitors Does the Jewish Land Require?
(Thoughts Out Loud)

by Mordechai Kaufman

At the time of the Ukrainian-Polish Wars in our area, when I was yet a small child and lived through this bi-national armed conflict as if in a dark fog, without memories and without details, my father once told me, how the Poles once seized a spy, as it happened a Pole from the same nation, and shot him for this near our house, which was in the vale of my birthplace, Nemirov.

This image made an extraordinary impression on my child's mind, and not a single detail of this has left my memory, concerning the execution of this traitor.

Well, such incidents have occurred among all nations, and so long as there will be people with lofty minds and traitorous hearts, national treason will not vanish from the face of the earth.

I was reminded of this theme of treason about a Pole, who served the Ukrainians and gave them military secrets to the detriment of the Polish occupation campaign in Eastern Galicia, because this week, I read a Yiddish-German weekly, from the Austrian capitol city of Vienna, about the publication of a book by the lofty minded Canaanite, shameful propaganda-smearer, and national traitor, Uri Avnery, "Living with the Arabs? – Israel between the Future and Zionism," which appeared this year in the Bertelsmann Zagbuch-Verlag (Spiegel Series). Even though the language, in which Avnery's pap was written, is not mentioned, I can imagine that this character has abandoned the Hebrew letters, and that the original is in Hebrew.

I have to force myself to excerpt several lines from this treasonous book against the Jewish people, especially against the Jewish state, because every adhering Jew and person would bridle to the point of spitting gall when it becomes necessary to engage such fallen souls. The author utters such awful thoughts as: " The Jews have driven the Arabs from Palestine" (the original German uses the words "*Die Juden haben die Araber aus Palestina vertrieben*") . And if this were not enough, this previously mentioned traitor writes about Zionism with such anti-Semitic sentiments as: "Zionism has made one cause with modern imperialism, one of the most provocative and hateful movements in the world." Such words, full of poison aimed at Zionism and towards the work of Jewish liberation, do not emanate from some other Jew-hater, who was, God forbid, educated in the Hitlerist schools of racism and Jew-hatred, but from a "Jewish" Deputy in today's Sixth Knesset, and uses the Jewish name: Uri Avnery. In accordance with his anti-Zionist outbreak and his loyalty to Arab murderers, such a character would be expected to be employed in today's fascist *"Deutscher Nazional und Soldaten Zeitung,"* which disseminates a zoological hatred against Jews in the official organ of Neo-Nazism in the West and East-Germany. Uri Avnery is also not a member of the traitorous communist band of the RK"Kh, at the head of which one can find traitors to the Land such as: Meir Willner and the hysterical Jewish Ruth Lubitsch, who are ready to murder Jews, if the latter day Kremlin would demand it of them.

If the Israeli authorities were not functioning in a democracy, which is, indeed, a foundation of the local life, but also is possessed of a great deal of neglect, and if the government and the justice department of the Jewish State were to give a suitable interpretation of Israeli democracy, a bald-faced anti-Jew and anti-Zionist dissolute like this Uri Avnery, would be brought up to trial for high-treason, especially in today's exceptional circumstances, in which the Jewish State finds itself, and it would not be difficult at all to take away the immunity of a Deputy from such a Canaanite character, bring him to the bar of justice, as a genuine criminal against the security of the State of Israel.

[Page 207]

Once again, it is possible to find such soft hearts among our Jews, who will say, what then is the difference between Israel and the politics of pursuit in the Soviet Union? Here, in the land of the Haidamak movement, authors and writers are punished because their works have been published outside of the country, and Israel is punishing an editor of a weekly periodical? How inappropriate is their point of view, and an author of a book in the German language, which mars the face of the Jewish State. With this kind of soft-hearted fool, it is entirely not possible to have a conversation. What sort of equivalence can one possibly find between democratic Israel and the bloodthirsty Red Dictator of the Kremlin satraps? The Daniels and the Sinyavskys are sentenced, because they have the temerity to raise their voices against wantonness and murder, but the Willners and Lubitsches and Avnerys, just like the satanic Yevseksiya in the entire Jewish world, raise themselves up with hatred for Israel and demonstrations against the core of the Jewish State, against the vanguard of the Jewish people, the world Zionist movement, and what it really means, and is unspeakable – to join with the most gruesome enemies of Jewish life and of Jewish freedom.

Uri Avnery's book that assaults the Jewish State contains a countless number of pro-Arab chapters, and in one of them, he says in a loud voice, that "the Jews created Israel with brutal violence," but there is not a single word about the assault on the newly-created Jewish State by seven Arab armies, each of which, jointly or severally, were ready to pull out each and every Jew in Israel by the roots, Avnery included, just as these same Arab nations today, inflamed by Soviet imperialism are prepared to do right now, may that hour not come.

The great anti-Israel front does not have its origins in Moscow, or in the Arab capitol cities, in has its roots in the Yevseksiya in every Jewish settlement and ends with the disinterested claque of the Canaanite Uri Avnerys and ends with the communist Willners and his ilk.

A new initiative needs to be undertaken: to root out national treason against the Jewish people, and the frightening treason against the State of Israel.

[Page 208]

Words to Remember...

by Frieda Starkman-Kaufman

(In Memory of My Beloved Parents)

R' Mordechai Kaufman with his wife, Frieda,
the daughter of R' Abraham Ber Starkman, ז"ל with their son

For the final time, beloved parents, I
Take my leave of you as I did once.
I had felt that never again in our lives –
Would you see your child with your own eyes.

* * *

Born, raise, doted on, loved,
In Jewish surroundings, in our home,
Suddenly, the fire of war, a global conflagration,
The house – burned down, the city – incinerated.

* * *

I also remember, and shed hot tears,
There is no one to feel, no one to hear –
The agonies and sorrow of a child,
Who survived the generational pain and wounds...

* * *

How oppressive is the thought,
That the dearest in life are no longer here,
The heart is so pained, there is such longing.
Never more to hear –
A word from them,
Not knowing where their graves are,
The most sacred of places,
When their bodies, in the final agony,
Gave up their souls with a sorrowful wail...

* * *

You raised ten children in joy and sorrow,
Now, your burial place is a secret.
When shall we recite the "*Kaddish*," light the little candle?
Your memory is united with that of other millions of martyrs!

[Page 209]

Scions of Cieszanow Are Tied to the State of Israel

Mordechai Kaufman, (Argentina)

(Dedicated to all the Loyal Members of the Cieszanow Émigrés)

R' Yitzhak Meir Liebeh's ז"ל, a scion of Lubliniec near Cieszanow. R' Yitzhak was an outstanding scholar from an aristocratic family.
תנצב"ה

Black clouds cover the blue skies of the Land where we were born, the Egyptian dictator, tied to the Red-Black Kremlin still persists in threatening to destroy our country, which was re-established after two thousand years of exile. All of our enemies return to their declarations to start a war anew with Israel, and their intent: to finish – God forbid – the killing, asphyxiation, and Jewish extermination that Hitler, may his name and memory be erased, began in the years 1939-1945.

The Jewish people in the Diaspora have endured many tribulations, and this is not the first time that cruel nations, who are godless and without good will and compassion, who lack faith in the core values of justice and righteousness, have consigned us to oblivion, destruction and to being torn down, but we have prevailed… despite the clouds filled with thunder and lightning that have darkened our lives, the nation has had the unique privilege of seeing the sun, and the light that is hidden behind it.

Even today, those of us who believe in the Zionist concept, see not only ominous clouds, we are able to see not only the light of the sun, but also to show the entire Jewish people, the rays of that sun, Our enemies have attacked Israel, they let the clang of their swords be heard; the sound of their airplanes, cannons, mortars and tanks resound throughout our beloved land, but Tzahal stands as a powerful force, and increases its physical and spiritual power from day-to-day, not only to protect the independence of our nation, but also to strike the enemy on its own soil, in his land.

Diaspora Jewry, day by day, and minute by minute, erects a fortified wall around the State of Israel, and those that are found in the Land of our Birth, in which are included all of the Émigrés from Cieszanow, my dear comrades, men and women alike, are tied about the State of Israel for three purposes:

A.   By giving a defined part of their financial assets through the trusted distribution channel '*HaMagbit HaMeukhedet*' – for the strengthening and enhancement of the State.

B.   The drafting of stout-hearted young men to serve the Country in all walks of her life.

C.   All our brethren in Israel give their beloved sons and daughters to all aspects of defending the homeland.

In the poem, 'Mikraei Zion,' the national poet, Chaim Nachman Bialik portrays for us, the enchanting power of the dream of redemption"

[Page 210]

'Lo, for with you, gathered from the corners of exile,
His bitter cry has aroused you all –
And here the great vision appeared,
And the tear will burst forward from its loyal source,
Great, pleasant, bright, warm.
To her we will pray profusely.

The tears of our nation will fall together also,
They will come in one skin from the ends of exile,
We have no mother of redemption – our redemption yet lives,
And how that great hour will arrive,
And it will raise the last from the dust –
The first to found the return.'

Many days have passed from the day when the national poet wrote these lines, as a memorial to the first Zionist Congress in Basel, many of the progenitors from that Zionist era saw with their own eyes the establishment of the State, but for a variety of reasons, the concept has become weakened, and a spiritual crisis pervades World Jewry, but the leader of the people stands at his post and shouts: **Is the sacrifice of six million Jews that were murdered solely because there were Jews not enough? Enough! No more will a Jew be cremated in a furnace, and no more will a Jew be sentenced to be murdered! The Guardian of the independence of Israel will never nod off or go to sleep!** I believe that a day will come, and it is not distant, that new, fresh forces, will ally themselves to the ranks of those who yearn for redemption, and they will step forward energetically, in all fields of work and endeavor, in order to advance the country of our birth, to push its borders outward, and to nullify the bitter exile and to fulfil the enchanting dream, the dream of freedom, a symbol of that stirring force. The yearning for redemption is a synthesis of our past dignity, and the greatness that awaits us in the future, a wonder and a miracle of the existence of our nation in the world.

In these difficult days – in the days of war against our many external enemies, and against the assimilation in the far reaches of Jewry and within our borders, the following objective stands before us: Victory in all aspects of our lives. The difficult struggle with our enemies – and with white blood – the sweat – in taming the swamp lands, the erection of cities, and kibbutzim, the nurturing of the kibbutzim, and labor settlements, with the lofty effort to establish the State of Israel, to produce bread from the desert…

And now, we will continue that struggle, for the establishment and continuity of our people and the Land of our birth. Under the gaze of those heroes who fell in the War of Independence, in all the ghettoes, in every rebellion against the Nazis, and in all the revolutions against anti-Semitic regimes, in each and every location, we return to our vow: to realize the agenda of the dream of redemption in which can be found: the freedom of our people, and the redemption of our Land.

We have received the mandate of history: to disperse the ominous clouds from the skies of Israel, to gird the forces of the people of Israel to have courage, and to go on to victory.

Good fortune to you, scions of Cieszanow, that you are participating this day in this national undertaking, whose name is: **From the Eternity of Israel – To a Brilliant Triumph**.

[Page 211]

Our Revered Women

Dr. David Ravid

A Triptych

Rachel Tepper ע"ה *Gitt'l Tepper עמ"ש* *Esther Tepper, ע"ה*

Mr. Mikhl Eichler and his Family

Mr. Eichler, may he have good health, was born in Cieszanow – and is today a prominent Canadian citizen, with his former wife Chana and their two little children who were killed by gentile murderers along with their mother.

God – Avenge the spilling of their innocent blood.

R' Chaim Joseph Markdorf and his wife

R' Chaim Joseph Markdorf, his wife Rachel and their daughter Faiga, exterminated by the murderous German bandits.

R' Chaim Joseph ז"ל, – A nice individual, a scholar, someone who lead prayer, and a donor to charity, and his wife was also blessed with a warm, Jewish heart.

May God Avenge Their Spilled Blo

Berish Eichler and his wife

Berish Eichler and his wife were both killed in the camp at Janów in Lemberg

ת.נ.צ.ב.ה.

Facsimile of the memorial stone in memory of those from our town that fell [during the Holocaust] in the Holocaust Cellar on Har Zion in Jerusalem. A gift of Aryeh Koenig ל"ז, of Antwerp.

G-d in Heaven

Pour out your wrath on the Nazi Germans and their helpers, the Poles, Ukrainians, and on all those peoples and nations that participated in the extermination of a third of the People of Israel, men, women, and children, in the years of the Holocaust 5639-57-04.

For they have consumed Jacob and laid waste to his essence.

Pour out your ire on them, and let the fire of your nostrils reach them, pursue them with anger and annihilate them from under the heavens, as is written: take heed nations of His people, for he shall avenge the blood of His people, and he will take vengeance upon those who have assaulted them.

Expiate the earth with them, and find a suitable resting place under your wings for the sacred souls that gave their lives in the Sanctification of Your Name.

Master of Mercy – bind their souls up in the bond of life, the Lord is their portion, and may they rest in peace on their biers.

Amen.

[Page 212]

Mr. Mordechai Eichler and his wife, Leah

Our landsleit in Canada, may they enjoy good health

Rachel Leah Schwartz

A genuine 'Yiddishe Mameh'
a righteous woman revered and loved.
May she rest in peace.

The Renner Family

father, Benjamin, Mother Dwora, and their three children:
Ben-Zion, Blume, and Michael.

The Weber Family

From right to left: Issachar Weber, his father, R' Leibusz and his wife Min'cheh, may they rest in peace.
In the middle: their child that saved herself.

The Bienenstock-Weber Family

Brother and sister
Mrs. Moll Bienenstock-Weber and her son, David,
and her brother, R' Abraham Weber.

The Eichler brothers

R' Eliezer and R' Zvi Hirsch Eichler, sons of R' Joseph ז"ל, from Cieszanow, were among the young intelligentsia and did a great deal for the benefit of the community during their lives.

R' Eliezer died of natural causes, and R' Zvi Hirsch fell at the hands of the Nazis ימ"ש.
ת.נ.צ.ב.ה.

[Page 213]

Each generation and its advocates,
Each generation and its sages,
Each generation and its compassionate women,
Each generation and its righteous women.

In our Jewish history, among the famous men – a series of famous women appear, who through their deeds, have adorned and beautified our nation.

I wish to present a small collection of famous women, as for example, the women of the Tanakh: Miriam, Deborah, Yael, Yehudit, Esther and later one from the time of the *Talmudic* Sages, such as 'Bruriah' the wife of the great Rabbi Meir, the famous women of the earl and late Middle Ages, who defended the honor of the people, such as the legendary 'Rachel' who in that tragic and famous year of *Ta"kh* was forced by one of Chmielnicki's Cossacks to agree to become his wife, and going with her so-called groom to the priest, past a river, threw herself off the bridge into the river and vanished forever into its depths, in order to rescue her honor, the essential thing being – the honor of her Jewish people.

Our history also displays for us the stories of thousands of such Jewish women – heroines, such as: the Golden 'Rosa' of Lemberg, Glikl of Hameln, and thousands of unknown women, and among them Ethel Koenigsberg ה"ע, who mindless of her own well-being, when the German and Ukrainian murderers came to take them – shielded her children with her own body, protecting their lives for a few more minutes, but the murderers tortured all of them to death, and their last words were:

Shema-Yisrael, we die for the honor of the tortured Jewish people.

Honor their memory.

May A Righteous Man Be Remembered for All Times!

Dr. David Ravid

We extend a heartfelt thanks to our brothers and sisters in Canada, for their warm participation in this great mitzvah of erecting a monument in the form of a '*Sefer HaZikaron*,' to the eternal memory of our beloved martyrs who lost their lives at the hands of the murderers of the Second World War: Hitler– Stalin ש"ימ.

We offer special thanks to our comrades: R' Abraham Weintraub, the brothers R' Paltiel and R' Luzer Sztam, R' Mikhl Eichler, R' Meir Willner and our cherished sister, Mrs. Yetta Eichler and others, for their moral and financial support, which literally, at the last minute, rescued our great work so full of our effort from failure.

May He, Who Dwells on High, Mete Out to Them Their Just Reward

[Page 214]
My Grandfather מוהר"ר Yitzhak HaKohen Glanzer, ז"ל

Zvi Elimelekh Glanzer
Member of the Committee

"So long as the elderly among the sages continue to age, wisdom accrues to them."

To memorialize the sacred and cruelly cut down lives of Cieszanow Jews, transports me far away in memory, to the home of my grandfather, מוהר"ר Yitzhak.

It was a house and a mainstay for sages open wide to all those in need. Despite the fact that he was engaged in Torah study, fulfilling the commandment 'and thou shalt study it by day and night,' he was also a community activist, and whoever needed to hear an explanation and receive advice, found in him a cocked ear, and one left him with a light feeling. He had a persuasive skill that enabled him to 'say little, but do much,' and achieved a great deal though being laconic.

Before the First World War, when the Cieszanow Rabbi, R' Simcha Issachar Ber ל"ז passed away, and his son, who remained after him was only of Bar Mitzvah age, and a problem ensued regarding a Teacher and Spiritual Director, until he could be able to assume the Rabbinate, my grandfather ל"ז was approached to temporarily assume the position of a Teacher and Spiritual Director. Despite the fact that commerce demanded his time, he did not refuse and was the Teacher and Spiritual Director for many years, and he spent this time in resolving questions and presiding over Jewish courts without taking any compensation.

I can aver with confidence, that he discharged his responsibility faithfully and to the satisfaction of all.

He was also the Head of the community and assumed considerable burdens on behalf of the community with the Mayor of the city, and the provincial officials, and with is approach and sagacity, he won favor and obtained that which was necessary.

I see before me an obligation also to recall my grandmother, Mrs. Reizel'eh ה"ע, 'You will be blessed by women in your tents' who in many instances lightened the burden on my grandfather, ל"ז, enabling him to carry out his obligations faithfully.

My grandfather passed away at an advanced age, and up to his final minutes, he was in possession of his faculties, and did not let go of his Torah study.

A Pity for Those We Have Lost

ת.נ.צ.ב.ה.

May Their Memory Be Blessed

[Page 215]

Names of the Holy and Pure Souls Most
of Whom Were Killed in Sanctification of The Name

[Pages 216-222]

Translator's Note:

The order in which these names appear has been made to conform to English alphabetization, and therefore does not follow the same order as they appear in the original Yiddish text. To assist the interested reader, each entry has been given a serial number that corresponds to its place in the original Necrology in Yiddish, found on pp. 309-319.

This Necrology contains many instances of names that appear to be duplicates. However, without the intimate knowledge of this community, it would be presumptuous for an uninformed third party to suggest that such duplications constitute errors. Accordingly, special care has been taken to assure that all of the entries in the original document were carried over into the translated version. Additionally, special care was taken to preserve 'nicknames' or 'names of endearment,' that were used to help better identify individuals in that community. While such nomenclature may not serve future generations quite in the same way, it is undoubtedly a sacred obligation to assure that they are brought forward for posterity, as they were used during their lifetimes.

A		
Abel	Sender	4
Abel	Shmuel	2
Abel	Shlomo	3
Abent	Brothers	1
Alter	Abraham	7
Alter	Meir	6
Angerst-Berger	Chaya	20
B		
Berger	Joseph	42
Berger	Michael	43
Berger	Rachel	45
Berger	Yehudit	44
Bern	Sarah & Family	60

Bessekhs	Tzivia & Children	41
Bessekhs	Baruch	40
Bienenstock	Chaim	35
Bienenstock	David	36
Bienenstock	Ethel	34
Bienenstock	Leibl	37
Blumenzweig	Shlomo	38
Blumenzweig	Ze'ev	39
Boxer	Abish	33
Braker	Charna	58
Braker	Miriam	59
Braker	Moshe	56
Braker	Yaakov	57
Brenner	Chava (Bluestein)	54
Brenner	Chaya (Hertzberg)	55
Brenner	Jonah	46
Brenner	Leah	52
Brenner	Mendl	50
Brenner	Rachel & Children	49
Brenner	Reizl & Daughters	47
Brenner	Yekhiel	51
Brenner	Zushya	48
Brenner	Zvi	53
Buchholz	Berish	21
Buchholz	Dwora	23
Buchholz	Faiga	22
Buchholz	Faiga'leh	29
Buchholz	Freida	26
Buchholz	Jonah	24
Buchholz	Jonah Mordechai	27
Buchholz	Neta	28

Buchholz	Shimon Meir	30
Buchholz	Zvi	25
Buchner	Beryl	31
Buchner	Reizl & Daughters	32

D

Dieler	Abraham David	96
Dieler	Dwora	95
Dieler	Ethel & Children	98
Dieler	Nehemiah Asher	94
Dieler	Saul	97
Dornberg	Chana Gitt'l & Children	93
Dornberg	Michael	92
Drucker	Avlah	102
Drucker	Chaya	101
Drucker	Frimet	106
Drucker	Golda	104
Drucker	Leah	108
Drucker	Leib	105
Drucker	Mina	107
Drucker	Myteh	100
Drucker	Reuven	103
Dumont	David & Family	99

E

Ebel	Sender & Family	338
Edelman	Chaim	5
Eichenbaum	Chana & Children	19
Eichenbaum	Zvi	18

Eichler	Berish Alter	9
Eichler	Chana Mirl	10
Eichler	Chana Mirl	14
Eichler	Eliezer	16
Eichler	Hirsch	12
Eichler	Hirsch	17
Eichler	Joseph	13
Eichler	Lejzor Chaim	15
Eichler	Yitzhak	11
Eisenmayer	Baruch	8

F

Feder	Abraham	339
Feder	Blume	347
Feder	Chana	342
Feder	Eliezer	344
Feder	Faiga	349
Feder	Gitt'l	348
Feder	Min'cheh	340
Feder	Moshe	345
Feder	Sender	343
Feder	Sholom	341
Feder	Yenta	350
Feder	Yitzhak	346
Fleischer	Faiga & Children	358
Frampol	Meir	367
Frankel	Bezalel & Family	359
Friedman	Chaya Dwora	364
Friedman	Michael	360
Friedman	Mollie	362

Friedman	Pessl	361
Friedman	Rachel-Zeiger	366
Friedman	Uri	363
Friedman	Zvi	365
Fudim	Sashi & Her Family	353
Furman	Nahum	351
Furman	Rache	352
Futsher	Chana Riva	354
Futshnik	Eliezer	355
Futshnik	Esther	356
Futshnik	Malka	357

G

Gams	Moshe	69
Geller	Ethel	68
Geller	Leib Ber	67
German	Abraham	84
German	Ben-Zion	88
German	Chana	85
German	Joseph	82
German	Miriam	83
German	Moshe Leib	87
German	Yekhezkiel	86
Gershtenfeld	Faiga	91
Gershtenfeld	Joachim-Meir	89
Gershtenfeld	Mollie	90
Glanzer	Mordechai & Wife	66
Goetz	Abraham	74
Goetz	Faiga	71
Goetz	Frieda	73

Goetz	Mollie	72
Goetz	Yaakov	70
Goetzl	Aharon & Family	79
Goetzl	Chana & Children	77
Goetzl	Shabtai	78
Goetzl	Shmuel	75
Goetzl	Ze'ev	76
Goldberg	Herman	64
Goldberg	Kalmus	65
Goldberg	Koppel & Family	61
Goldberg	Lemel	62
Goldberg	Sarah & Family	63
Griener	Azriel	80
Griener	Dr. & Family	81

H

Halberstam	Rabbi Yekhezkiel	114
Halberstam	Rebbetzin Rosa Blume & Children	115
Hammer	Bileib	120
Hammer	Chaim	117
Hammer	Rachel	119
Hammer	Rivka	118
Hammer	Sali	121
Helman	Yaakov & Family	116
Hertzberg	Hella & Family	124
Hertzberg	Nissan & Family	123
Hertzberg	Zushya & Family	122
Hoffman	Frieda	111
Hoffman	Golda	112
Hoffman	Pinchas	109

Klapper	Mina	394
Klapper	Yaakov	393
Klapper-Goldberg	Sala	390
Koenig	Aryeh Leibusz	404
Koenig	Elkanah	403
Koenig	Moshe	401
Koenig	Yuta	402
Koenigsberg	Ethel	406
Koenigsberg	Mordechai	407
Koenigsberg	Moshe	405
Koenigsberg	Pinchas Leibusz	408
Koren	Et'keh	386
Koren	Frieda	385
Koren	Lyushka	384
Koren	Menik	387
Koren	Moshe	382
Koren	Serkeh	383
Krieg	Joseph Hirsch	410
Krieg	Pinchas	411
Kupperman	Anschel	380
Kupperman	Gershon	379
Kupperman	Shlomo	381
Kupperstuck	Chana	378

L

Langenthal	Basha	268
Langenthal	Chaim Israel	269
Langenthal	Hirsch	270
Langenthal	Joseph	272
Langenthal	Roch'cheh	266

Langenthal	Sarah Breindl	271
Langenthal	Yitzhak	267
Langenthal	Yuta & Husband	273
Lehrer	Abraham Yitzhak	297
Lehrer	Asher	280
Lehrer	Azriel	283
Lehrer	Baylah	292
Lehrer	Brana	284
Lehrer	Chana Esther	289
Lehrer	Charna	282
Lehrer	Chaya	294
Lehrer	Feivel	305
Lehrer	Gershon	299
Lehrer	Gita	276
Lehrer	Leah	298
Lehrer	Leib	288
Lehrer	Malka	295
Lehrer	Masha	290
Lehrer	Meir	274
Lehrer	Mindl	278
Lehrer	Mittl	285
Lehrer	Mordechai	286
Lehrer	Moshe	296
Lehrer	Nathan	281
Lehrer	Nathan	301
Lehrer	Ozer	293
Lehrer	Pessia	304
Lehrer	Rachel	303
Lehrer	Rivka	275
Lehrer	Rivka	300
Lehrer	Shlomo	291

Lehrer	Shmuel	302
Lehrer	Shmuel Zeinvil	277
Lehrer	Simcha	287
Lehrer	Yehuda	279
Lempel	Abraham	262
Lempel	Lejzor	261
Lempel	Yitzhak Eizik	263
Lempfelz	Akiva	265
Lempfelz	Sarah	264
Lichtenfeld	Eliezer	259
Lichtenfeld	Faiga Tzipa	260

M

Mager	Chaim	306
Mager	Chana	311
Mager	Manli	307
Mager	Nachman	308
Mager	Reizl	309
Mager	Rivka	310
Markdorf	Chaim Joseph & Wife	318
Markdorf	Feiga	320
Markdorf	Rachel	319
Mendel	Shlomo & Family	316
Mensch	Leibusz & Family	317
Mintz	Abraham	315
Mintz	Chaim	313
Mintz	Esther	312
Mintz	Feiga	314

N

Nadel	Ethel	324
Nadel	Hadassa	323
Nadel	Hana'leh	321
Nadel	Shimon	322
Najman	Chana	328
Najman	Hodel	327
Najman	Menachem Mendl	326
Najman	Yitzhak & Family	325

R

Rabfogel	Abraham	426
Rabfoge	Chana	416
Rabfogel	Chana	425
Rabfogel	Chana Riva	421
Rabfogel	Chaya	420
Rabfogel	Ethel	423
Rabfogel	Gitt'l	418
Rabfogel	Leah	422
Rabfogel	Matityahu	417
Rabfogel	Mordechai	415
Rabfogel	Mordechai	424
Rabfogel	Tova	419
Ratz	Ala	414
Ratz	Frieda	412
Ratz	Ruth	413
Renner	Benjamin	435
Renner	Dwora	436
Rubin	Meir	428
Rubin	Rabbi Aryeh Leibusz	427

Ruchenstreich	Moshe	434
Ruzhenchuk	Khuli	432
Ruzhenchuk	Moshe	431
Ruzhenchuk	Neshi	430
Ruzhenchuk	Tova	433
Ruzhenchuk	Yitzhak	429
S		
Schmid	Aryeh Leibusz	505
Schmid	Chana	502
Schmid	Sarah	506
Schmid	Shmuel	503
Schmid	Wolf	501
Schmid	Yehoshua	504
Schneider	Abraham & Family	519
Schneider	Akiva & Wife	518
Schneider	David	524
Schneider	Lejzor	525
Schneider	Mordechai	517
Schneider	Mordechai	522
Schneider	Reizl	521
Schneider	Yukl	520
Schneider	Zvi Hirsch	523
Schreiber	Chaim Israel	540
Schreiber	Eydl	550
Schreiber	Joseph ben David	548
Schreiber	Krein'cheh	537
Schreiber	Malka bat David & Family	549
Schreiber	Meir	542
Schreiber	Mordechai & Family	545

Schreiber	Mordechai ben David	547
Schreiber	Riva	541
Schreiber	Shayndl	546
Schreiber	Shifra & Children	543
Schreiber	Wolf & Family	538
Schreiber	Yitzhak & Wife	544
Schreiber	Zvi	539
Schuldiner	Aharon	451
Schuldiner	Hanoch	455
Schuldiner	Rivka	454
Schuldiner	Yaakov	456
Schuldiner	Yehoshua	453
Schuldiner	Zivia & Children	452
Schwartz	Dov	450
Schwartz	Faiga	449
Schwartz	Rachel Leah	459
Serber	Beryl	331
Serber	Golda	332
Serber	Hirsch	330
Serber	Mollie	336
Serber	Mordechai	333
Serber	Moshe	335
Serber	Rivka	337
Serber	Ze'ev	334
Shalatiner	Moshe & Family	437
Shapfel	Faiga Esther	447
Shapfel	Genendel	444
Shapfel	Hella	448
Shapfel	Hirsch Leib	445
Shapfel	Joseph	442
Shapfel	Malka	446

Shapfel	Meir Tuvia	443
Shapfel	Miriam	440
Shapfel	Pinchas	441
Shapfel	Yekhezkiel	439
Shapfel	Zissel	438
Shapiro	Feivel	527
Shapiro	Rachel	526
Shapiro	Sarah	528
Shargil	Aryeh	536
Shargil	Yehoshua Heschel & Family	534
Shargil	Zelig	535
Shechter	Kayla & Daughters	494
Shechter	Shmuel	493
Shmukler	Chana	496
Shmukler	Hirsch	500
Shmukler	Michael	497
Shmukler	Mollie	498
Shmukler	Nathan	499
Shmukler	Shimon & Family	495
Shulman	Berish	457
Shulman	Mollie Dwora	458
Singer	Abraham Yaakov	202
Singer	Anna	204
Singer	Bluma	203
Singer	Chaya Gitt'l	211
Singer	David	214
Singer	Gershon	206
Singer	Golds	215
Singer	Hessie	212
Singer	Leib	200
Singer	Malka	208

Singer	Malka	217
Singer	Pearl	213
Singer	Rachel Baylah	210
Singer	Rivka	219
Singer	Sarah	205
Singer	Tova	201
Singer	Wolf	209
Singer	Yaakov	207
Singer	Zvi	218
Singer	Zvi Yaakov	216
Sofer	Hirsch	329
Stanger	Lula	478
Starmer	Dwora	490
Starmer	Eizik & Family	492
Starmer	Ethel	489
Starmer	Hen'cheh	491
Starmer	Joseph	488
Steinberg	Chana & Children	468
Steinberg	Yitzhak	469
Steinberg	Zvi	470
Steinbruch	Chaim Leib	477
Steinbruch	David	476
Steinbruch	Esther	472
Steinbruch	Frieda	473
Steinbruch	Gitt'l	474
Steinbruch	Yitzhak	471
Steinbruch	Zivia & Children	475
Sternlicht	Joseph	486
Sternlicht	Leib	484
Sternlicht	Lipa	487
Sternlicht	Mini'cheh	483

Sternlicht	Yaakov	485
Striegel	Sasha	479
Striegel	Wolf	480
Striegler	Mottl	481
Striegler	Rivka	482
Sznycer	Aharon	508
Sznycer	Dwora	510
Sznycer	Esther	511
Sznycer	Leah	509
Sznycer	Mikhl	516
Sznycer	Raphael & Family	514
Sznycer	Sarah	507
Sznycer	Tzipa & Family	515
Sznycer	Yaakov Moshe & Family	512
Sznycer	Yitzhak & Family	513
Szpritzer	Beniek	532
Szpritzer	Fala	533
Szpritzer	Leah	529
Szpritzer	Meir	531
Szpritzer	Zelig	530
Sztam	Aharon Yitzhak	460
Sztam	Chaya Yenta	461
Sztam	Leah Zissl	462
Sztrukh	Eliyahu	467
Sztukhammer	Frieda	466
Sztukhammer	Leah	463
Sztukhammer	Sarah	465
Sztukhammer	Yehoshua	464

T

Waxman	Eliyahu	180
Waxman	Elka	172
Waxman	Esther	186
Waxman	Faiga	187
Waxman	Hirsch	182
Waxman	Joseph	161
Waxman	Joseph	170
Waxman	Leib	191
Waxman	Leib Ari	168
Waxman	Meir	171
Waxman	Min'cheh & Children	167
Waxman	Mordechai	178
Waxman	Moshe	165
Waxman	Moshe	177
Waxman	Pearl	179
Waxman	Rachel	192
Waxman	Rosa	164
Waxman	Sarah & Family	175
Waxman	Shayndl	169
Waxman	Sholom	162
Waxman	Sholom	188
Waxman	Yaakov	184
Waxman	Yehoshua	183
Waxman	Yitzhak	173
Waxman	Yitzhak Eizik	189
Waxman	Yuta	190
Waxman	Zelda	176
Waxman	Zelig	163
Weber	Abraham	131
Weber	Faiga	133
Weber	Issachar	135

Weber	Leibusz	129
Weber	Mini'cheh	130
Weber	Pinchas	136
Weber	Yehoshua	132
Weber	Yuta	134
Weinberg	Moshe & Children	146
Weinberg	Moshe David	147
Weinberg	Ze'ev	148
Weinig	Meir	160
Weinig	Yaakov	159
Weintraub	Saul	193
Weissberg	Faiga	156
Weissberg	Gitt'l	152
Weissberg	Hanoch	154
Weissberg	Lejzor	158
Weissberg	Mordechai	151
Weissberg	Moshe Baruch	153
Weissberg	Reizl & Daughters	150
Weissberg	Yaakov	155
Weissberg	Yekel'eh	157
Weissberg	Ze'ev	149
Wint	Abraham	142
Wint	Gitt'l & Family	143
Winter	Chaim Israel	145
Winter	Rivka Rachel	144
Wolf	Chaim	125
Wolf	Shayndl	126
Wolfang	Bran'cheh	127
Wolfang	Joseph	128
Wubar	Chana	140
Wubar	Chaya	138

NAME INDEX

www.ingramcontent.com/pod-product-compliance
Lightning Source LLC
Chambersburg PA
CBHW050410110426
42812CB00006BA/1848